A Research Agenda for Entrepreneurship and Context

Elgar Research Agendas outline the future of research in a given area. Leading scholars are given the space to explore their subject in provocative ways, and map out the potential directions of travel. They are relevant but also visionary.

Forward-looking and innovative, Elgar Research Agendas are an essential resource for PhD students, scholars and anybody who wants to be at the forefront of research.

Titles in the series include:

A Research Agenda for Management and Organization Studies
Edited by Barbara Czarniawska

A Research Agenda for Entrepreneurship and Context
Edited by Friederike Welter and William B. Gartner

A Research Agenda for Entrepreneurship and Context

Edited by

FRIEDERIKE WELTER

Institut für Mittelstandsforschung (IfM) Bonn and University of Siegen, Germany

WILLIAM B. GARTNER

Copenhagen Business School, Denmark and California Lutheran University, USA

Elgar Research Agendas

 Edward Elgar
PUBLISHING

Cheltenham, UK • Northampton, MA, USA

Published by
Edward Elgar Publishing Limited
The Lypiatts
15 Lansdown Road
Cheltenham
Glos GL50 2JA
UK

Edward Elgar Publishing, Inc.
William Pratt House
9 Dewey Court
Northampton
Massachusetts 01060
USA

Paperback edition 2017

A catalogue record for this book
is available from the British Library

Library of Congress Control Number: 2016938595

This book is available electronically in the **Elgar**online
Business subject collection
DOI 10.4337/9781784716844

ISBN 978 1 78471 683 7 (cased)
ISBN 978 1 78471 684 4 (eBook)
ISBN 978 1 78471 685 1 (paperback)

Typeset by Servis Filmsetting Ltd, Stockport, Cheshire
Printed and bound in Great Britain by TJ International Ltd, Padstow, Cornwall

Contents

Contributors

Howard E. Aldrich, PhD, is Kenan Professor of Sociology, the University of North Carolina, Chapel Hill, USA and Fellow, Sidney Sussex College, Cambridge University. His main research interests are entrepreneurship, entrepreneurial team formation, gender and entrepreneurship, and evolutionary theory. His 1979 book, *Organizations and Environments*, was reprinted in 2007 by Stanford University Press. His book, *Organizations Evolving* (Sage, 1999), was co-winner of the Max Weber Award from the OOW section of the American Sociological Association. His latest book, *An Evolutionary Approach to Entrepreneurship: Selected Essays*, was published by Edward Elgar in 2011. In October 2014 he received an honorary doctorate from Mid Sweden University.

Ted Baker is the George F. Farris Chaired Professor of Entrepreneurship at Rutgers Business School and Senior Fellow at the Bertha Centre for Social Innovation and Entrepreneurship at the University of Cape Town. His research explores entrepreneurship under resource constraints, focusing in particular on bricolage and improvisation as constructs useful for understanding resourceful behaviour and organizational resilience. His recent work builds on the social psychology of identity to explain founders' responses to adversity and the dynamics of joint organizing efforts in multi-founder ventures. He believes that entrepreneurship research became legitimate too quickly, too complacently and with too little self-reflection and echoes the call for a critical turn among entrepreneurship scholars.

Malin Brännback, DSc, BSc (Pharm), is Dean and Chair of International Business at Åbo Akademi University where she received her doctorate in management science in 1996. She was vice rector of Åbo Akademi University 2010–2014 and Visiting Professor in Entrepreneurship at Stockholm University School of Business 2012–2014. She also holds a BSc in pharmacy. Prior to her return to Åbo Akademi University in 2003, she served as Associate Professor in Information Systems at University of Turku, and Professor of Marketing at Turku School of Economics. She has published widely on entrepreneurship, biotechnology business, and knowledge management. She has co-authored with Alan Carsrud several books: *Understanding the Entrepreneurial Mind – Opening the Black Box* (Springer, 2009), *Understanding Family Businesses* (Springer, 2012) and *Fundamentals for Becoming a Successful Entrepreneur* (Pearson, 2016). She is on the review board of *Journal of Small Business Management*. Her current research interests are in entrepreneurial intentionality, entrepreneurial cognition, entrepreneurial growth and performance in technology entrepreneurship and family business.

Alan L. Carsrud, PhD, EcD (hc), is Visiting Research Professor and Docent at Åbo Akademi University, Finland and in 2013 Visiting Professor at Universidad del Desarrollo, Chile. In 2012 he retired as Loretta Rogers Chair of Entrepreneurship Research at Ryerson University in Canada. He served on the faculties of University of Texas at Austin, University of Southern California, Durham University, University of California, Los Angeles, Bond University and Florida International University. He has 200+ journal articles and chapters in entrepreneurship, family business, social and clinical psychology as well as seven books on entrepreneurship and family business. His entrepreneurship research is in technology, cognitive factors (motivation and intentions), growth, leadership, education, and family business. He co-founded *Entrepreneurship & Regional Development* and is Associate Editor of the *Journal of Small Business Management*. He is Managing Director of Carsrud & Associates helping create firms as diverse as biotechnology, software, wineries and airlines.

Simone Chlosta is Research Coordinator at the Institut für Mittelstandsforschung (IfM) Bonn, Germany. After her apprenticeship as Aviation Clerk, she worked for several years as Sales Manager for the Frankfurt airport. Afterwards, she studied psychology at the University of Frankfurt, UC Berkeley, and UW Madison. She completed her PhD thesis about 'the context-dependency of personality in entrepreneurship' in summer 2009 (*summa cum laude*). She then worked as lecturer for the EBS University, teaching entrepreneurship, organizational behaviour and leadership. In 2011 Simone Chlosta successfully launched her own start-up and returned to university in 2013 as Postdoctoral Researcher in entrepreneurship and SME management at the University of Siegen. Her research interests are contextual and processual entrepreneurship, SME management, psychology of entrepreneurship and academic entrepreneurship.

Sarah Drakopoulou Dodd, PhD, is a Professor of Entrepreneurship at the Hunter Centre for Entrepreneurship, Strathclyde Business School. Her research has focused on the impact of social factors on the quality and quantity of entrepreneurship. She is interested in investigating why people from different cultures start new ventures and how the world around them affects this process. She has published in several journals including *Journal of Business Venturing, Entrepreneurship Theory and Practice* and *Family Business Review*.

Denise Fletcher is Professor of Entrepreneurship and Innovation at the University of Luxembourg where she is Academic Director of the Management Group and Study Director for the Masters in Entrepreneurship and Innovation programme. Prior to this she held a Readership role at the University of Sheffield, UK. Utilizing theories from relational sociology, Denise's academic work centres on explaining how time, context, action and interaction cohere in the production of entrepreneurial forms of work in owner-managed, spousal, sibling, team-based or family enterprises. She has published widely in the small business and entrepreneurship journals and is also involved in running a small business with her partner.

William B. Gartner holds a joint appointment with Copenhagen Business School as Professor of Entrepreneurship and the Art of Innovation, and California Lutheran University as Professor of Entrepreneurship. He is the 2005 winner of the Swedish Entrepreneurship Foundation International Award for outstanding contributions to entrepreneurship and small business research. His recent book *Entrepreneurship as Organizing: Selected Works of William B. Gartner* (2016) is published by Edward Elgar. His current scholarship focuses on entrepreneurial behaviour, entrepreneurship as practice, the social construction of the future, and the hermeneutics of value, possibility and failure.

Stephen Lippmann, PhD, is Associate Professor of Sociology and faculty affiliate of the Institute for Entrepreneurship at the Farmer School of Business at Miami University in Oxford, Ohio, USA. His main research interests are entrepreneurship, and organizational dynamics in cultural industries. His work has appeared in *Academy of Management Review, Social Science History* and *Journal of Business Venturing.* He received his PhD in Sociology from the University of North Carolina, Chapel Hill, USA.

E. Erin Powell is Assistant Professor of Management at Clemson University. After completing her PhD in Technology Management at North Carolina State University, she did a postdoc as the Hugh W. Pearson 1958 Family Visiting Assistant Professor of Business, Entrepreneurship and Organizations at Brown University. Her current research bridges multiple levels of analysis by using social psychological theories of identity to study how founders attempt to fulfil heterogeneous motivations and become who they want to be through entrepreneurship. In addition, her ongoing empirical focus is on the development of a general theory of entrepreneurial resourcefulness. Her research has appeared in the *Academy of Management Journal.*

Tobias Pret is a Doctoral Researcher at the Hunter Centre for Entrepreneurship, Strathclyde Business School. His research explores the ways in which embeddedness in different contexts affects the practices of entrepreneurs. He is particularly interested in investigating the impact of creative communities, households and rural environments on entrepreneurial processes. His work has appeared in *International Small Business Journal* and *International Journal of Management Reviews.*

Eleanor Shaw, PhD, is a Professor of Entrepreneurship and Head of the Hunter Centre for Entrepreneurship at Strathclyde Business School. Her research interests include female entrepreneurship, entrepreneurial philanthropy and networking. She is also interested in entrepreneurial contexts and research methods which enable a wider and deeper understanding of entrepreneurial actions and behaviours. Her recent publications include contributions to *Human Relations, British Journal of Management* and *Entrepreneurship Theory and Practice.*

Paul Selden completed his PhD degree in 2008 at Nottingham Trent University, UK. The focus of his doctoral thesis was a cognitive constructivist approach to the temporality of creative entrepreneurial decision-making processes. Since then he has continued to pursue an interest in the entrepreneurial experience of time into the areas of practical narrative, the relational causality of action–context relationships, the creation of entrepreneurial opportunities, the nature of context, entrepreneurship as an artificial science, entrepreneurship as a complex emergent system, as well as entrepreneurship theory development and modes of explanation.

Erik Stam is Full Professor at the Utrecht University School of Economics, where he holds the chair of Strategy, Organization and Entrepreneurship. Next to this he has been co-founder and Academic Director of the Utrecht Center for Entrepreneurship. He held positions at Erasmus University Rotterdam, the University of Cambridge, the Max Planck Institute of Economics (Jena, Germany), and the Netherlands Scientific Council for Government Policy (WRR). He is editor of *Small Business Economics: An Entrepreneurship Journal*. He is interested in how socio-economic contexts (at the societal and organizational level) affect new value creation by individuals, and the consequences of this entrepreneurship for the performance of firms and society. Next to his scientific work he is often consulted by governments, start-ups and corporates on innovation and entrepreneurship.

Chris Steyaert is Professor for Organizational Psychology at the University of St Gallen, Switzerland. He has published in international journals and books in the area of organizational theory and entrepreneurship. His current interests concern creativity, multiplicity (diversity) and reflexivity in organizing change, intervention and entrepreneurship.

R. Daniel Wadhwani is Fletcher Jones Professor of Entrepreneurship and Associate Professor of Management at University of the Pacific. He also holds appointments as a Visiting Professor in the Department of Management, Politics, and Philosophy at Copenhagen Business School and the Department of Economics at Kyoto University. A historian by training, Dan uses historical sources, methods, and reasoning to examine the foundations of entrepreneurial action and the origins and evolution of organizations and markets. He is co-editor of *Organizations in Time: History, Theory, Methods* (Oxford University Press, 2014), which examines the epistemic, theoretical and methodological opportunities and challenges of integrating historical research and reasoning into management and organizational research.

Friederike Welter heads the Institut für Mittelstandsforschung, Bonn, the oldest policy-oriented small business and entrepreneurship research institute in Germany, and holds a professorship at the University of Siegen, Germany. Prior to this, she worked at Jönköping International Business School in Sweden, at the University of Siegen and at the RWI Essen, a policy-related research institute. Her research interests include entrepreneurial behaviour and entrepreneurship/SME policies in different contexts, with emphasis on former socialist countries, and women's entrepreneurship. Currently, she is particularly interested in theories of contexts as well as how to contextualize entrepreneurship policies. Friederike has published widely in leading international journals and is Senior Editor of *Entrepreneurship Theory and Practice.*

Mike Wright is Professor of Entrepreneurship and Head of the Innovation and Entrepreneurship Group at Imperial College Business School, Director of the Centre for Management Buyout Research, which he founded in 1986, Associate Director of the Entrepreneurship Research Centre and a Visiting Professor at the University of Ghent. He is currently co-editor of *Strategic Entrepreneurship Journal* and of *Academy of Management Perspectives.* He has published over 50 books and more than 400 articles in leading international journals such as *Academy of Management Journal, Academy of Management Review, Strategic Management Journal, Journal of Management Studies, Review of Economics and Statistics, Entrepreneurship Theory and Practice, Journal of International Business Studies, Journal of Business Venturing, Journal of Management, Research Policy* and *Organization Studies,* among others. His research focuses on entrepreneurial ownership mobility, academic entrepreneurship, returnee entrepreneurs, habitual entrepreneurs, technology transfer, family firms, venture capital, private equity, emerging economies, state capitalism and related topics.

1 The context of contextualizing contexts

Friederike Welter, William B. Gartner and Mike Wright

Why context is interesting: personal viewpoints

Friederike: For me, context has always played a role, implicitly and more recently, explicitly. I see it as a theme running through my research career and life, influencing the topics I study and how I do research. When I started my research career, it was in a policy-oriented research institute outside academia, in multicultural teams and with the theme of entrepreneurship in post-Soviet countries (or, even earlier, for my doctoral thesis collecting data on informal ventures in Nigeria – see Welter [2016]). I have worked and lived in so many different and diverse contexts, which again and again made me aware of the role of context in creating differences between entrepreneurs and their behaviour. It also has made me more and more intolerant of our universalized claims for entrepreneurship across the world.

I have set out my context ideas explicitly in Welter (2008, 2011), where I took stock of what I had learned from my research in different contexts since the early 1990s and developed my insights into a few ideas on how contextualization could further entrepreneurship research. The 2011 paper focused on showing why context mattered, what context is in entrepreneurship research and what contextualizing entrepreneurship (research) means. I reviewed the multiplicity and intersectionality of contexts, going beyond the business context and looking at social contexts (households, families and community), the spatial context of neighbourhoods, communities and regional cultures and the institutional contexts. Also, I see close links between the context theme and gender (Welter, Brush and de Bruin 2014), context and entrepreneurship policies (Welter and Smallbone 2011b) and resourcefulness/entrepreneurial behaviour across contexts (Welter and Smallbone 2011a; Welter and Xheneti 2013). To sum up, for me, contextualization is about recognizing differences. Thus, a contextualized understanding of entrepreneurship questions our tendency for an 'all-are-alike' approach. Thus, context matters as it contributes to and determines differences in entrepreneurship.

Currently, I am particularly interested in what to do with this insight: how can we contextualize theories, especially theory-building? And what does context mean for entrepreneurship policies? How can we incorporate temporal and historical contexts? How are process and contexts linked and how to make sense of this? How to

1

theorize that entrepreneurs also influence contexts? And, on a more practical level, how to conduct meaningful contextualized empirical research?

Bill: My interest in contextual perspectives in entrepreneurship stems from my initial experiences of interviewing entrepreneurs for my dissertation (Gartner 1982). A retrospective sense-making of that research effort can be found in Gartner (Gartner 2008). The dissertation spawned two articles, a theoretical paper in which I offered the insight that there is a great amount of variation in the kinds of: entrepreneurs, processes, organizations, and, environments that might be observed when looking at new venture start-ups (Gartner 1985), and an empirical paper (Gartner, Mitchell and Vesper 1989) where an attempt was made to show how specific start-ups might be grouped across these four dimensions. What often gets lost in looking at entrepreneurial phenomena is the uniqueness of each situation. I believe that we tend, as scholars, to look for generalizable insights from our data, and, therefore, overlook the many differences that exist among the various start-ups in our studies. My initial struggle was in trying to figure out whether any kind of generalizable findings might be ascertained from the cases in my dissertation. It seemed, at one level, each start-up case was so different from the others that no apparent logic could be offered for finding a basis for generalizing insights from one case to another. Characteristics of these individuals were often so different. They had different backgrounds, different interests, and different ways at looking at the situations they were in. The kinds of business they started varied across so many industries, and the ways that these new businesses entered their markets were often very different as well. And, the ways that these new firms came into existence was never described in the same way. And, finally, the environments in which these new businesses were founded were never exactly the same: different industries, different locations, different networks of individuals, different types of customers and suppliers. The aphorism that came out of this attempt at finding similarities among was 'There is no average in entrepreneurship' (Gartner, Mitchell and Vesper 1989, p. 184).

So, I have tried to carry this viewpoint forward: entrepreneurship is about variation and that the differences among entrepreneurial situations are likely to be as significant as the variation (in the characteristics of the situation) that might exist between entrepreneurial and non-entrepreneurial situations. I think there is often a misreading of the article '"Who is an entrepreneur?" is the wrong question' (Gartner 1988) that would suggest I do not believe that the characteristics of entrepreneurs play a factor in determining aspects of the development of new ventures. I think a more accurate reading of that article is that I believe that the characteristics of entrepreneurs matter, but only in that those characteristics are linked to specific entrepreneurial situations, and, for the most part those specific entrepreneurial situations vary so widely that finding a common individual characteristic would seem to be pointless. Context matters. Assuming that a 'one-size-fits-all' kind of entrepreneur exists, who could act entrepreneurial in all situations, would seem to be very unlikely. I think the only way one might find characteristics of individuals that have strong correlations to their situations, is to narrow the context of these situations. There is a person–situation fit (Shaver and Scott 1991) that needs to be accounted for.

Where I believe there might be some way of finding commonalities among start-up situations is to look at the kinds of activities these individuals engage in. And, even in looking at start-up activities, I believe my research has shown that there are various sequences of behaviours, rather than one set formula of entrepreneurial activity (Carter, Gartner and Reynolds 1996; Gartner, Carter and Reynolds 2004).

So, finding commonalities among entrepreneurial situations: difficult. And, I believe the reason that a growing focus on 'context' has occurred, is that when researchers look closely at the situations where entrepreneurship occurs, they see 'difference' rather than similarities. Context matters because entrepreneurial situations are so very different.

Friederike: Was Hjorth, Jones and Gartner (2008) the first Special Issue on context in entrepreneurship?

Bill: I think this special issue was an attempt to offer a 'counter-narrative' to 'taken-for-granted' assumptions about the nature of entrepreneurship. The idea of context addressed in the special issue introduction as important to consider was due to the reason that the situations that are assumed to be entrepreneurial have been 'taken-for-granted', yet upon closer inspection most situations in which entrepreneurship occurs appear to be very different from one-another. The papers that are presented in that special issue are examples of various contexts that are not necessarily 'taken-for-granted'.

But, if I were to look for an effort where context was fundamental to expressing differences in the nature of entrepreneurial phenomena, then, it would be much earlier: The *Journal of Business Venturing* Special Issue on Qualitative Methods (Gartner and Birley 2002). If one looks at that issue of the journal, then, there is a variety of contexts (Nigeria, Sri Lanka, the life histories and social contexts of a start-up, metaphors used in the media) that were not typical, at this point, of entrepreneurial situations, currently explored in most mainstream entrepreneurship journals. One observation from our efforts to shepherd those special issue articles to publication was that the entrepreneurship field needed to recognize a larger body of research across a wider range of sources, contexts and genres. We offered the idea of the 'critical mess' as a metaphor for collecting different information about different kinds of entrepreneurships as a way to enrich our understanding of the entirety of entrepreneurship as a phenomenon.

Mike: My positions on the role and nature of context in entrepreneurship have been set out, inter alia in Zahra and Wright (2011), Autio et al. (2014) and Wright et al. (2014). In these papers, I have sought to articulate the multiple dimensions of contexts, notably institutional, geographical, technological, industrial, organizational, temporal and social. I also take the view that context is dynamic and continually evolving and that we need to take account of this both in developing and testing theory. These different contexts have implications for the nature and extent of entrepreneurship and entrepreneurial forms.

I think that I've come to these views because, over time, looking at different types of entrepreneurs (management buyouts, serial entrepreneurs, returnee entrepreneurs, academic spin-offs, entrepreneurship in family firms) in various contexts, that we have a very fragmented understanding of context and that there has been very little work to join the dots. This is a major challenge as the interplay of different dimensions of context and different types of entrepreneurs is complex but unless we start to address this challenge our insights will remain limited and policy prescriptions may be faulty. Erkko Autio is doing work that tries to address configurations of context but I'm not sure that this fully addresses all dimensions or the variety of entrepreneurial types.

Contexts matter: why all of a sudden and which ones?

For some time, entrepreneurship scholars have indicated that context matters (Davidsson 2003; Ucbasaran, Westhead and Wright 2001) – picking up a theme which gained importance in general management research at the turn of the century (Bamberger 2008; Johns 2001) and which, to some extent, can be traced back to the German historical school as represented by Gustav Schmoller in the nineteenth century (Schmude, Welter and Heumann 2008) and to German historical sociologists such as Max Weber (Jones and Wadhwani 2006). Already in 2006, Geoffrey G. Jones and Daniel Wadhwani argued that 'historical research may help management researchers to understand how entrepreneurship needs to be understood within the context of time and place'. Since our 2011 context papers (Welter 2011; Zahra and Wright 2011) this theme has been taken up by several entrepreneurship scholars. For example, van Gelderen and Masurel (2012) edited a book on entrepreneurship and context which drew attention to 'the various meanings and roles, as well as the importance of context in entrepreneurship studies' (p. 1). Spedale and Watson (2013) show how we can move beyond the artificial separation of 'context' and 'individual' and instead arrive at a more realistic picture of entrepreneurial actions. De Bruin and Lewis (2015) and Shaw and de Bruin (2013) suggest that consideration of context can advance research on social entrepreneurship. Chalmers and Shaw (2015) elaborate on methodological challenges in contextualizing. Su, Zhai and Landström (2015) illustrate how context (in this case the Chinese context) is reflected in some of the themes Chinese entrepreneurship researchers study. McKeever, Jack and Anderson (2015) highlight the complex and recursive interrelationship between contexts and entrepreneurs, drawing our attention to the dynamics of a context-perspective on entrepreneurship, whilst Korsgaard, Ferguson and Gaddefors (2015) emphasize the links between contexts and opportunity creation of rural entrepreneurs.

Friederike: Why is it that context has (re-)emerged in entrepreneurship research as one of the hot topics? I am still puzzled as to why all of a sudden there's this huge interest in all things context. And don't we risk a superficial and diluted discussion around this? One where context becomes just another of these 'must tick-this-off when submitting to a journal' box?

Bill: Well, one just needs to look at who is writing about context. These authors are non-US authors, for the most part. It is mostly a European discussion. I have a USA background, but, now, I'm at Copenhagen Business School (CBS), in a European context, where, the discussion of context is part of a normal discussion of what entrepreneurship is. So, I think that one of the reasons that context matters, now, more, is that the discussion is occurring because of individuals who are outside of the North American 'taken-for-granted' assumptions about what kinds of contexts matter. I'm going to address this more, later, in a different way.

Mike: I'm not sure why the sudden surge in interest in context. To some extent I feel we've been like Moliere's Bourgeois *Gentilhomme*: '*il y a plus de quarante ans que je dis de la prose sans que j'en susse rien*' – we've been researching context without realizing or acknowledging it for years. Perhaps we, at last, have recognized that evidence and theories based in the US are not necessarily applicable elsewhere – or maybe I should say, US reviewers and journals have come to accept that this is not the case. From that beginning, I think it has opened up a search for dimensions of that context. I guess also that authors have begun to theorize the different relationships between different context and entrepreneurial activities, rather than just applying hypotheses developed in the US into other contexts.

Friederike: Anyway, there seems to be general agreement now in the field that context is important. But, do we agree on which context/s to take into account? Re-reading our context writings (Welter 2011; Welter, Brush and de Bruin 2014; Welter and Xheneti 2013; Zahra and Wright 2011; Zahra, Wright and Abdelgawad 2014), my feeling is 'No, we don't agree'. To me it looks a bit like you, Mike and I have different understanding of what context is/should be in entrepreneurship research. Mine seems to be broader and encompassing more than the institutional, business, industry and organizational contexts – probably more 'weird' contexts for an entrepreneurship researcher as they are 'outside' the business world. Or do I misinterpret? Is our understanding more similar than I envisage? Complementing each other? I stand to be corrected . . .

Mike: The recent paper I did with other colleagues in *Research Policy* extends some of the contextual aspects (Autio et al. 2014). My 2013 *Journal of Management Studies* paper with Hoskisson et al. also deepens the variety of context in emerging economies (Hoskisson et al. 2013). I'm quite open to a range of different approaches to context beyond the ones I've looked at so far . . . and I'm also open to a broad definition of what entrepreneurial activity means beyond start-ups.

Friederike: Isn't it interesting that most of our context thinking stems from research in 'other' contexts, such as emerging market economies? For me proof that we need to leave our comfort zones in order to recognize what fits and what not.

Bill: One of the ideas that I want to have pondered is this: the generalizability of difference. We don't really have much thought about differences and how we make sense of differences in our findings. We are always looking for commonalities and generalizable insights. I think we have some difficulty presenting the generalizability of difference. We are somewhere in the discussion between 'all contexts are unique' and 'all contexts are similar'. Hmmm. I'm thinking, now, about what the 'context of contexts' would be about. We are contextualizing context, and, I think, that inherently orients one more towards 'contexts are unique'. Anyway, I'm going to play more, later, with this idea about difference, and, what it means to talk about variation in the nature of entrepreneurship, as a phenomenon.

How to contextualize theories

[T]here is a need to theorize context rather than leave it as some kind of kitchen sink dumping ground standing behind all our foreground theories and explanations. (Pollitt 2013b, p. 95)

Mike: For me, an issue with context heterogeneity is that we haven't particularly done a great deal to examine the interactions between different types of context, which may highlight conflicts and complementarities. So, how do the different dimensions of context interact with each other? Further, what are the most common and effective configurations? How do contextual dimensions interact with other levels of analysis, notably, firm, team and individuals?

Friederike: The configuration idea definitely needs to be discussed further. When I read your suggestion to discuss 'configurations of contexts', my first reaction was – this won't work. Can we really elaborate configurations of context(s)? Isn't that contradicting the dynamics of contexts and temporal aspects? I am more comfortable with seeing contexts as something which is fluid and changeable – although there may be elements that are more stable than others. Difficult to disentangle; and I believe also a challenge to research empirically.

When it comes to interactions, we need to pay much more attention to the multiplicity of contexts. An individual works in particular contexts (a firm, an industry, a culture, a region, a community), she is influenced by each of these contexts, interprets and make sense out of her contexts and simultaneously provides the contexts for others (as boss, as colleague, as entrepreneur, as family member and so on). I really like what Clarke (2013, p. 22) suggests, namely 'thinking contextually', which to him 'certainly demands more than a conventional approach to naming or even describing contexts before the real business of analysis takes place'. He points out that by thinking contextually we will refute 'mono-causal and linear accounts of agency and action' (Clarke 2013, p. 31). For me, his ideas highlight a fundamental issue in regards to the interactions between contexts: those can be all sorts of things – contexts can supplement or complement, but also contradict or antagonize each other. And that at different levels! And of course, we shouldn't forget the agency of entrepreneurs – they can change and influence contexts, especially so, if we accept contexts as something which is also interpretative and constructed.

Bill: So, can we say that discussions of context sensitize one to looking for differences in the phenomenon? What is particular to this situation and how is it similar or not to other situations? We so yearn for generalizability. Yes? That what I find in my data might have some relevance to other situations? That I can offer some insights that others might find useful? Maybe 'generalizability', now, needs to be 'contextualized' to a great degree. Maybe we need to offer more specific descriptions of what the situations, are, that we find our results applicable to. There is a sense, then, of humility in our findings. For example, contextualizing our findings, then, means that, in an obvious example, insights from Silicon Valley may not transfer to any other part of the world. Lessons from Silicon Valley may be lessons useful to no one else outside of that location. When we contextualize 'high growth firms', then, those firms might be very, very different depending on where they are located, when they were started (so, time and history are critical as aspects of context), and, who–why–when–what–how become important variables in the discussion. And, the idea of 'high growth firms' is itself, an idea that comes out of a particular context and value system where 'high growth firms' may be given more prominence than other kinds of firms.

Friederike: I couldn't agree more! This is always an issue when governments want good practice examples of what works elsewhere in fostering small firms and entrepreneurship . . . I always tell them that they cannot transfer policies, but may have a close look at the constitutive elements of such policies. A particular good example is the very successful German *Mittelstand* – over the past years, we have had several delegations from around the world, visiting our institute and each of them asking for the recipe of fostering a vibrant *Mittelstand* in their own countries . . . contexts! You can't take the German small business sector outside its context and you can't understand it without looking at the social, historical, temporal, institutional and organizational contexts.

Bill: So, to contextualize is also to consider what we value and find important to focus on. I think that when we introduce, for example, studies of firms in Africa, then, we have to celebrate the differences in cultural, political, regulatory, competitive and so on, ways that entrepreneurship occurs. What relevance does the Silicon Valley model have for anyone else? It is unique to that location. What is generalizable about that context? And, then, what is generalizable about contexts in Eastern Europe, or the Middle East, or South Asia?

For me, this gets back to 'critical mess' arguments I have made – that our field just needs more evidence, more data, about various entrepreneurships that exist (Gartner 2006). We simply do not know enough about the variation in entrepreneurial phenomena that exist in this world. I will offer this straw dog that: we simply generalize our own particular situation as similar to other contexts – and they are not the same. Difference matters. And, we may just need to spend more time publishing articles where these differences (no matter how small or trivial we might, at this point, perceive them to be) are described and presented. Hmmm. I could poke a little at the problem of requiring most articles to have some theoretical underpinnings as diminishing chances for publishing articles where the insights are about uniqueness and difference. Aren't theories about generalizability? If X happens, then, we will see Y? And, aren't we, then, looking always for more X's in this world? But, what if there is only one X to Y? What if there are different situations and relationships that are truly unique? What can we learn from that?

So, this comes down to my hope for theories of difference. I assume, on some level, that entrepreneurial situations have, in some facet of themselves, difference (be it in time, location, motivation, strategy, resources and so on) that makes each situation, unique. How do we pay attention to that? And, then, how do we celebrate those differences and talk about them in a way that could actually be generalizable?

Friederike: Maybe a first step towards theories of difference is acknowledging that contexts are something which is not simply 'out there', but which is also created by us. Remember, Bill, that in our recent workshop on the future of entrepreneurship research at the University of Siegen, we discussed that context is also something which is 'inside' a person or stems from the person's understanding of context (which contexts matter, for example, for an entrepreneur, which ones are considered important by an entrepreneurship scholar? Is there a fit or a misfit between both groups?). That means language and interpretations of context matter – interestingly something which is taken up in commonplace definitions of context.[1] We touched upon contexts and identity building and the construction of contexts by individuals and so on. I believe these issues are under-researched at the moment when it comes to entrepreneurship research, although this is important because it also influences how we theorize and empirically research contexts.

Interestingly, the social construction of context has been widely discussed in other disciplines, notably so in informatics – I only came across these articles by chance, through a very general literature search on 'context' (isn't it telling also: we don't talk to each other across disciplinary boundaries?). Much of what has been written there resonates with my understanding of the 'subjectivity' of context. Akman (2000) has published a really interesting review, highlighting how our understanding and interpretation of words, sentences and situations are not only influenced by the respective contexts, but also create these contexts. So, no two contexts are alike as we individually reinterpret and make sense of them.

Another issue is whether we can stretch existing theories to incorporate context specificities – for me, this also is a step towards Bill's idea to develop theories of differences. I certainly think we can use and stretch existing theories to incorporate differences – we just need to be willing! Most of our theories stem from Western contexts, maybe even from the US context. So, they give us a very narrow picture of how entrepreneurs behave, what they do, how they use resources and which resources they draw on, how they grow their businesses and so on. I see two ways forward: One is to take back to mainstream entrepreneurship what research on different contexts brings to the table. The research on women's entrepreneurship is, for me, an excellent example of this: In that field, we have suggested a framework which allows us to theoretically grasp the multiplicity of contexts and their interactions (Brush, de Bruin and Welter 2009) – why not use those frameworks for all of entrepreneurship? The same holds true for research on ethnic/minority entrepreneurship, where Kloosterman and colleagues have developed the framework of mixed embeddedness arguing for a close look at the interactions of migrants within their economic, social and institutional contexts (Kloosterman, Van der Leun and Rath 1999). And, secondly, there are several theories by now, that already contextualize or would allow for contextualizing. For example, concepts like bricolage (Baker and Nelson 2005), entrepreneurial resilience and resourcefulness (Corbett and Katz 2013; Misra and Kumar 2000; Powell 2011) have a lot to say about (successful) resource acquisition in different social, spatial and institutional contexts – but there may be a tendency to see those approaches as too narrow and restricted to a specific target group (those in need – those who can't do resource acquisition properly. . .).

Mike: These latter theories also give rise to research agendas on the limitations of the context they explore. For example, for me bricolage doesn't have much to say about scaling up challenges relating to entrepreneurship.

Friederike: But by now bricolage has been explored in many different contexts. Anyway, besides working on theories of difference, I think we also need to show that, and how, contextualizing is not the 'enemy of big generalizations' (Pierre 2013). Somehow, these two issues go hand in hand for me. So, we need to discuss what does generalization mean once we contextualize? Pollitt (2013c) talks about scale/levels on which contextual factors operate. Public policy research uses micro, meso, macro frameworks to disentangle context factors, focusing mainly on meso research as a level where 'a considerable degree of generalizing can be achieved and yet contextual peculiarities can still be given a place. Middle-level generalizations, it is claimed, can be transferred (cautiously) between similar contexts, once those contexts are defined and integrated into the relevant explanatory theory' (Pollitt 2013a, p. 416). Can we transfer this to entrepreneurship research? That seems to be difficult because entrepreneurship is something which depends on both persons, that is, the micro level, and their wider contexts at meso and macro level. Maybe one idea would be to identify contexts that are more or less there 'forever' – and others that are more short-lived. In a way, this is also something that goes in the direction of configurations of contexts? Not sure yet . . . but Pollitt (2013b, p. 94) also suggests that we can do something he labels 'contextualized generalizations'. And I think this is exactly what Mike is asking us to discuss now.

Mike: Maybe we need to think in terms of the interaction of exogenous and endogenous dimensions of context then? I think that the individual dimension of context is not just about the way they perceive context but also has something to do with the variety of individual entrepreneurial goals. Entrepreneurs do not all have the same goals and their different goals provide different contexts for their entrepreneurial behaviour.

Can we tease out what aspects of entrepreneurship transcend context and which aspects are context-dependent? I think we should also explore not just whether theories and evidence from one context translate to another context, and which context, but also the dark side. That is, is transferring inappropriate theories and evidence 'neutral' or does it have negative consequences?

Friederike: Big questions! Again, for me this has a lot to do with generalizability. Maybe looking at each of the contexts in turn will help: When we look at individual behaviour, is there something universal across cultures and countries? Difficult to say, because we also know that, for example, what we would consider illegal entrepreneurship may be considered legal or tolerated elsewhere. But the fundamentals of how individuals think and behave are similar, or? Cognitions may differ because meanings and interpretations matter; they in turn are context-dependent and they also change over time. Ok, I admit this is not yet really helpful in answering your questions – but then, your questions set out some of the challenges researchers will have to tackle when developing context theories.

Mike: Perhaps betraying my training as an economist, I also think we need to consider the 'so what?' question. In other words, does analysis of different dimensions of context matter for understanding the performance outcome of entrepreneurial ventures rather than just their creation? This is reminiscent to me of all the work on the contingency theory of organizations in the 1970s and 1980s – lots of work on the contingent (that is, contextual) effect on the structure of organizations but very little on performance effects. Interestingly, this work did start out by looking at structural (exogenous) factors but subsequently looked at endogenous issues like internal culture of organizations.

How to contextualize in practice

Mike: How does one research these interdependencies of context and these different levels? What are the roles of qualitative and quantitative work (and which sorts)? What are the challenges and how can they be overcome?

Friederike: Multi-level modelling? I am not an expert on that, but have listened to and reviewed several papers over the past years, which set out multi-level models as one way to deal with the interdependencies of contexts and its manifold, cross-level nature. I'd personally go for in-depth work at different levels and with different methods, for example, participant observations, interviews or focus groups and many more. We may actually learn a lot here from anthropology. And, I see a great opportunity for contextual research because we need both more 'quantitative' and 'qualitative' work – we finally can start reconciling both research approaches and look for their contributions in their own rights.

One of the challenges – or advantage? – for our empirical research is that we can't decontextualize ourselves. We are shaped by our contexts (also see Zahra 2007), and we often don't see this. How to tackle this? What does it mean for our research? Hjorth, Jones and Gartner (2008, p. 82) talk about contextualized research as research that is grounded deeply in the context of disciplines, drawing on and simultaneously contributing to social and human sciences. So, can we suggest that contextualized research is one which per nature (definition) is interdisciplinary/multidisciplinary? Together with the multi-level approaches, this would have implications for empirical research – make it more complicated and complex and at the same time fascinating. I do think the entrepreneurship field is ideally suited for contextualized (interdisciplinary) research because we ourselves stem from so many different disciplines. And we could become so much more relevant (again) (Baker and Welter 2015) . . .

Another question I recently have been asked is 'How do you develop contextualized hypotheses?' A tricky issue, same can be said for the issue of 'theorizing context'. In my eyes, many of us seem to misunderstand what 'theorizing context' means in practice. In papers submitted to ET&P or elsewhere, I too often see a section on 'the research context' or 'the context in'. When it comes to hypotheses development, researchers often tag 'in China', 'in Germany', 'in the tech industry' and similar onto hypotheses. This is not contextualizing – we definitely need to push this further. Context research from other disciplines argues for 'greater precision' in identifying contexts and operationalizing it, because without 'some precision it is hard for contexts to enter into theories. They tend to remain a passive "background"' (Pollitt 2013a, p. 416). How can we achieve similar precision for entrepreneurship research? I think through deep engagement with contexts and then integration into our research as a lens, not as a simple variable. For hypotheses development, this would mean engaging with the relevant contexts and trying to tease out why one may expect different results because of these contexts.

Something else arises as a challenge from that – variables/measurements of contexts: If we accept that contexts are also constructed, this asks for contextualized variables (measurements), contradicting research which normally would assume that variables are the 'same kind of "thing" across a wide range of contexts, and to vary in value (quantity) but not in essence' (Pollitt 2013a, p. 418). We have grappled with this in a project studying trust in different cultures: does a Russian entrepreneur talk about the same thing compared to a German entrepreneur? How can we solve this? Pollitt (2013a, p. 419) suggests a more 'nuanced and inclusive approach', trying to reconcile the usual approach where we apply the same measures/variables across all contexts with what he labels 'radical contextualism', reflecting a qualitative and interpretative narrative.

Bill: Well, I will continue to beat the drum on this: If differences matter, then, the goal becomes discerning what the differences actually are, and, why these differences would matter. As Mike suggests, we have to ask 'So what?' Indicating that, 'everything is unique', does not provide much insight into suggestions for practice. I assume that we believe that one of the values of gaining knowledge and insight through research is to inform others about more viable or plausible ways of acting in this world. So, then, the challenge is not in assuming that all contexts are inherently different (due to time, place, culture, and so on) but, that, one might find that some characteristics of the context can also be comparatively understood. I think this can be a bit tricky to facilitate. For example are we aiming for comparative efforts in a similar vein as Hofstede's (1984) dimensions for comparing cultures? Does his work contextualize or decontextualize the ability to generate insights? So, while Hofstede's dimensions of culture might be characteristics that we would want to comparatively contextualize, our ability to understand it comparatively, outside of the specific contexts of what culture actually is, in the context of a specific culture, can be problematic. And, yet, we must try.

Moving forward

Stop. For a moment:

Look. Listen. Pay attention.

What did you find here?

NOTE

1 Merriam-Webster defines context as '1: the parts of a discourse that surround a word or passage and can throw light on its meaning; 2: the interrelated conditions in which something exists or occurs: environment, setting'. See: www.merriam-webster.com/dictionary/context (accessed 26 November 2015).

References

Akman, Varol (2000), 'Rethinking context as a social construct', *Journal of Pragmatics*, **32** (6), 743–759.

Autio, Erkko, Martin Kenney, Philippe Mustar, Don Siegel and Mike Wright (2014), 'Entrepreneurial innovation: The importance of context', *Research Policy*, **43** (7), 1097–1108.

Baker, Ted and Reed E. Nelson (2005), 'Creating something from nothing: Resource construction through entrepreneurial bricolage', *Administrative Science Quarterly*, **50** (3), 329–366.

Baker, Ted and Friederike Welter (2015), 'Bridges to the future', in Ted Baker and Friederike Welter (eds), *The Routledge Companion to Entrepreneurship*, London: Routledge, pp. 3–17.

Bamberger, Peter (2008), 'From the editors: Beyond contextualization: Using context theories to narrow the micro–macro gap in management research', *Academy of Management Journal*, **51** (5), 839–846.

Brush, Candida G., Anne de Bruin and Friederike Welter (2009), 'A gender-aware framework for women's entrepreneurship', *International Journal of Gender and Entrepreneurship*, **1** (1), 8–24.

Carter, Nancy M., William B. Gartner and Paul D. Reynolds (1996), 'Exploring start-up event sequences', *Journal of Business Venturing*, **11** (3), 151–166.

Chalmers, Dominic M. and Eleanor Shaw (2015), 'The endogenous construction of entrepreneurial contexts: A practice-based perspective', *International Small Business Journal*, published online before print 21 September 2015, doi: 10.1177/0266242615589768.

Clarke, John (2013), 'Contexts: Forms of agency and action', in Christopher Pollitt (ed.), *Context in Public Policy and Management: The Missing Link?*, Cheltenham, UK and Northampton, MA, USA: Edward Elgar Publishing, pp. 22–34.

Corbett, Andrew C. and Jerome A. Katz (eds), (2013), *Entrepreneurial Resourcefulness: Competing With Constraints*, Bingley: Emerald.

Davidsson, Per (2003), 'The domain of entrepreneurship research: Some suggestions', in J.A. Katz and D.A. Shepherd (eds), *Cognitive Approaches to Entrepreneurship Research*, Amsterdam: JAI, pp. 265–314.

De Bruin, Anne and Kate V. Lewis (2015), 'Traversing the terrain of context in social entrepreneurship', *Journal of Social Entrepreneurship*, **6** (2), 127–136.

Gartner, William B. (1982), *An empirical model of the business startup, and eight entrepreneurial archetypes*. Unpublished Dissertation, Seattle, WA: University of Washington.

Gartner, William B. (1985), 'A conceptual framework for describing the phenomenon of new venture creation', *Academy of Management Review*, **10** (4), 696–706.

Gartner, William B. (1988), '"Who is an entrepreneur?" is the wrong question', *American Journal of Small Businesses*, **12** (4), 11–32.

Gartner, William B. (2006), 'A "critical mess" approach to entrepreneurship scholarship', in Anders Lundström and Sune Halvarsson (eds), *Entrepreneurship Research: Past Perspectives and Future Prospects* (Vol. 2), Hanover, MA: NOW, pp. 73–82.

Gartner, William B. (2008), 'Variations in entrepreneurship', *Small Business Economics*, **31** (4), 351–361.

Gartner, William B. and Sue Birley (2002), 'Introduction to the special issue on qualitative methods in entrepreneurship research', *Journal of Business Venturing*, **17** (5), 387–395.

Gartner, William B., Nancy M. Carter and Paul D. Reynolds (2004), 'Business startup activities', in William B. Gartner, Kelly G. Shaver, Nancy M. Carter and Paul D. Reynolds (eds), *Handbook of Entrepreneurial Dynamics: The Process of Business Creation*, Thousand Oaks, CA: Sage pp. 285–298.

Gartner, William B., T.R. Mitchell and K.H. Vesper (1989), 'A taxonomy of new business ventures', *Journal of Business Venturing*, **4** (3), 169–186.

Hjorth, D., C. Jones and W.B. Gartner (2008), 'Introduction for "recreating/recontextualising entrepreneurship"', *Scandinavian Journal of Management*, **24** (2), 81–84.

Hofstede, Geert (1984), *Culture's Consequences: International Differences in Work-Related Values*, Newbury Park: Sage.

Hoskisson, Robert E., Mike Wright, Igor Filatotchev and Mike W. Peng (2013), 'Emerging multinationals from mid-range economies: The influence of institutions and factor markets', *Journal of Management Studies*, **50** (7), 1295–1321.

Johns, Gary (2001), 'In praise of context', *Journal of Organizational Behavior*, **22** (1), 31–42.

Jones, Geoffrey and R. Daniel Wadhwani (2006), *Entrepreneurship and Business History: Renewing the Research Agenda*, Harvard: Division of Research, Harvard Business School. Available at: http://hbswk.hbs.edu/item/entrepreneurship-and-business-history-renewing-the-research-agenda (accessed 15 June 2016).

Kloosterman, R., J. Van der Leun and J. Rath (1999), 'Mixed embeddedness: (In)formal economic activities and immigrant businesses in the Netherlands', *International Journal of Urban and Regional Research*, **23** (2), 252–277.

Korsgaard, Steffen, Richard Ferguson and Johan Gaddefors (2015), 'The best of both worlds: How rural entrepreneurs use placial embeddedness and strategic networks to create opportunities', *Entrepreneurship & Regional Development*, **27** (9–10), 1–25.

McKeever, Edward, Sarah Jack and Alistair Anderson (2015), 'Embedded entrepreneurship in the creative re-construction of place', *Journal of Business Venturing*, **30** (1), 50–65.

Misra, Sasi and E. Sendil Kumar (2000), 'Resourcefulness: A proximal conceptualisation of entrepreneurial behaviour', *Journal of Entrepreneurship*, **9**, 135–154.

Pierre, Jon (2013), 'Context, theory and rationality: An uneasy relationship?', in Christopher Pollitt (ed.), *Context in Public Policy and Management: The Missing Link?*, Cheltenham, UK and Northampton, MA, USA: Edward Elgar Publishing, pp. 124–130.

Pollitt, Christopher (2013a), 'Context: What kind of missing link?', in Christopher Pollitt (ed.), *Context in Public Policy and Management: The Missing Link?*, Cheltenham, UK and Northampton, MA, USA: Edward Elgar Publishing, pp. 415–422.

Pollitt, Christopher (2013b), 'First link', in Christopher Pollitt (ed.), *Context in Public Policy and Management: The Missing Link?*, Cheltenham, UK and Northampton, MA, USA: Edward Elgar Publishing, pp. 88–97.

Pollitt, Christopher (2013c), 'Preface: Context – A missing link?', in Christopher Pollitt (ed.), *Context in Public Policy and Management: The Missing Link?*, Cheltenham, UK and Northampton, MA, USA: Edward Elgar Publishing, pp. xv–xx.

Powell, Erin E. (2011), *Weathering the gale: Toward a theory of entrepreneurial resourcefulness and resilience*. Dissertation, North Carolina State University. From: http://proquest.umi.com/pqdlnk?did=2485153441&Fmt=2&clientI d=79356&RQT=309&VName=PQD (accessed 25 April 2016).

Schmude, Jürgen, Friederike Welter and Stefan Heumann (2008), 'Entrepreneurship research in Germany', *Entrepreneurship Theory and Practice*, **32** (2), 289–311.

Shaver, Kelly G. and Linda R. Scott (1991), 'Person, process, choice: The psychology of new venture creation', *Entrepreneurship Theory and Practice*, **16** (2), 23–43.

Shaw, Eleanor and Anne de Bruin (2013), 'Reconsidering capitalism: The promise of social innovation and social entrepreneurship?', *International Small Business Journal*, **31** (7), 737–746.

Spedale, Simona and Tony J. Watson (2013), 'The emergence of entrepreneurial action: At the crossroads between institutional logics and individual life-orientation', *International Small Business Journal*, **32** (7), 759–776.

Su, Jing, Qinghua Zhai and Hans Landström (2015), 'Entrepreneurship research in China: Internationalization or contextualization?', *Entrepreneurship & Regional Development*, **27** (1–2), 50–79.

Ucbasaran, Deniz, Paul Westhead and Mike Wright (2001), 'The focus of entrepreneurial research: contextual and process issues', *Entrepreneurship: Theory and Practice*, **25** (4), 57–78.

van Gelderen, Marco and Enno Masurel (eds), (2012), *Entrepreneurship in Context*, Abingdon: Routledge.

Welter, Friederike (2008), 'Entrepreneurship in its context(s): a review'. Paper presented at the NSF-DFG Conference 'Contextualizing Economic Behaviour', New York, NY.

Welter, Friederike (2011), 'Contextualizing entrepreneurship – conceptual challenges and ways forward', *Entrepreneurship Theory and Practice*, **35** (1), 165–184.

Welter, Friederike (2016), 'Wandering between contexts', in David Audretsch and Erik Lehmann (eds), *The Routledge Companion to Makers of Modern Entrepreneurship*, London: Routledge, forthcoming.

Welter, Friederike and David Smallbone (2011a), 'Institutional perspectives on entrepreneurial behavior in challenging environments', *Journal of Small Business Management*, **49** (1), 107–125.

Welter, Friederike and David Smallbone (eds), (2011b), *Handbook of Research on Entrepreneurship Policies in Central and Eastern Europe*, Cheltenham, UK and Northampton, MA, USA: Edward Elgar Publishing.

Welter, Friederike and Mirela Xheneti (2013), 'Reenacting contextual boundaries – Entrepreneurial resourcefulness in challenging environments', in Andrew C. Corbett and Jerome Katz (eds), *Entrepreneurial Resourcefulness: Competing with Constraints* (Vol. 15), Bingley: Emerald, pp. 149–183.

Welter, Friederike, Candida G. Brush and Anne de Bruin (2014), 'The gendering of entrepreneurship context', Working Paper, 1/2014, Bonn: IfM Bonn.

Wright, Mike, James J. Chrisman, Jess H. Chua and Lloyd P. Steier (2014), 'Family enterprise and context', *Entrepreneurship Theory and Practice*, **38** (6), 1247–1260.

Zahra, Shaker A. (2007), 'Contextualizing theory building in entrepreneurship research', *Journal of Business Venturing*, **22** (3), 443–453.

Zahra, Shaker A. and Mike Wright (2011), 'Entrepreneurship's next act', *Academy of Management Perspectives*, **25** (4), 67–83.

Zahra, Shaker A., Mike Wright and Sondos G. Abdelgawad (2014), 'Contextualization and the advancement of entrepreneurship research', *International Small Business Journal*, **32** (5), 479–500.

2 Understanding entrepreneurial cognitions through the lenses of context

Malin Brännback and Alan L. Carsrud

Introduction

The concept of contexts is indeed complex, as we can see in this very book. Welter (2011) identifies spatial, temporal, institutional, social, and societal contexts. This can also be expressed as contexts that are cultural, linguistic, economic, or interpersonal. But, rather than arguing about which nomenclature is more appropriate, we will, through this chapter, make a case of the necessity of paying attention to the contexts of what we study (see also Chapter 7 by Fletcher and Selden and Chapter 9 by Chlosta). We want to stress this as we think contexts are not adequately described, observed, and paid attention to. We argue that contexts fundamentally impact every step in any research in social sciences, from the formation of research questions, choice of research approach, and method to the interpretation of results and suggestions for future research.

For example, can you define yourself independent of your relationships with others? Try defining a mother without discussing children. Using another example, can you think of any human behaviour that occurs outside a context? Try discussing Larry Page and Sergey Brin, the co-founders of *Google*, without discussing the impact of being graduate students at Stanford University and operating in Silicon Valley. Very clearly our answers to both of these questions are a short and very blunt *no*. We must remember that the basis of all communication and interpersonal relationships is embedded in specific contextual circumstances that shape intrinsic meanings, and this is especially the case with entrepreneurial cognitions.

While we think contexts are not adequately paid attention to in entrepreneurship research, we can also illustrate an area where context 'is everything'. Such an area would be biotechnology. The authors of this chapter have, for over a decade, been involved in biotechnology entrepreneurship. In this, the word 'biotechnology' is used to distinguish this kind of entrepreneurship as a special case of technology entrepreneurship. Take, for example, two reports written for the Finnish National Technology Agency (TEKES) in 2001 and 2005, and a book chapter in 2008. These were titled 'Finnish pharma cluster – vision 2010' (Brännback et al. 2001), 'Pharma development in Finland today and in 2015' (Brännback et al. 2004), and 'Strategy and strategic thinking in biotechnology entrepreneurship' (Carsrud et al. 2008). The very titles are highly context-specific with respect to place (spatial), industry (institution and economy), culture (societal), and temporality (texts written a decade before 2010 and 2015). At the same time as these reports are highly context-specific, something else takes place; they intentionally or unintentionally include some readers (those with an interest) and exclude others (those with no interest). This is to illustrate that, while contextualizing is important (we still think it is more important than not), it is problematic and also becomes a balancing act of inclusion and exclusion. It is a little bit like gravy: some love a lot of gravy, others do not want any, or want very little.

The myth of a single model of entrepreneurship

Even Steve Blank, the famous serial technology entrepreneur and investor, has admitted that the *Lean Start-up Model* (a customer-first model of starting firms) that he developed does not work in contexts that are different from Silicon Valley. Yet this model has been widely copied around the world as if context does not matter. The access to markets in Australia is very different from the access to markets in the United States, thus the business models developed in one are not going to be the same as the other, because the entrepreneurs perceive their environments very differently. However, the *Lean Start-up Model* assumes that would-be entrepreneurs have equal access to sophisticated customers, willing investors with plenty of money among other things. Blank readily admits this only occurs in Silicon Valley, as our example of *Google* above reflects. Clearly the entrepreneurial environment is going to vary from location to location.

What this also suggests is that an entrepreneur in Silicon Valley will have cognitions, motivations, expectations, and goals that reflect the unique context or environment in which they operate. These mental mind-sets will be very different from those held by an entrepreneur in a context where these resources are different or lacking. Yet when we look at research on this topic of entrepreneurial hot-beds, we see too many studies which seem to inadequately deal with context. Many completely ignore context as a factor, or they approach context as factors, which have to be controlled for as sources of error variance (Brännback et al. 2014). Age, religious beliefs, political orientation, gender, location, education levels, quality of research universities nearby, and firm size are all ways to measure various aspects of context and are frequently lumped together as control variables. Often, these demographic and geographic variables continue to be misused, despite warnings from decades ago (Carsrud et al. 1993).

The role of context

This continued lack of concern about context seems to be true in both entrepreneurship and family business research. For example, just because social norms don't seem to impact entrepreneurial intentions in American samples, this does not hold true for samples of entrepreneurs in, say, Finland, Germany, or the UK or elsewhere, like Turkey (Elfving et al. 2009; Sabah et al. in press). We firmly believe that, by understanding the importance of context, we can significantly inform both the practice of and research about entrepreneurship. From our experience, when we are confronted with research results that are somehow surprising or do not make sense upon first glance, we can find adequate explanations by looking at the context.

You should be asking: when was the research data collected? Where was the study done? How was the data collected? Who were the subjects of the study in terms of age, gender, and so on? If research was conducted in the middle of a recession, finds will be different than if the work was conducted during a boom period. Research on entrepreneurs in the United States will show different patterns from that conducted in the Middle East. Even the methods used will have an impact, as we all should be sensitive to common method variance. We believe the impact of context holds whether we choose to study success, failure, growth, entrepreneurial finance, women entrepreneurship, leadership succession, technology entrepreneurship, family business, or any other facets of entrepreneurial behaviour and cognitions.

The realization that context is important for understanding economics and human behaviours is not new, nor is it even revolutionary. While psychology often emphasizes cognitive processes over context it has rarely found context not to be an influencing factor. In the academic literature, contexts have been identified as spatial, temporal, institutional, social, and societal. The issue was brought back to the attention of the entrepreneurship research community through the article 'Contextualizing entrepreneurship – conceptual challenges and ways forward' (Welter 2011) and by noting the role of context in entrepreneurial intentions (Elfving et al. 2009). Some refer to these kinds of context-impacted cognitions as being 'grounded cognitions'. There is evidence that task context supports the flexible control of goal-directed cognitions which, in turn, are critical for entrepreneurial behaviour to be exhibited. Such grounding insures that these behaviours are functional and appropriate to that given context.

Context, cognition and behaviour

The key question remains: do we really understand the role of context and how various contexts impact our understanding of entrepreneurship, entrepreneurial cognitions, and eventually entrepreneurial behaviour? Our answer to this question is: *not very well, if at all.* To be honest, the title of this chapter is nearly a tautology, as understanding is, in itself, a cognitive process. Understanding how we *understand context* could therefore offer an alternative.

For the sake of illustration, let us start with a context most of us think we are very familiar with – a territorial or geographical context. We have all seen a world map

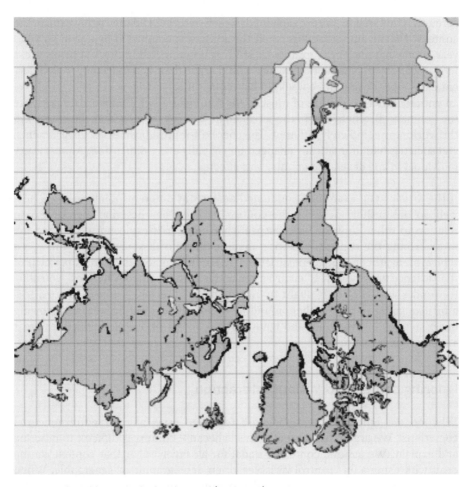

Source: Adapted from Brännback and Carsrud (2009, p. 76).

Figure 2.1   Map of the world upside-down

like the one in Figure 2.1. We have known it since our early childhood. It gives us a sense of safety and stability. Or does it? Take a look at the map – is it the familiar one? Or is it 'different'? Can you quickly find Poland, New York State, Stockholm, or Kuala Lumpur? It is difficult when the orientation changes from its normal context. You are not used to reading maps where north is at the bottom and east and west have flipped. After the advent of the Global Positioning System (GPS), most people who have cell phones or GPS devices do not know how to read maps anymore except to know where to turn on a road to get to a destination, and with Google self-driving cars that too may not be necessary.

Now, the next thing we want you to do is to take the latest issue of any entrepreneurship journal and pick any three articles. Go through every one of these articles carefully. How well is context explained in each of these? Did they really explain the context? Do the authors tell us when the study was conducted by a date, in what year, or at what place? For example, a study was conducted in the first three weeks in May of 2008 in New York City. We would argue that the same study with differ-ent dates, like the first three weeks in December of 2008 in New York City, will give an entirely different picture of most of the findings. Why? The first date is before the Lehmann Brothers' crash, the second date is three months after the crash, and the world was completely different. The context for most businesses, governments, and societies had dramatically changed on virtually every dimension. Almost every individual in any developed country was affected.

If the articles you examined conducted analysis at different points in time, how well do the authors describe the context and do they describe the context in relation to other contexts? We suspect that most articles do not do a good job in describing the context. Likewise, much is made of R squares, but when, in a typical study, the independent variables are accounting for less than 25 per cent of the variance and the rest is 'error variance due to the control variables', you start to wonder what we really ought to be looking at in terms of impact factors. It is a bit like going to the Parthenon and being totally focused on a flower growing out of a crack in the stones and ignoring the context of one of civilizations great architectural treasures.

Ignoring context–cognitions interaction

Why do we ignore context in most research, especially on entrepreneurial cognitions? We argue that, partially, this is because context is difficult to describe and explain. We assume context is equal for all involved, or that context can be dealt with using a few control variables, often demographic or geographic. When it is not, we simply do not understand why something did not have an impact. We recently have seen studies on entrepreneurial passion in which it was assumed that entrepreneurs are male and so are investors. The context of passion in male entre-preneurs may be very different from female entrepreneurs, and that perception will differ based on the gender of the investors as well. Thus, different contexts (gender of the entrepreneur) could find differential impacts of passion on investment deci-sions of investors who likewise have a gender context.

Another reason context is often ignored is because most studies in entrepreneur-ship are based on statistical analysis and quantitative modelling. It is awfully hard, if not impossible, to translate a context into a set of easily measured variables. So, we solve that issue with controlling simple demographic factors like age and firm size. Sometimes we see other control variables such as industry, gender, income level, and marital status, and in the limitation of the study section there is some-thing about an overly long questionnaire and low response rates. We rarely see discussions about religious beliefs impacting cognitions and behaviours, but obvi-ously they do. Including a short section describing the known context, and then including a discussion that takes in the implications of context on results, would help in understanding context. We may discover that we need to be researching the impact of context on entrepreneurial cognitions rather than assuming they are unimportant or irrelevant.

Social networks as context

While there has been much work on the role of networks in entrepreneurship, there is still much to be done, as networks clearly vary among entrepreneurs and not all networks are the same (Brännback 2003; Brännback et al. 2008). We certainly have examined the strength of weak ties in terms of context, but we have not really fully appreciated the impact of the networks in which one is embedded in as an entrepreneur.

For example, Centola (2015) has shown recently that if one's networks are too tightly interconnected, then that individual does not have social contact with people in other networks. They also have difficulty influencing those outside their group. That is, their context is very different from those individuals who have looser network boundaries. These are individuals who may have differences in various demographic factors, but still have similar activities and characteristics with others in their network. These looser network boundaries allow people to adopt new ideas and spread them to other groups.

However, when group boundaries do not exist at all, individuals have been shown to have nothing in common with those nearby and thus have very little influence over one another. The role of the boundaries of networks might well explain how some new ventures move into new markets easier than others. The point we want to make is that networks as a context for entrepreneurial activity still has a lot of research potential.

Research methods as context

We are suggesting that our research methods seem to have become a context in itself, irrespective of whether those methods are the best fit with our research questions. We are all familiar with the old saying 'if your only tool is a hammer, the world is going to be full with nails', and the *marteau du jour* seems to be structural equation modelling (SEM) regardless of whether it is the best approach. Fundamental to SEM is the assumption that relationships are linear and occur in some pre-set order. The notion of reciprocity of impact becomes problematic in SEM. Take, for example, efficacy impact intentions which then impact behaviours, which, in turn, impacts efficacy. This fails to accept that cognitions of efficacy occur within the context of people's behaviours. What we are saying is that our research methods often assume a context or order to events that may not be accurate.

The same goes for using case method in teaching. Here we are trying to generalize a case to learn a principle that may or may not occur again under a similar context. Understood this way, the method can become a contextual constraint that does not help us advance our understanding about various phenomena – rather, it produces just the opposite. If we study cases based on Silicon Valley entrepreneurs, and we are not in that location, how can we specify what we are to gain from that case to the context in which we are presently?

Context as a cognitive map

Context is essential for making sense of what we encounter. It serves as a form of cognitive map. Context becomes particularly important when we encounter something new, perhaps something we have never seen before. It can help us navigate by offering us a potential cognitive map based on past experiences, or assumptions we have generalized about a new context. The problem is that these maps may not be very accurate or even correct (as described above). Maps also have a nasty tendency of being stable, that is, humans are not very good at adjusting their cognitive maps to changes. Even when there are major events that occur, one's cognitive maps are often slow to change. They are in many ways beliefs and are not as malleable as, say, attitudes. We often try to stick to our old cognitive maps as long as possible until we are absolutely certain that the old one will no longer work.

Our existing cognitive maps are the result of what we like to call 'past experience and education'. To further complicate matters, past experience may be only partially relevant. Past experience in the same industry can be extremely beneficial, as we can assume that such a person knows key players and probably has a very good network (Brännback and Carsrud 2008; Brännback et al. 2009). But, if that past experience is based on how to manage and operate a large, multinational firm, it may not give much appropriate guidance for someone about to create a small firm (Brännback and Carsrud 2009). They hold a great map, but not for the current context.

This is because the individual's cognitive map lacks any experience in how to create a venture, or how to function in the resource-constrained small firm reality. In a newly created venture almost everything is new, and the challenge becomes the selection of open-ended possibilities and very limited financial resources. Likewise, experience in one sector of high technology does not allow for generalizations across different sectors or industries within high technology – for example, ICT and biotechnology or ICT and medical device, or food industry and biotechnology (Brännback and Carsrud 2008; Brännback et al. 2001, 2004; Carsrud et al. 2008). Often, cognitive maps are very dependent on the context of the industry, especially when dealing with regulations, market penetration strategies, and even potential investors (Carsrud et al. 2008).

Contextual maps for researchers

Entrepreneurs use cognitive maps to navigate the contexts in which they find themselves, and we also believe this is true of entrepreneurship researchers. We have long thought that any entrepreneurship professor should have created something, preferably a firm – even a research centre or a research group will do – as long as it is something. We have some research evidence that this experience, as well as the educational background (engineering versus business management), has an impact on how professors teach the topic. This may also be true about the types of research questions one choses to study in entrepreneurship. If you have had no experience of starting a venture, you are going to see things differently than if you had started something. This is a first-hand way of understanding how a person in the process of creating something understands the contextual reality.

The real paradox comes when a person, with 20 years of managerial experience, decides to undertake the considerable challenges in completing a PhD thesis in entrepreneurship. While their experience will help in asking questions of practical relevance, there are still huge methodological and theoretical challenges ahead. The context of scientific work is very different, even if the research is conducted on a topic that the researcher knows in great detail. The process of recontextualizing practice to fit a scientific context, and then again to a practical context, can sometimes become overwhelming.

How context is created

One way to look at context and how it is created and transmitted is to examine what influences contextual meaning, through behaviours, language, and symbols, as shown in Figure 2.2. These are impacted by conscious and unconscious beliefs as well as values. Contextual conflicts appear when there exist inconsistencies between behaviours, language, and symbols. The words we use imply context. Terms like *assertive*, *dominate*, and *powerful* have different implications when they are associated with men than with women. Likewise, terms like *caring*, *nurturing*, and *sensitive* have different meanings when applied to women rather than to men. When the language comes into conflict with the observed behaviours we have contextual conflicts. We admire *assertive behaviours* in entrepreneurs, but is this equally true if they are female entrepreneurs versus male? If a male entrepreneur wears a suit, is it seen the same way as if a female entrepreneur wore a pant suit? Here, the suit is a symbol, and provides signals for status. Sometimes, context has multiple sources, and can often provide mixed signals as to meaning.

Entrepreneurial success as context

Let us now look at cognition and context through the lenses of success. That is, what do we mean by success? How do we define success? Can we really define

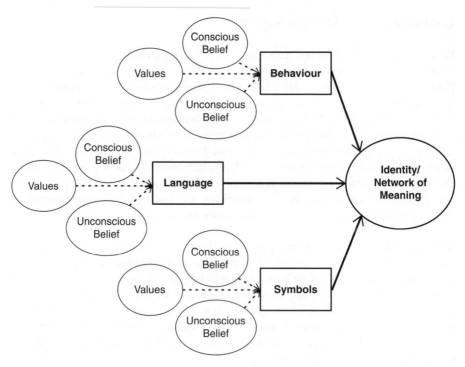

Source: Authors.

Figure 2.2   Factors influencing the creation of contextual meaning

success? To us, success is contextual; the definition of success will depend upon the context and obviously vary across individuals. How one defines success, we argue, depends almost entirely on the person doing the defining, and the values and conscious and unconscious beliefs they have with regards to success. Perceptions surrounding success will vary from person to person and culture to culture. Thus, success and failure in the eyes of an American will probably be very different from someone operating a new venture in the rural Andes.

We believe that the most important person to consider when looking at success is the individual entrepreneur and their perceptions of their success. The individual entrepreneur has a unique context. We have seen this rarely thought of as important to most researchers; it is as if the researcher is best able to define success, usually as revenues or sales, or even growth. In discussing the context of successful entrepreneurs, we need to be careful not to define success in solely a monetary fashion, or in terms of a given society's common conceptions of success. It is important that we respect the definitions that entrepreneurs have made for themselves. In this regard, we are taking a rather existential approach to success as a contextual concept. Then there is the contextual reality that some entrepreneurs see success as increasing their quality of life. Thus, an individual may adopt a lifestyle form of entrepreneurship, which is perfectly appropriate. Measuring success must take this context into account. This context is very different from the context of those focused on becoming wealthy (Brännback and Carsrud 2016).

Conclusions

Context matters, and digging deeper into the role of context in human perception, especially with respect to entrepreneurship, is long overdue. Entrepreneurship as a field of research is problematic since it is highly applied – and contextual. Even if it is about creating a venture – something that, in a sense, seems simple – the entire process is highly complex, particularly from a contextual perspective. While some of the problems an entrepreneur stumbles across may seem generic (finding customers, running out of cash, etc.), the way an entrepreneur solves these problems may differ across contexts and culture. As an 'outsider' to a particular context, interpretation of what is critical and significant can become difficult and sometimes overwhelming – it just does not make sense. The field of entrepreneurship research has been dominated by quantitative research methods, whose aim is to reduce the noise caused by context. Yet, this noise is, to our minds, absolutely vital for obtaining a deeper understanding of the phenomenon at study. To us, there are really no shortcuts here. If the field of entrepreneurship is to advance knowledge and our own understanding, we must do a better job of accounting for context and contexts.

Suggested readings

Komisar, R. (2000), *The Monk and the Riddle*, Boston, MA: Harvard Business School Press. This book offers a different look at entrepreneurship in that it challenges the dominant mental model of entrepreneurship of sacrificing your life to make a living. Rather, it rests on a mantra Alan and I like to promote; *choose a job that you love and you will never have to work a day in your life*. This is in fact the mental model we have found to be the prevailing model among successful entrepreneurs. This book also tells the story of many wanna-be entrepreneurs and how they come with what they think is a *brilliant idea* and how that idea needs to be moulded. Here, the wanna-be entrepreneur *wants to put FUN into funerals*, which perhaps seems like a strange way to approach the mere concept AND context of funerals as perceived by most people. It is usually not a FUN thing. It is about wanna-be entrepreneurs' struggle to understand the context he wants to create his venture in which seems to clash with his concept of a *brilliant business idea*. We have suggested this book to many real entrepreneurs in our classes. They have first found it an odd suggestion, but those who have read it have all come back and said *Yes, it is exactly like this, the best book they have had to read so far*. We hope you enjoy it.

Huff, Anne S. (1990), *Mapping Strategic Thought*, Chichester, UK: Wiley & Sons. This book gives you tools for delving into how people think about different strategic issues, and how to use these tools to construct bigger pictures, that is, understand contexts of various sorts. This book is an edited volume and offers the readers many different aspects of cognition in different contexts that are highly applicable to entrepreneurs and researchers madly trying to understand how entrepreneurs think about and construct their realities. If I think of books that have been important in my academic career, this is one of the major eye-openers into the field of managerial cognition. This book, together with the next, really spells out how differently we can look at, talk about, argue about, and perceive the same contexts we are active in.

Mintzberg, H., B. Ahlstrand, and J. Lampel (1998), *Strategy Safari*, London: Prentice Hall. If strategy is a safari, so too is entrepreneurship. Not only is the title of this book great, but it really shows the complexities of strategy theory. So too is entrepreneurship theoretically and especially in practice. The book offers several schools of thought. As a doctoral student in 1995 I participated in a course where Mintzberg used the manuscript to this book. The exercise we were given was to *pick one* school of thought that we thought firms used. Needless to say, this was ridiculous, as a firm does not 'use one particular school of thought'. Real life is far more complex, depending on *context and cognition*. What was missing from this manuscript was the last school of thought, in which Mintzberg offers his school of thought, which is a mixture of all the others. The take away was, of course, that schools of thought are good pedagogic tools, where we simplify at first to help us understand and learn so that then can add on complexities to deepen our understanding. The down side is that, when we present things as 'schools of thought', we tend to lock the minds of people and the schools become thought-constraining truths that are hard to challenge.

Koehn, N.F. (2001), *Brand New, How Entrepreneurs Earned Consumers' Trust from Wedgewood to Dell*, Boston, MA: Harvard Business School Press. In this book the development of six companies are described. It is about six entrepreneurs who worked systematically to build sustainable businesses and how those endeavours were anything from linear. It is how they understood their contexts and navigated their ventures to become ones which carry brands that are still valued by consumers worldwide. Each chapter contains rich contextual descriptions of the external realities of society in which these ventures were created, and how the entrepreneurs perceived opportunities and dealt with the challenges they faced.

Finally, we would like to recommend people to read biographies of anything from Peter the Great to Jack Welsh, and perhaps even less known people. In these books you find stories of people who have lived in very different contexts. Some of us find them interesting precisely for this reason; we learn something of these contexts, but perhaps even more so, we want to learn something about how these people have navigated in these contexts, implicitly through their cognitive capacities.

References

Brännback, Malin (2003), 'R&D collaboration: The role of *Ba* in knowledge-creating networks', *Knowledge Management Research and Practice*, **1** (1), 28–38.

Brännback, Malin and Alan L. Carsrud (2008), 'A decade of do they see what we see? A Nordic tale about perceptions of entrepreneurial opportunities, goals and growth', *Journal of Enterprising Culture*, **16** (1), 55–89.

Brännback, Malin and Alan Carsrud (2009), 'Cognitive maps in entrepreneurship: Researching sense making and action', in Alan Carsrud and Malin Brännback (eds), *Understanding the Entrepreneurial Mind: Opening the Black Box*, Heidelberg: Springer Verlag, pp. 75–96.

Brännback, Malin and Alan Carsrud (2016), *Fundamentals for Becoming a Successful Entrepreneur: From Business Idea to Launch and Management*, Old Tappen, NJ: Pearson.

Brännback, Malin, Alan Carsrud, and Niklas Kiviluoto (2014), *Understanding the Myth of High Growth Firms: The Theory of the Greater Fool*, New York, NY: Springer Verlag.

Brännback, M., Alan Carsrud, and William Schulze (2008), 'Exploring the role of Ba in family business context', *Journal of Information and Knowledge Management Systems*, **38** (1), 104–117.

Brännback, Malin, Alan L. Carsrud, Leif Nordberg, and Maija Renko (2009), 'Cognitive maps and perceptions of entrepreneurial growth: A quasi experimental study between technology entrepreneurs, corporate managers, and students', *Journal of Enterprising Culture*, **17** (1), 1–24.

Brännback, Malin, Markku Jalkanen, Kalevi Kurkela, and Esa Soppi (2004), 'Securing pharma development in Finland today and in 2015', *TEKES Technology Review*, 163/2004.

Brännback, Malin, Pekka Hyvönen, Hannu Raunio, Maija Renko, and Riitta Sutinen (2001), 'Finnish pharma cluster – vision 2010', *TEKES Technology Review*, 112/2001.

Carsrud, Alan, Malin Brännback, and Maija Renko (2008), 'Strategy and strategic thinking in biotechnology entrepreneurship', in Holger Patzelt and Thomas Brenner (eds), *Handbook of Bioentrepreneurship*, Heidelberg: Springer Verlag, pp. 83–99.

Carsrud, Alan L., Connie Marie Gaglio, and R. Kernochan (1993), 'Demographics in entrepreneurship research: Guidelines for the use of demographic data', in Jerome Katz and Robert Brockhaus, Sr. (eds), *Advances in Entrepreneurship, Firm Emergence, and Growth*, Volume I, Greenwood, CT: JAI Press, pp. 49–82.

Centola, Damon (2015), 'The social origins of networks and diffusion', *American Journal of Sociology*, **120** (5), 1295–1338.

Elfving, Jennie, Malin Brännback, and Alan Carsrud (2009), 'Towards a contextual model of entrepreneurial intentions', in Alan Carsrud and Malin Brännback (eds), *Understanding the Entrepreneurial Mind: Opening the Black Box*, Heidelberg: Springer Verlag, pp. 23–34.

Sabah, S., Akin Koçak, and Alan Carsrud (in press), 'The impact of family, culture, religion, and nationalism on new venture creation: Exploratory cases of Turkish entrepreneurial family firms', *Journal of Small Business Management*.

Welter, Friederike (2011), 'Contextualizing entrepreneurship – conceptual challenges and ways forward', *Entrepreneurship Theory & Practice*, **35** (1), 165–183.

3 'After' context

Chris Steyaert[1]

At Context there is no place to park. (Bruno Latour 2005, p. 167)

Context enthuses

If it is true, as Theodore Schatzki (2002, p. 60) claimed a long time ago, that '[t]he expression "context" has assumed virtually mythic allure in recent decades of social and humanistic theory', it seems as if the debate on context in entrepreneurship studies is far more recent (Zahra 2007; Zahra, Wright and Abdelgawad 2014) and uphill (Welter 2011). The pleas in favour of contextualized approaches of entrepreneurship (Chalmers and Shaw 2015; Welter 2011) come at a moment where context has elsewhere been heavily criticized, even actually is discarded. Such a changed context makes the current debate in entrepreneurship studies even more stimulating and sweet: 'Nothing works better than a little creative de(con)struction', notes the entrepreneurship scholar promptly.

In this chapter where I engage with some of these more critical remarks (Felski 2011; Latour 2005) and mostly will question and (and try to) reframe the idea of contextualization – asking the question whether there is an 'after' to context? – let me start with some opening reflection and – ironically enough – with a short personal contextualization, a little storytelling. Such opening should illustrate that to consider context as part of empirical research in entrepreneurship studies cannot be done without theorizing the notion of context itself (Welter 2011) and to align accordingly the paradigmatic and practical position of researchers as 'understanding context is largely shaped by the ontological and epistemological stances assumed by researchers' (Chalmers and Shaw 2015, p. 2).

The notion of context has kept me busy ever since I got involved with the linguistic turn (Steyaert 2004) and learned to consider the empirical data I generated as text. Interpreting a text was first of all an issue of considering the feasible 'con-texts' transpiring in the text. A text became to me a living meshwork where one could delve into and trace storylines, genres, and discourses, but also intonations, hesitations and translations. Like a story, a text became a ball of string full of knots, impossible to unravel but irresistible not to try so and to rearrange (Steyaert 2007a). Conceptually, I became equipped with a Bakhtinian view

(Steyaert 2004) on context. His triad of concepts – addressivity, heteroglossia and dialogue (see below) – helped me to somehow disentangle the complexities of text interpretation and to understand how a text is a living, creative process of constantly reinventing, in the way the Argentinian writer Jorge Luis Borges described this in *Seven Nights* (1984, pp. 76–77):

> When the book lies unopened, it is literally, geometrically, a volume, a thing among other things. When we open it, when the book surrenders itself to its reader, the aesthetic event occurs. And even for the same reader the same book changes, for we change; we are the river of Heraclitus, who said that the man of yesterday is not the [wo]man of today, who will not be the [woman or] man of tomorrow. We change incessantly, and each reading of a book, each rereading, each memory of that rereading, reinvents the text. The text too is the changing river of Heraclitus.

Text and context became related as inter-text. Simultaneously, I was (re)reading Eco's *Name of the Rose*, a book (Eco 1984 [1980]) that performs the linguistic turn in fiction form. It offers plural readings as many as the name of the rose itself can assume 'because the rose' – so says Eco (1984, p. 506) in a postscript – 'is a symbolic figure so rich in meanings that by now it hardly has any meaning left': as love story, as *Bildungsroman*, as a history of religious struggle, as a tale of a lost book on Comedy (by Aristotle) and so on. Of course – especially with the movie adaptation in the back of our mind (Annaud 1986), we remember it as a historical murder story, where the Franciscan friar William of Baskerville and the Benedictine novice Adso of Melk remind us respectively of Arthur Conan Doyle's character of Sherlock Holmes, in his book *The Hound of the Baskervilles*, paired with his assistant 'Watson', together trying to solve the mystery of the various murders. In the blind librarian Jorge from Burgos, we recognize indeed Jorge Luiz Borges, once director of Argentina's National Library who had a major influence on Eco (not least on his use of the library (and knowledge) in the form of a labyrinth). But above all, Eco, professor in semiotics – Umberto de Bologna as he calls himself in the novel – practices his understandings of language in a fictional form; there is a crucial dialogue (Eco 1984, p. 306) between Brother William and his pupil Adso where intertextuality could not be better explained in academic fashion:

> It seemed to me, as I read this page, that I had read some of these words before, and some phrases that are almost the same, which I have seen elsewhere, return to my mind. It seems to me, indeed, that this page speaks of something there has been talk about during these past days. . . .. But I cannot recall what. I must think it over. Perhaps, I'll have to read other books.

> (Adso:) Why? To know what one book says you must read others?

> (William:) At times this can be so. Often books speak of other books. Often a harmless book is like a seed that will blossom into a dangerous book, or it is the other way around: it is the sweet fruit of a bitter stem. In reading Albert, couldn't I learn what Thomas might have said? Or in reading Thomas, know what Averroës said?

True, I said amazed. Until then I had thought each book spoke of the things, human or divine, that lie outside books. Now I realized that not infrequently books speak of books: it is as if they spoke among themselves. In the light of this reflection, the library seemed all the more disturbing to me. It was then the place of a long, centuries-old murmuring, an imperceptible dialogue between one parchment and another, a living thing, a receptacle of powers not to be ruled by a human mind, a treasure of secrets emanated by many minds, surviving the death of those who had produced them or had been their conveyors.

Like a generative novel, a good contextual analysis creates multiplicity (Steyaert 2012).

Context performs

Contexualization implies relating text-with-context. In narrative and discursive studies (Hjorth and Steyaert 2004), language is studied in its use, in how it is performed. Conversation, talking, writing, any discursive practice happens in situ. Text and context imply each other, in a dynamic, intertextual play. Thus, if you work with discourse analysis (Gee 2014) or narrative analysis (De Fina 2008) one has to deal with contextualization *tout court*. For instance, storytelling lives and becomes alive from its relationship to context, which gives it oxygen, cues, genres, and many other things: in short, a linguistic-material apparatus. Narrative analysis cannot happen in a social vacuum (Atkinson, Delamont and Housley 2008) as stories (of all kind) are highly context-sensitive, being told in relationship to and drawing upon their social, linguistic and cultural context. Thus, it is not 'just' researchers that can contextualize their studies, but contextualization has to be part of the study object itself, as this allows understanding how storytelling (and other forms of speaking and acting) is enabled through contextualization. Contextualization is not something we can only do as researchers (see Chapter 7 by Fletcher and Selden) but it is central to how we understand the entrepreneurial process as contextualized, as always in situ and mediated. Context is then not from the outside, exogenously, 'brought in' by researchers but part of (constituting) the entrepreneurial process.

As said, the literary theorist Bakhtin (1984) provides very apt conceptual tools to understand this. Language is itself a 'con-text' as it is featured by heteroglossia, by the simultaneous presence of several, co-habiting, social 'languages'. Speaking is heteroglot as language is shot through with a mixture of social and historical 'back-vocals' which echo social backgrounds and reverberate past uses. Furthermore, we all speak with accents and intonations, which colour our voices and point at the worlds we have crossed and mixed during our lives. In the notion of addressivity, Bakhtin shows also how every utterance is coloured by the (horizon of the) addressee – an entrepreneur pitching to a financer sitting at the other end of the table or the imagined client that might one day enter one's business. In conversation, we are able to take into account the contours of the audiences we address. That is why Bakhtin considers language as dialogical and utterances as inter-texts since

[t]he life of the word is contained in its transfer from one mouth to another, from one context to another context, from one social collective to another, from one generation to another generation. In this process the word does not forget its own path and cannot completely free itself from the power of those concrete contexts into which it has entered. When a member of a speaking collective comes upon a word, it is not as a neutral word of language, not as a word free from the aspirations and evaluations of others, uninhabited by others' voices. No, [s]he receives the word from another's voice and filled with that other voice. The word enters his [her] context from another context, permeated with the interpretations of others. His [her] own thought finds the world already inhabited. (Bakthin 1984, p. 201)

Of course, a discursive practice is only one form of practice and conversation one form of interaction. Therefore, with an increasing interest in practice-based approaches in entrepreneurship studies, we can see an expansion of the range of endogenous approaches that study the real-time functioning of context as part of ongoing interactions. For instance, Chalmers and Shaw (2015) examine episodes of situated social interaction in the form of question and answer interactions between pitchers of entrepreneurial ideas and jury members, drawing upon conversation analysis and ethnomethodology. Together with the conversation analyst Schegloff (1997), the authors emphasize that priority must 'be afforded to those contextual factors that are oriented to by actors themselves in a specific social interaction' (Chalmers and Shaw 2015, p. 4). It is thus up to analysts to document how actors recognize features of context as they fade in and out of relevance for a particular episode of interaction. In turn, this interaction episode forms the context for a following episode, so that context is incrementally produced.

Therefore, context cannot be a priori fixed as if experts or researchers would know in advance what institutional or cultural factors determine how a specific interaction unfolds. This endogenous position of conversation analysis thus criticizes often the ways in which critical discourse analysis is said to be done where 'a lot of a priori contextualization goes on' (Blommaert 2001, p. 15), turning context into mere background. In return, conversation analysis with its preference for single instances of talk is often criticized for not being able to accommodate translocal phenomena, where issues are made relevant post hoc in later sequences (see Blommaert 2001): meanings can emerge after several interactions – for instance, a series of meetings – have taken place or ideas can be reviewed after some interaction already finished – for instance, when one discusses with a colleague how a certain meeting had evolved.

With others (Chalmers and Shaw 2015), I would like to see that the field of entrepreneurship studies subscribes more to linguistic and practice-based approaches. That is not just a matter of underlining the important role of qualitative methods (which have been recognized as one of the institutional barriers; see Bamberger 2008; Welter 2011), but also deepening out the practical ways in which we respect texts, interactions and practices as primary sources of data generation and understand the everyday talk, conversation and interaction through which we enact our lives, as a core 'unit of analysis' to study entrepreneurship: if it is often stressed that every text has/is a context, we should also realize that there is no context without text; in a similar vein, practices do not happen in vacuum, outside arrangements which, in their turn, cannot exist outside the performance of practices (Schatzki 2002). So could we show a little more enthusiasm for the text-part in the word context – in all its forms and performances – as entrepreneurship studies' (most) important unit of analysis? Here, the possibilities of narrative, discursive, dialogical, conversational and other (sociolinguistic) forms of interaction could be significantly increased, in order to study directly contextualized (entrepreneurial) performance (see Blommaert 2001, 2015).

Let me give an example. Narratives form often 'frequently rehearsed performances' (Atkinson, Delamont and Housley 2008, p. 101), which are subtly adapted to but also inspired by constant forms of recontextualization. Stories allow entrepreneurship scholars to dig in all kinds of urban or rural milieus, giving voice to less known or to-be-expected stories of entrepreneurial endeavours. For instance, we could study the entrepreneurial companies that have invented the concept of messenger bikers: this would give insight in the micro-stories of couriers who as independent contractors 'identify with an entrepreneurial spirit and are driven to hustle and earn as much as possible' (Pupo and Noack 2014, p. 342). This comes with a precarious employment situation based on 'believing that their entrepreneurial status provides them with a degree of freedom that has usually been absent from their work experience' (Pupo and Noack 2014, p. 337). We could engage with the entrepreneurial imagination that instigated this 'new' form of 'delivery' companies that became initiated in the 1980s, recontextualizing the possibilities of the biker as messenger, an activity which is as old as the bike itself (and thus would inquire a history of the meaning and use of biking); we could study how the concept of the biker messenger has travelled to various contexts, where it has become increasingly used in certain countries but not at all in other countries. We could contemplate how to study this through contextualized research and undertake, as Fincham (2006) did, an ethnography by becoming temporarily a biker oneself. We could follow the quasi-legal trajectories that these bikers ride throughout the city, and how they develop a different urban knowledge, far removed from what the city planners had drawn on their maps.

Context challenges

So if we have already such a quite broad repertoire of contextual understandings in linguistic and practice-based approaches where contextualization is studied in vivo, the question needs to be asked why there is so little reference to these contributions in the current hammering on the importance of context in entrepreneurship studies. In my view, this has to do with the fact that many scholars vow for a 'context light' version, not taking seriously the challenges that come with context (as inter-text). More particularly, it challenges us to take on different epistemological and ontological stances, which seems to be the elephant in the room that several (mainstream) scholars refuse to acknowledge. After all, the notion of context was invented to turn analysis away from its universalistic ambitions and to overcome the problems of contingency theory – with its quasi-endless series of contingent factors that could interfere in the generalizability of causal relations. Contextualization became the core operation and thought-mode of interpretive scholars and of textual analysts. For instance, in developing a processual theory through a narrative approach (Steyaert 1997), which was also specified as a narrative-contextualist epistemology inspired by Pepper's world hypothesis of contextualism (Steyaert and Bouwen 1997), I took issue with the many levels and entitative variables that scholars interested in entrepreneurial processes seemed able to a priori claim. Therefore, I argued that '[a] full process theory would consist of one process, by transcending the distinction between micro (for example, the entrepreneur) and macro (for example, the environment) models of entrepreneurship and becoming a [kind of] meso-approach where interactions are described in their sociocultural context' (Steyaert 1997, p. 17). What contextual description then means, remained rather 'vague' at the time as processes-in-context were situated 'within a larger context—a framework of events, circumstances, situations, settings, and niches' (Steyaert 1997, p. 18).

Furthermore, I made a plea that entrepreneurship studies should be oriented along the ideas of local knowledge (Geertz 1983), where entrepreneurship scholars would generate 'knowledge-in-context', 'always local, situated in a local culture and embedded in organizational sites' (Steyaert 1997, p. 29). Later on, what knowledge-in-context could mean became more specified in a special issue (see Steyaert and Katz 2004): in connecting entrepreneurship to the societal context, a political understanding of context became obvious in the form of a geopolitics of everyday entrepreneurship. The idea was to stimulate the research agenda of entrepreneurship by visiting surprising and unexpected, geographical sites (we avoided the term contexts; see Schatzki 2002) ranging between narrow scenes and wider landscapes, by relocating the understanding of entrepreneurship in a multi-discursive space, and by zooming in on the minutiae and detail of everyday sociality that constitutes entrepreneurial processes.

Contextualization can thus not be done without also considering the paradigmatic infrastructure that comes with it. However, it seems that several discussions on context in entrepreneurship studies remain inconsequential as contextualization remains part of the grand agenda of 'advancement' (Zahra et al. 2014) grounded in a neo-positivistic research ideology, so that we can read statements of the following kind: 'considering context could guide theory building and enhance our theories' predictive powers' (Zahra and Wright 2011, p. 72). How come contextualization enhances predictability? Is this not contingency thinking covered up as context? Why are we serving old wine in new bottles (see Chapter 1 by Welter, Gartner and Wright)?

There is thus an urgent task for entrepreneurship scholars to make the discussion on the meaning and use of context(ualization) more controversial, giving the concept the force it could have for entrepreneurship research, namely to be more about the assumptions underlying its research practices. If Zahra (2007) complains that entrepreneurship scholars too often borrow concepts from other disciplines without acknowledging how to do this in a reflexive way, this is above all true for the 'theories' and understanding of context itself. So, if Felski (2011, p. 573) qualifies context as 'an endlessly contested concept' (in literary and cultural studies) it should not lose its potential to bring some controversy to the ways in which we imagine entrepreneurship research rather than to become assimilated in neo-positivist research ideals. Indeed, this is also what Welter (2011, p. 177) argues for, that the discussion on context in entrepreneurship studies should be developed by 'working with disciplines like anthropology, sociology, and others [– and here I would add literary theory and cultural studies], which possess some of the tools and concepts entrepreneurship scholars need to explore the variety, depths, and richness of contexts'.

In my experience, there is (still) very little desire to engage with such fundamental debates in entrepreneurship studies. For instance, I mentioned earlier that con-textualization is foremost a notion that can be studied if one adopts a linguistic turn perspective, but I cannot find a footnote on the idea that context is first of all text(ual) in the articles that are considered dominant readings of this issue in entrepreneurship studies. Therefore, I need to ask the question if context can 'really' matter, if it can make a difference for how we enact entrepreneurship research, paradigmatically, practically, reflexively or if we are just going to hide behind it. That is also why Welter underlines the need to develop 'theories of context', which I think we need to respond to by exploring many more current conceptualizations of how context is being debated in 'other' fields. What if one of the most important debates about context is currently to 'drop' the notion altogether? Can we accommodate such a stance in how the field of entrepreneurship studies 'thinks' about context?

Context stinks

Here is another slogan: 'Context stinks!' Indeed, at the very moment, where entrepreneurship scholars seem to agree that context is no longer 'optional' (Felski 2011, p. 573) – even for entrepreneurship studies – the notion gets frontally tackled. Could it be said with more denigration than in the way the Dutch architect Rem Koolhaas who as 'persuasive polemicist' (Filler 1996) likes controversy has formulated it: 'context stinks' (see Latour 2005, p. 148; Latour and Yaneva 2008, p. 87; Koolhaas and Mau 1995). With the idea that context could be done away with, it is underlined that context

> stinks only because it stays in place too long and ends up rotting. Context would not stink so much if we could see that it, too, moves along and flows just as buildings do. What is a context in flight? It is made of the many dimensions that impinge at every stage on the development of a project: 'context' is this little word that sums up all the various elements

that have been bombarding the [architectural] project from the beginning—fashions spread by critiques in architectural magazines, clichés that are burned into the minds of some clients, customs entrenched into zoning laws, types that have been taught in art and design schools by professors, visual habits that make neighbors rise against new visual habits in formation, and so on. And of course, every new project modifies all the elements that try to contextualize it, and provokes contextual mutations. (Latour and Yaneva 2008, pp. 87–88)

Indeed, Koolhaas's denunciation of context would not be so notorious by now, if not taken up by Bruno Latour and how he 'finished it off' with a wink: 'context is simply a way of stopping the description when you are tired or too lazy to go on' (Latour 2005, p. 148). In *Re-assembling the Social*, Latour (2005) undertakes a notorious attempt – a dialogue resembling the earlier William–Adso interaction – to convince a doctoral student (in Organization Studies) to question the need for context as crucial, and to even let go of it. After all, context is a symbol for the power of scientists to explain to laypersons their limited access to their own understanding of their lives, by 'putting them in context' and thus by putting them 'in prison' (Latour 2005, p. 116). So on the question of the student 'But you always need to put things into a context, don't you' (Latour 2005, p. 144), Latour answers:

I have never understood what context meant, no. A frame makes a picture look nicer, it may direct the gaze better, increase the value, allows to date it, but it doesn't add anything to the picture. The frame, or the context, is precisely the sum of factors that make no difference to the data, what is common knowledge about it. If I were you, I would abstain from frameworks altogether. Just describe the state of affairs at hand.

Refusing to choose between the Scylla of objectivist and the Charybdis of interpretive sociology, Latour proposes a third, descriptive form that re-instates the symmetry between objects and subjects: objects 'might look a bit more complicated, folded, multiple, complex, and entangled' (Latour 2005, p. 144) than what objectivists have to say, while there is more than human meaning as interpretivists would have it, as we have to acknowledge materiality and the non-human. Therefore, actor–network theory or ANT's tenet is 'that actors themselves make everything, including their own frames, their own theories, their own contexts, their own metaphysics, even their own ontologies. So the direction to follow would be more descriptions I am afraid' (Latour 2005, p. 147). Latour wants to get done with the micro–macro distinction that so has dominated and divided the history of sociology, so he wants to keep (descriptions of) the social 'flat'. Tracing these associations then turns social science work into a 'slowciology' (Latour 2005, p. 165). So, there is no context or society (that controls human practices) to fall back on. Instead,

the social just is the act and the fact of association, the coming together of phenomena to create multiple assemblages, affinities, and networks. It exists only in its instantiations, in the sometimes foreseeable, sometimes unpredictable ways in which ideas, texts, images, people, and objects couple and uncouple, attach and break apart. (Felski 2011, p. 578)

Therefore, the strategy indeed is

> to slow down at each step, to forego theoretical shortcuts and to attend to the words of our fellow actors rather than overriding them – or overwriting them – with our own. The social, in other words, is not a preformed being but a doing, not a hidden entity underlying the realm of appearance, but the ongoing connections, disconnections, and reconnections between countless actors. (Felski 2011, p. 578)

From this angle, it does not make sense to analyse spatial and temporal dimensions separately (see Chapter 5 by Lippmann and Aldrich), as these

> interconnections are temporal as well as spatial; woven out of threads criss-crossing through time, they connect us to what comes before, enmeshing us in extended webs of obligation and influence. Time is not a tidy sequence of partitioned units, but a profusion of whirlpools and rapids, eddies and flows, in which objects, ideas, images, and texts from different moments swirl, tumble, and collide in ever-changing combinations and constellations. New actors jostle alongside those with thousand-year histories; inventions and innovations exist alongside the very traditions they excoriate. (Felski 2011, p. 578)

Can we keep hiding behind the notion of context?

So, 'who, in their right mind ... could feasibly take issue with the idea of context as such', asks Rita Felski (2011, p. 573). What smells does it produce that we should run away from it as quickly as possible, now that entrepreneurship scholars recognize context 'as being of acute analytical importance' (Chalmers and Shaw 2015, p. 3)? What if we accept Latour's premise that referring to context is a form of laziness (or tiredness), which we should try to overcome? Do we have to let go of the context-debate(s), completely? Have we to give up context as a 'place-holder', because 'at Context, there is no place to park' (Latour 2005, p. 167). I think we have to admit that the problems are manifold, tough and hard to contain, as one problem brings along more problems. For instance, if we agree to question 'any notion of history or context as a stable ground' (Felski 2011, p. 574) or go along with the warnings 'against the perils of an overcontextualization that wreaks violence on the distinctiveness' (Felski 2011, p. 574) of its object, how can we proceed? Do we need to follow a complete overhaul in our thinking as Latour does or can we also weaken the smell a little by reconfiguring understandings of context?

As suggested in the 'context performs' section, there are other forms of processual theorizing (than ANT; see Steyaert 2007b) that can help us to overcome the understanding of history or context as 'a box' (Felski 2011) or as 'a bucket' (see Chalmers and Shaw 2015) so that we can account 'for the transtemporal movement and affective resonance of particular texts' as Felski proposes (2011, p. 574). Translated to entrepreneurship: even if entrepreneurship is as much a form of history-breaking as history-making, we have to study the movements and translations of an entrepreneurial idea (text), why its texts appeal and why they resonate as new forms of doing and thinking things. After all, entrepreneurial endeavours cannot be reduced to being histories, they are about futures. Entrepreneurial performances are not residues of histories; they are imaginative translations, and follow surprising trajectories based on mutations. Can we account as much for their singularity as for their worldliness? That is a core issue to overcome: 'The singular disadvantage of the "context concept" is that it inveigles us into endless reiterations of the same dichotomies: text versus context, word versus world, literature versus society and history, internalist versus externalist explanations' (Felski 2011, p. 576). Therefore, Felski thinks we have to invest in 'transhistorical methodologies or the tracing of cross-temporal networks' (p. 577) in a similar vein as Blommaert (2001) suggested to work with a processual understanding of context in the form of text trajectories and data histories.

But there is more to overcome, according to Felski. Besides context's bias towards historical origin, another issue lies 'in the tacit beliefs about agency, causality, and control that steer acts of contextualization, in cultural studies as elsewhere . . . we inflate context, in short, in order to deflate text' (Felski 2011, pp. 581–582). Felski thinks there is an imbalance between the powers of context versus text. So Felski follows Latour's re-distribution of agency across human and non-humans, texts and objects. An actor is not just a human performer, but anything that can modify a state of affairs by making a difference (see Latour 2005, p. 71). An actor, however, is never alone (in terms of agency – what we often claim about the entrepreneur), as actors 'only become actors via their relations with other phenomena, as mediators and translators linked in extended constellations of cause and effect' (Felski 2011, p. 583). Of course, this redistribution in no way implies that we re-install again the agency of an individual actor like the entrepreneur or the stories s/he tells: 'The glory of the "text" is not to be defended by rescuing it from the slavering jaws of "context"' (Felski 2011, p. 584).

If there is some specialness and distinctiveness to an entrepreneurial endeavour, this comes by how its connections have become assembled and all those that have become attached. So besides translations, we need to study how attachments and attractions are solicited and sustained. Indeed, any entrepreneurial text written is a co-acted performance, an assemblage of many heterogeneous elements that become attached across time and space, over and over again. Therefore, context should not be used as a (static) place-holder we try to hide behind: context should not stop the description of an entanglement but actually support its realization. In that sense, context dissolves as it becomes woven into and spirals along with the unfolding of entrepreneurial becomings.

NOTE

1 I thank Friederike Welter and Bill Gartner as editors of this book for setting up such an inspiring context to write this chapter as well as for the feedback they provided. My colleagues – especially Tim Lehmann, Christoph Michels, Julia Nentwich and Bernhard Resch – at the Research Institute for Organizational Psychology gave me excellent back-up to write this text.

Suggested readings

Blommaert, J. (2001), 'Context is/as critique', *Critique of Anthropology*, **21** (1), 13–32. This article provides excellent arguments about the pitfalls through which both critical discourse analysis and conversation analysis (mis)treat context and (self) undermine its critical potential. The author also gives some inspiring suggestions to reclaim some forgotten contexts such as the use of text trajectories – the ways in which a text shifts across contexts – and data histories – the ways in which data are socio-historically situated.

Chalmers, D.M. and E. Shaw (2015), 'The endogenous construction of entrepreneurial contexts: A practice-based perspective', *International Small Business Journal*, published online before print 21 September 2015, doi: 10.1177/0266242615589768. The authors provide a well-argued and philosophically founded rationale for the use of a contextualized approach. Drawing upon ethnomethodology and conversation analysis, they steer in the direction of an endogenous understanding of entrepreneurial contexts and illustrate this through an empirical analysis of (video recorded) business plan pitch question and answer interactions.

Felski, R. (2011), '"Context stinks!"', *New Literary History*, **42** (4), 573–591. Drawing on Bruno Latour's argument that referring to context is a form of (empirical) tiredness or laziness as one stops the descriptions, Rita Felski applies these ANT-inspired ideas to the analysis of literary texts. Anyone interested in (empirical) text interpretation in entrepreneurship studies needs to read this already classic article. Hopefully, the stink then disappears from certain misguided approaches to context in entrepreneurship studies.

Schatzki, T.R. (2002), *The Site of the Social. A Philosophical Account of the Constitution of Social Life and Change*, University Park, PA: The Pennsylvania State University Press. In this conceptually erudite book, context is made centrepiece to explain the philosophical foundation of sociality and change through the idea of site ontologies. It is explained with empirical examples that a site-context is composed of a mesh of orders – seen as arrangements of entities – and practices – seen as organized activities. Theodore Schatzki's proposal thus relates and confronts 'theories of arrangements' (drawing upon Latour, Callon, Foucault, Deleuze and Guattari, and others) with 'practice theories' (referring to Bourdieu, Dreyfus, Giddens and others).

References

Annaud, Jean-Jacques (1986), *The Name of the Rose*, Columbia Pictures.

Atkinson, Paul, Sara Delamont and William Housley (2008), *Contours of Culture. Complex Ethnography and the Ethnography of Complexity*, Walnut Creek: Altamira Press.

Bakhtin, Mikhail M. (1984), *Problems of Dostoevsky's Poetics*, edited and translated by C. Emerson, Manchester: Manchester University Press.

Bamberger, Peter (2008), 'From the editors: Beyond contextualization: Using context theories to narrow the micro–macro gap in management research', *Academy of Management Journal*, **51** (5), 839–846.

Blommaert, Jan (2001), 'Context is/as critique', *Critique of Anthropology*, **21** (1), 13–32.

Blommaert, Jan (2015), 'Chronotopes, scales, and complexity in the study of language in society', *Annual Review of Anthropology*, **44**, 105–116.

Borges, Jorge Luis (1984), *Seven Nights*, New York: New Directions.

Chalmers, Dominic M. and Eleanor Shaw (2015), 'The endogenous construction of entrepreneurial contexts: A practice-based perspective', *International Small Business Journal*, published online before print 21 September 2015, doi: 10.1177/0266242615589768.

De Fina, Anna (2008), 'Who tells the story and why? Micro and macro contexts in narrative', *Text & Talk*, **28** (3), 421–442.

Eco, Umberto (1984 [1980]), *The Name of the Rose*, New York: Harcourt.

Felski, Rita (2011), '"Context stinks!"', *New Literary History*, **42** (4), 573–591.

Filler, Martin (1996), 'The master builder', *The New York Times*, 17 March.

Fincham, Benjamin (2006), 'Back to the "old school": Bicycle messengers, employment and ethnography', *Qualitative Research*, **6** (2), 187–205.

Gee, James Paul (2014), *An Introduction to Discourse Analysis. Theory and Method*, London: Routledge.

Geertz, Clifford (1983), *Local Knowledge*, New York: Basic Books.

Hjorth, Daniel and Chris Steyaert (eds) (2004), *Narrative and Discursive Approaches in Entrepreneurship*, Cheltenham, UK and Northampton, MA, USA: Edward Elgar Publishing.

Koolhaas, Rem and Bruce Mau (1995), *S, M, L, XL*, New York: Monacelli Press.

Latour, Bruno (2005), *Re-assembling the Social: An Introduction to Actor–Network Theory*, Oxford: Oxford University Press.

Latour, Bruno and Albena Yaneva (2008), 'Give me a gun and I will make all buildings move. An ANT's view of architecture', in R. Geiser (ed.), *Explorations in Architecture: Teaching, Design, Research*, Basel: Birkhäuser, pp. 80–89.

Pupo, Norene and Andrea M. Noack (2014), 'Organizing local messengers: Working conditions and barriers to unionization', *Canadian Journal of Sociology*, **39** (3), 331–358.

Schatzki, Theodore R. (2002), *The Site of the Social. A Philosophical Account of the Constitution of Social Life and Change*, University Park, PA: The Pennsylvania State University Press.

Schegloff, Emanuel A. (1997), 'Whose text? Whose context?', *Discourse & Society*, **8** (2), 165–187.

Steyaert, Chris (1997), 'A qualitative methodology for process studies of entrepreneurship: Creating local knowledge through stories', *International Studies of Management and Organization*, **27** (3), 13–33.

Steyaert, Chris (2004), 'The prosaics of entrepreneurship', in Daniel Hjorth and Chris Steyaert (eds), *Narrative and Discursive Approaches in Entrepreneurship*, Cheltenham, UK and Northampton, MA, USA: Edward Elgar Publishing, pp. 8–21.

Steyaert, Chris (2007a), 'Of course that is not the whole (toy) story: Entrepreneurship and the cat's cradle', *Journal of Business Venturing*, **22** (5), 733–751.

Steyaert, Chris (2007b), '"Entrepreneuring" as a conceptual attractor? A review of process theories in 20 years of entrepreneurship studies', *Entrepreneurship & Regional Development*, **19** (6), 453–477.

Steyaert, Chris (2012), 'Making the multiple: Theorizing processes of entrepreneurship and organization', in Daniel Hjorth (ed.), *Organizational Entrepreneurship*, Cheltenham, UK and Northampton, MA, USA: Edward Elgar Publishing, pp. 151–168.

Steyaert, Chris and René Bouwen (1997), 'Telling stories of entrepreneurship. Towards a narrative-contextual epistemology for entrepreneurial studies', in Rik Donckels and Asko Miettinen (eds), *Entrepreneurship and SME Research: On its Way to the Next Millennium*, Ashgate: Aldershot, pp. 47–62.

Steyaert, Chris and Jerome Katz (2004), 'Reclaiming the space of entrepreneurship in society: Geographical, discursive and social dimensions', *Entrepreneurship and Regional Development*, **16** (3), 179–196.

Welter, Friederike (2011), 'Contextualizing entrepreneurship – Conceptual challenges and ways forward', *Entrepreneurship Theory and Practice*, **35** (1), 165–184.

Zahra, Shaker A. (2007), 'Contextualising theory building in entrepreneurship research', *Journal of Business Venturing*, **22** (3), 443–452.

Zahra, Shaker A. and Mike Wright (2011), 'Entrepreneurship's next act', *Academy of Management Perspectives*, **25** (4), 67–83.

Zahra, Shaker A., Mike Wright and Sondos G. Abdelgawad (2014), 'Contextualization and the advancement of entrepreneurship research', *International Small Business Journal*, **32** (5), 479–500.

4 Let them eat bricolage? Towards a contextualized notion of inequality of entrepreneurial opportunity

Ted Baker and E. Erin Powell

Entrepreneurial opportunity and the 'nexus'

For almost 20 years, the notion of 'opportunity' has been of central importance in entrepreneurship research (Venkataraman 1997) and it has been a rich topic within strategy and management theory more generally for much longer (Gartner et al. in press). Shane and Venkataraman (2000, p. 218) argued that 'entrepreneurship involves the nexus of two phenomena: the presence of lucrative opportunities and the presence of enterprising individuals', clarifying that entrepreneurial opportunities are 'those situations in which new goods, service, raw materials and organizing methods can be introduced and sold at greater than their cost of production' (Shane and Venkataraman 2000, p. 220). These have become the dominant and even default notions of opportunity and how opportunity relates to entrepreneurship in our field (Baker and Welter 2015), with almost 8000 Google Scholar citations as of mid-2015.

Echoing earlier comments by Zahra and Dess (2001), Baker, Gedajlovic and Lubatkin (2005) criticized this definition and the framework in which it is embedded for its explicit and implicit de-emphasis of the social context in which entrepreneurship takes place. They argued that this 'undersocialized' approach made it inadequate for supporting cross-national studies of entrepreneurship. Specifically, Baker and colleagues (2005, p. 495) noted that:

> Both economists (Smith 1909/1776) and sociologists (Durkheim 1982; Weber 1947) have long used the phrase, "division of labor" to refer to the manner in which the specialized productive roles of individuals are distributed in a national marketplace, as well as the processes by which individuals are prepared for their roles.

They argued that the division of labour – and in particular, structured and stratified differences in how members of different groups were prepared for and sorted into roles – were key to understanding international differences in *creating* the so-called nexus of lucrative opportunities and enterprising individuals that Shane and Venkataraman (2000) make key to entrepreneurship.

The division of labour and the degree to which it is stratified across a variety of dimensions strongly affects individual biographies, often largely through the circumstances of birth. For example, they shape who has access to what prior experiences and is thereby positioned to create or discover opportunities (Shane 2000), peoples' opportunity costs and risks for undertaking entrepreneurial actions (www.gemconsortium.org) and the social and financial resources people can bring to bear (Evans and Jovanovic 1989). One's life and career experiences are also shaped by the division of labour in ways that affect one's individual characteristics (Kohn and Schooler 1969, 1978, 1983), including how 'enterprising' one is likely to be. From this perspective the 'nexus' is generated in major part by the fundamental structuring of the division of labour and is itself largely epiphenomenal. To focus on it leads us to a too narrow view of the field of entrepreneurship research, ignoring both causes and consequences of the process that generate the joint distribution of individuals and opportunities.

Increasingly, for example, the 'nexus' of enterprising individuals and *not-so-lucrative* opportunities seems closer to the core of what many of us, as entrepreneurship researchers, care about and perhaps especially as the legitimacy of our field has grown beyond the need to self-impose a narrowly distinctive domain (Baker and Welter 2015; Gartner et al. in press). More to the point, by minimizing focus on the determinants of the joint distribution of people and opportunities for entrepreneurship, the currently dominant framework for understanding opportunity radically decontextualizes this concept. In so doing, it renders our field less attuned to and less capable of dealing productively with what we describe below as inequality of entrepreneurial opportunity. We have had far too little to say about the question, 'entrepreneurial opportunity for whom?'

Inequality of opportunity

Concern with issues of social and economic inequality has grasped the popular imagination. Even fairly forbidding tomes describing and analysing increasing socioeconomic inequality and declining mobility have become non-fiction bestsellers (for example, Piketty 2014; Stiglitz 2015). In the United States, the so-called 'disappearance of the middle class' and the spectre of the 'top one percent' gaining an increasing share of riches increasingly haunt political and social media discourse and have energized activities such as the 'occupy movement'.

Many European countries have done more than the US to curb income inequality both through redistribution and typically apparently also in part at the cost of higher levels of exclusion of immigrants (recent experience with Syrian refugees notwithstanding): 'I do think there is a trade-off between inclusion and equality', said Gary Becker, a professor of economics at the University of Chicago and a Nobel Laureate. 'I think if you are a German, you are better off than your American equivalent, but if you are an immigrant, you are better off in the US' (quoted in Stille 2011).

Concern with inequality spans pretty much every level of comparison imaginable. Globally, the country in which you are born is probably the largest single determinant of how much money you will make. For example, 'More than one-half of variability in income of world population classified according to their household per capita in 1% income groups (by country) is accounted for by these two characteristics': country of residence and income distribution within that country (Milanovic 2015, p. 452). This creates large contrasts. For example, 'Only about 40% of the Chinese population is richer than the poorest Germans' (Milanovic 2015, p. 454). Less obvious perhaps, levels of inequality differ dramatically across and even within regions in many nations, for example at the county level in the United States (Moller, Nielsen and Alderson 2009). In most cities around the world, it takes only a little effort to observe stark differences between rich and poor. In nations with high Gini coefficients (a standard measure of income inequality) such as South Africa or Honduras, the contrasts are hard to avoid or ignore. Much of this inequality is, of course, structured by ethnicity, gender, age, class, caste, religious affiliation, immigrant status and other demographic characteristics.

Individuals and cultures differ in the extent to which their personal and political values lead them to concern with 'equality of outcomes' (roughly speaking, what is measured by income and wealth distributions) versus equality of opportunity (one aspect of which is captured by mobility from one socioeconomic stratum to another). For example, it is a truism that in the US many people are comfortable with relatively high levels of income and wealth inequality as long as perceived mobility chances are high: my ability and that of my children to greatly improve our lot in life through hard work. Most concerning to many US observers is what appears to be a fundamental challenge to the 'American Dream': the United States now has one of lowest rates of social mobility – the likelihood of move up to a higher social class or income level – among peer nations. A very similar concern, perhaps more focused on equality of outcomes, resonates with Europe's generally lower Gini coefficients but more exclusionary policies toward foreign born 'others' and more recently in terms of divisions between have and have-not members of the Eurozone. The greatest inequality and lowest chances for mobility are, perhaps unsurprisingly, found neither in the US nor Europe, but in poorer regions. To a substantial (though perhaps decreasing) extent, mainstream entrepreneurship research has often ignored such places and local scholars have had little voice in our journals.

We present these stylized facts about rising inequality and immobility neither to support nor to refute any specific underlying claims. Scholars continue to disagree about the details. Rather, our purpose is to juxtapose rising inequality and shrinking mobility against the apparent lack of concern with how we think about inequality – or fail to think about it – in entrepreneurship research. We argue that the dominant, radically decontextualized conception of opportunity in entrepreneurship steers us away from concern with differences in what we label 'inequality of entrepreneurial opportunity'. This is unfortunate, both because it artificially narrows and impoverishes our theories of entrepreneurship, but also because it deters our engagement with one of the most pressing social issues of our time and of the foreseeable future.

Entrepreneurship research as apologia?

An important theme in contemporary entrepreneurship research celebrates entrepreneurship as a tool or mechanism for overcoming the sorts of constraints that are faced by people in disadvantaged circumstances. In very broad terms, Rindova, Barry and Ketchen's (2009) description of 'entrepreneuring as emancipation' provides an invigorating and powerful connection to what makes entrepreneurship exciting for many of us. It allows people to overcome a wide variety of constraints and challenges as they accomplish things that surprise and delight us. Increasingly, entrepreneurship is seen as a means of 'identity fulfillment' (Ruef 2010) and 'becoming'. Closely related, ideas about entrepreneurial resourcefulness and 'bricolage' promote the idea that entrepreneurs are sometimes able to 'create something from nothing', escaping a wide variety of disadvantages in accomplishing their goals.

Unfortunately, however, in a context of increasing inequality and limited mobility the notion of entrepreneurship as emancipation and the celebration of bricolage and resourcefulness threaten to become apologias for the declining equality of opportunity and outcomes. The transcendence implied by the possibilities of identity fulfilment can disguise the objective disadvantages an entrepreneur may face. Primers on how to cope with disadvantage can serve as default justifications and paths to acceptance for that disadvantage. At worst these ideas become ideological tools allowing us to say (or at least to believe) 'well, if they face unequal opportunities, let them emancipate themselves'. To horribly abuse something Marie Antoinette never said: 'Let them eat bricolage!'

Relatedly, as Baker and Welter (2015, pp. 8–9) argued, entrepreneurship is sometimes viewed, perhaps especially by policymakers, as a 'panacea': 'Your economy has become less competitive and innovative? . . . look at entrepreneurship – that is the solution! . . . Women, immigrants, youth and disabled persons are excluded from the labour market? Get them to open their own businesses'. Rather than dealing with systemic issues including but not limited to inequality and socioeconomic immobility, the answer may too often become, 'Why not try entrepreneurship policies? There is something in it for everybody. . . .'.

For example, Jones and Ram (2015) provide a critical evaluation of 'Entrepreneurship as ethnic minority liberation', taking to task the 'widespread feeling, especially among policymakers' (Ram and Smallbone 2003), that self-employed business ownership is a virtually assured antidote to the discrimination suffered by racialized minorities in Western urban society. They contrast the celebration of South Asian immigrants to Britain as entrepreneurial achievers to the denigration of other ethnic groups, quoting Kundnani (2000, p. 7) to note that such comparisons become the basis for claims that if one disadvantaged minority group can succeed through entrepreneurship, 'then the others are just not trying hard enough'. They go on to add evidence that most South Asian immigrant entrepreneurs in Britain work backbreaking hours for low returns. Accordingly, as the next generation in these families gain access to other opportunities they are apparently 'voting with their feet' (Jones and Ram 2015, p. 401) and pursuing professional careers rather than entrepreneurship.

Dannreuther and Perren (2015) go much further in their attempt to 'rekindle past academic resistance to the hegemony of entrepreneurial discourse'. Their insightful, if self-admittedly one-sided, narrative paints entrepreneurship as an all but purely ideological concept used as a tool by those in power to victimize those to whom opportunity is denied. To these authors, most readers of this chapter – researchers engaged in the empirical study of entrepreneurship – would be seen as more or less unwitting tools of this hegemony: 'Policy, corporate and academic functionaries provide "convenient facts" for the elites to strengthen their hegemony by providing "facts" to litter entrepreneurial rhetoric. In reciprocation the functionaries receive resources through grants, consultancy fees and legitimacy through having influence, or, in today's catchphrase, "impact"' (Dannreuther and Perren 2015, p. 384).

While we strenuously disagree with the strident excess and absolutism of Dannreuther and Perren's (2015) argument, they do have a point: when we simply accept things as they are and build conceptual frameworks that make it easier to 'hear no evil, see no evil and speak no evil', we risk becoming apologists for power and privilege whether we want to or not. A fuller awareness of what puts people into positions of having to emancipate themselves or to create something from nothing can inform our research in a way that celebrates the emancipatory potential of entrepreneurship without ignoring the context in which this takes place and which it can serve both to challenge but also to reproduce. We believe that it is time to reconceptualize the notion of entrepreneurial opportunity in a manner that points us toward grappling in theoretically interesting and practically useful ways with inequality of entrepreneurial opportunity.

Reaching back: toward a reconceptualization of entrepreneurial opportunity

We suggest broadening and contextualizing the concept of entrepreneurial opportunity promulgated by Shane and Venkataraman (2000). To do this, we reach back to embrace an older and more broadly useful definition of entrepreneurial opportunity that can easily contain the Shane and Venkataraman (2000) approach as a special case and thereby preserve the benefits of their definition when it proves useful. Stevenson and Jarillo were not trying to promote the idea of a distinctive domain for entrepreneurship research but were instead trying to extend existing themes in entrepreneurship research to embrace 'corporate' entrepreneurship. Therefore, they did not need to delimit a narrow form of entrepreneurial opportunity as distinctly different from other sorts of opportunity. Instead, they proffered a more general definition of opportunity as: 'a future situation which is deemed desirable and feasible' (Stevenson and Jarillo 1990, p. 23).

For the purpose of answering the question, 'opportunity for whom?' this definition has a number of features going for it (Gartner et al. in press). First, it generalizes human desires and entrepreneurial motivation beyond economic gain to include whatever 'future situation' people may desire. Second, it also allows generalization beyond the 'individual' to encompass situations in which desirability points not just to what one person wants but rather to something joint or shared, perhaps among members of a founding group (Powell and Baker 2015). Third, like the Shane and Venkataraman (2000) framework it is agnostic with regard to organizational form and can incorporate multiple meanings of entrepreneurship including new venture creation and corporate activities. Fourth, matching the common sense of many entrepreneurship researchers, but unlike the dominant framework, it easily encompasses virtually all new venture creation efforts, including both so-called 'opportunity' and 'necessity' entrepreneurship (GEM), as involving 'opportunities'. Importantly, this reincorporates most of the mass of 'informal sector' entrepreneurial activity as well as 'social entrepreneurship' into the domain of entrepreneurship. Fifth, it is easy to see that the Shane and Venkataraman (2000) definition 'fits' as a special case with this broader framework for the study of opportunity and entrepreneurship.

Most importantly, as Stevenson and Jarillo (1990) go on to point out, their definition renders opportunity 'relativistic' because desirability and feasibility vary across people, and for the same people over time and depending on their 'current position and future expectations'. This 'relativistic' stance invites consideration of the determinants – for any individual or group of potential founders – of what shapes their desires and both their perceptions and the reality of what is feasible. These characteristics virtually scream out the need for researchers to contextualize their work and the definition provides an effective basis to do so. We argue, therefore, that the Stevenson and Jarillo (1990) definition provides a superior foundation for developing a contextualized understanding of entrepreneurial opportunity.

Where do we go from here?

Welter (2011) notes that context can be viewed as an overall lens informing work on entrepreneurship or as a discrete variable locating a study in a specific context. In addition, she points out that an adequate conceptualization of context in entrepreneurship requires that we attend to top down processes through which context affects entrepreneurial action and also to bottom up processes through which entrepreneurial action either changes or reproduces context. Taken together with the fact that context – as we described above for the myriad contexts of inequality and mobility – can be assessed at levels of analysis ranging from those structured by global relations among nations to those structured by race and gender in a single community or even family, the task of contextualizing work in entrepreneurship, and perhaps especially work on entrepreneurial opportunity, can seem a bit overwhelming.

We suggest two tactics for beginning to sort this out. While these tactics are focused on the notion of entrepreneurial opportunity, they are likely to be more general strategies that could apply to other concepts as well. First, dropping all concern with trying to carve a distinctive scholarly domain for entrepreneurship, we suggest embracing the substantial bodies of work on inequality that are a central focus of research in important branches of economics and sociology. In particular, while management scholars have drawn extensively from organizational sociology, they have attended much less to the very extensive corpus of sociological research in social stratification (Grusky 2014; Lippman, Davis and Aldrich 2005). Our main point is that in terms of contextualizing inequality of entrepreneurial opportunity, substantial and sophisticated theories and empirical work have long been available and should be – indeed should have already been – broadly embraced by entrepreneurship scholars. Stratification research spans an extraordinary range of contextual levels and comparisons – as described above, from the global to the family – and this literature both can and should inform our understanding of inequality of entrepreneurial opportunity. What this literature does not explore adequately is how these structural and related cultural and institutional sources of advantage and disadvantage shape the lived experience of entrepreneurs and would-be entrepreneurs around notions of what is feasible and desirable in the contexts in which they find themselves.

Second, and unsurprisingly, recent reductive conceptualizations have not stopped some researchers from doing work that explores entrepreneurship among people who engage in entrepreneurship even when the opportunities they face are far from 'lucrative'. A number of entrepreneurship scholars have demonstrated that they are also more interested in contextualized notions of entrepreneurial opportunity and entrepreneurial action. Several strands of work – some of them longstanding, some much newer – in effect address the highly contextualized question: 'opportunity for whom?'

Here, we point briefly to a few such strands in the literature. This is not a literature review. We intend only to provide illustrations of what has been done and where additional foundational work may be required. Some of the relevant research focuses on groups of people represented by the demographic and other characteristics along which the contours of disadvantage are structured. For example, the topic of 'gender and entrepreneurship' has been a longstanding theme, perhaps especially in sociologically influenced research (Brush, de Bruin and Welter 2009; Yang and Aldrich 2014).

Interesting bodies of work investigate so-called 'ethnic' entrepreneurship (Aldrich et al. 1981; Aldrich, Jones and McEvoy 1984; Aldrich and Waldinger 1990; Chaganti and Greene 2002), including ethnic enclaves (Auster and Aldrich 1984; Portes and Jensen 1989), as well as minority entrepreneurship in urban areas (Robinson, Robinson and Blockson 2007) and entrepreneurship in post-Soviet nations and other transitional contexts (Stark 1996; Smallbone and Welter 2001). Also compelling is the surge of interest in 'informal sector entrepreneurship' and entrepreneurship in poor communities (Castells and Portes 1989; Webb et al. 2009). Much of this work is even – implicitly or explicitly – critical of the status quo that structures advantaged and disadvantaged access to opportunities. This begins to address questions of opportunities *for whom* by directly addressing opportunities *not* for whom. For example, Al-Dajani and Marlow (2015, p. 343) build on several pertinent literatures to 'critically evaluate the potential of entrepreneurship to enable women to challenge disempowering patriarchal structures embedded within the Global South'. Most of this work investigates topics that would be rendered as contextual background noise or categorized as non-entrepreneurship in the currently dominant framework for understanding entrepreneurial opportunity.

Much of this research uses methods that seek to develop close understanding (Weber 1947) of the desirable and the feasible and how these may become intertwined in the lives of entrepreneurs. It explores entrepreneurs in various positions within the joint distribution of individuals and opportunities. For example, Sarasvathy's (2008) use of 'talk aloud protocols' led to the understanding of themes of 'affordable loss' that provide non-obvious insights into the experience of what is desirable and feasible among a group of experienced entrepreneurs. Baker and colleagues (2003) showed that among entrepreneurs engaged in strategic improvisation, what was feasible became desirable. In contrast, Powell and Baker (2014) show how some founders facing prolonged adversity enacted the adversity as opportunity such that what was desirable became feasible. By explicitly adopting Stevenson and Jarillo's definition of opportunity, Baker and Nelson (2005, p. 358) were able to show the intertwining of 'what seemed desirable and what seemed feasible' among entrepreneurs engaged in bricolage. A body of work by Welter and her colleagues studying entrepreneurship in post-Soviet Eastern Europe provides close insights into entrepreneurs' strategies for dealing with a complex and changing opportunity context. A rapidly expanding set of papers on entrepreneurial narrative (Gartner 2007; Hjorth and Steyaert 2004; Lounsbury and Glynn 2001), provides insights into how stories in many different forms help entrepreneurs and those with whom they work and interact make sense of the desirable and the feasible (also see Chapter 3 by Steyaert and Chapter 12 by Gartner). Many of these studies specify the context in which individuals engage in entrepreneurial action toward what is desirable and feasible. However, there have been limited attempts to date – mostly in traditional demographically focused topics such as gender and race – to develop connections between this work and the frameworks developed in the economics and sociology literatures on structural and related cultural and institution sources of advantage and disadvantage.

To summarize, there exists a substantial body of research developing sophisticated *etic* (roughly, from an outside observer's perspective) perspectives on inequality of opportunity that is directly relevant to but largely ignored by most entrepreneurship scholars. A smaller body of active research is attempting to develop *emic* (roughly, from the subject's insider perspective) understandings of the nature of entrepreneurial opportunity. Unfortunately, these two literatures remain largely separate. We argue that a reconceptualization of entrepreneurial opportunity, starting with 'a future situation which is deemed desirable and feasible' (Stevenson and Jarillo 1990, p. 23) as a framework is likely to help provide a foundation for allowing these literatures each to inform the other, while more generally expanding the scope of inquiries and scholarly conversation across levels of analysis, contexts and epistemologies.[1] Little of the work focused on specific contexts has been explicitly comparative across opportunity contexts. Nor, for example, has much work in entrepreneurship taken a life course perspective (Baker and Aldrich 1996; Elder 1974) toward understanding changes related to age, period and cohort in access to opportunities. Much more such work is necessary if we are to develop a robustly grounded understanding of the varied meanings of opportunity as these are experienced and constructed by entrepreneurs.

From our perspective, the literature on founder identity, especially to the extent that this comes to incorporate entrepreneurial narrative and life course perspectives, provides a particularly promising path to marrying the Weberian emphasis on empathic understanding to the Durkheimian treatment of social facts as things. Understanding processes of founder identity construction and change call for understanding of life course dynamics. These processes also involve construction and promulgation of sometimes competing narratives that help both founders and stakeholders – past, present and future – to orient themselves toward defending or changing what is deemed desirable and feasible (Powell and Baker 2014). Social psychological theories of identity are explicitly oriented toward understanding the co-determination of individual and structural elements in social life (Stryker 1980; Tajfel 1978). They are therefore particularly well-suited for joining emic and etic perspectives, and for understanding the emergence of new social structures – including new organizations – from individual and group action (Fauchart and Gruber 2011; Powell and Baker 2015). It seems to us that these activities are at the core of entrepreneurial action. It is also worth pointing out that much of the work in entrepreneurship from a social cognitive perspective, on topics such as optimism, intentions and self-efficacy (Hmieleski and Baron 2009) bears fairly obvious ties to notions of desirability and feasibility. Individual differences among entrepreneurs that are captured by such concepts can be incorporated within the rich understandings of being and becoming comprehended by the social psychologies of identity.

We conclude by noting that despite our real concerns about academic work on entrepreneurial emancipation, resourcefulness and overcoming adversity serving as apologias for inequality of entrepreneurial opportunity, we continue to believe that such research speaks to the heart of what makes entrepreneurship transcendent, exciting and meaningful. By combining this work with a realistic grasp of context, concerns about such research comforting the powerful and afflicting the afflicted can be ameliorated. More importantly, such research requiring us to reach back, renew and contextualize an old definition of entrepreneurial opportunity will help us to understand when and how resourcefulness, responses to adversity, and commitment to emancipation serve as means to overcome structural disadvantage, and when and how they serve to reproduce it. Questions of context matter in both theoretical and highly practical ways.

NOTE
1 We thank a reviewer for this point.

Suggested readings

Grusky, David (ed.) (2014), *Social Stratification: Class, Race, and Gender in Sociological Perspectives*, 4th edn, Boulder, CO: Westview Press. This reader provides a relatively comprehensive overview of the massive body of sociological research on stratification. It includes a selection of classic works that provide grounding for contemporary studies. While few people will read this book from cover to cover, it is structured in a manner that makes it easy to get a good sense of the field and then to dig much more deeply into specific areas.

Powell, E.E. and T. Baker (2014), 'It's what you make of it: Founder identity and enacting strategic responses to adversity', *Academy of Management Journal*, **57** (5), 1406–1433. This paper applies an identity lens to the life experiences that bring founders to their ventures in order to understand the richness and heterogeneity of entrepreneurial motivations that exist even within a narrowly defined industry segment. Entrepreneurs facing persistent resource constraints and adversity make the desirable feasible by enacting definitions of the situation that allow them to use their ventures to become who they want to be. Context itself is rendered as both an objective constraint and also as a broad canvas upon which founders' identity aspirations play out.

Stevenson, H.H. and J.C. Jarillo (1990), 'A paradigm of entrepreneurship: Entrepreneurial management', *Strategic Management Journal*, **11** (5), 17–27. This paper introduces the definition of opportunities in terms of what is desirable and feasible in the future using clear, direct and unadorned prose. Perhaps because the authors implicitly accept the legitimacy of entrepreneurship research as they seek to extend it into the management of existing businesses, the definition melds common sense and an impressive underlying sense that people can want very different things and entrepreneurship can serve as a vehicle for creating and becoming many different things.

References

Al-Dajani, H. and S. Marlow (2015), 'Empowerment, place and entrepreneurship: Women in the global south', in T. Baker and F. Welter (eds), *The Routledge Companion to Entrepreneurship*, New York: Routledge, pp. 343–357.

Aldrich, H. and R. Waldinger (1990), 'Ethnicity and entrepreneurship', *Annual Review of Sociology*, **16**, 111–135.

Aldrich, H.E., J. Cater, T.P. Jones and D. McEvoy (1981), 'Business development and self-segregation: Asian enterprise in three British cities', in Ceri Peach, Vaughan Robinson and Susan Smith (eds), *Ethnic Segregation in Cities*, London: Croom Helm, pp. 170–190.

Aldrich, H.E., T.P. Jones and D. McEnvoy (1984), 'Ethnic advantage and minority business development', in Robin Ward and R. Jenkins (eds), *Ethnic Communities in Business: Strategies for Economic Survival*, Cambridge: Cambridge University Press, pp. 189–210.

Auster, E. and H.E. Aldrich (1984), 'Small business vulnerability, ethnic enclaves, and ethnic enterprise', in R. Ward and R. Jenkins (eds), *Ethnic Communities in Business: Strategies for Economic Survival*, Cambridge: Cambridge University Press, pp. 39–54.

Baker T. and H.E. Aldrich (1996), 'Prometheus stretches: Building identity and cumulative knowledge in multiemployer careers', in Michael B. Arthur and Denise M. Rousseau (eds), *The Boundaryless Career*, New York: Oxford University Press, pp. 132–149.

Baker, T. and R. Nelson (2005), 'Creating something from nothing: Resource construction through entrepreneurial bricolage', *Administrative Science Quarterly*, **50** (3), 329–366.

Baker T. and F. Welter (2015), 'Bridges to the future of entrepreneurship research', in T. Baker and F. Welter (eds), *The Routledge Companion to Entrepreneurship*, London: Routledge, pp. 3–17.

Baker, T., E. Gedajlovic and M. Lubatkin (2005), 'A framework for comparing entrepreneurship processes across nations', *Journal of International Business Studies*, **36**, 492–504.

Baker, T., A. Miner and D. Eesley (2003), 'Improvising firms: Bricolage, retrospective interpretation and improvisational competencies in the founding process', *Research Policy*, **32**, 255–276.

Brush, C., A. de Bruin and F. Welter (2009), 'A gender-aware framework for women's entrepreneurship', *International Journal of Gender and Entrepreneurship*, **1**, 8–24.

Castells, M. and A. Portes (1989), 'World underneath: The origins, dynamics, and effects of the informal economy', in A. Portes, M. Castells and L.A. Benton (eds), *The Informal Economy: Studies in Advanced and Less Developed Countries*, Baltimore, MD: Johns Hopkins University Press, pp. 11–37.

Chaganti, R. and P.G. Greene (2002), 'Who are ethnic entrepreneurs? A study of entrepreneurs' ethnic involvement and business characteristics', *Journal of Small Business Management*, **40** (2), 126–143.

Dannreuther, C. and L. Perren (2015), 'The rhetoric of power: Entrepreneurship and politics', in T. Baker and F. Welter (eds), *The Routledge Companion to Entrepreneurship*, New York: Routledge, pp. 376–390.

Durkheim, E. (1982), *The Rules of the Sociological Method*, edited by Steven Lukes and translated by W.D. Halls, New York: The Free Press.

Elder, Glen H., Jr. (1974), *Children of the Great Depression: Social Change in Life Experience*, Chicago, IL: University of Chicago Press (Reissued as 25th Anniversary Edition, Boulder, CO: Westview Press, 1999).

Evans, D.S. and B. Jovanovic (1989), 'An estimated model of entrepreneurial choice under liquidity constraints', *Journal of Political Economy*, **97** (4), 808–827.

Fauchart, E. and M. Gruber (2011), 'Darwinians, communitarians, and missionaries: The role of founder identity in entrepreneurship', *Academy of Management Journal*, **54**, 935–957.

Gartner, W.B. (2007), 'Entrepreneurial narrative and a science of the imagination', *Journal of Business Venturing*, **22**, 613–627.

Gartner, W.B., B.T. Teague, T. Baker and R.D. Wadhwani (2016, in press), 'A brief history of the idea of opportunity', in C. Leger-Jarniou and S. Tegtmeier (eds), *Research Handbook on Opportunity Formation*, Cheltenham, UK and Northampton, MA, USA: Edward Elgar Publishing.

Grusky, David (ed.) (2014), *Social Stratification: Class, Race, and Gender in Sociological Perspective*, 4th edn, Boulder, CO: Westview Press.

Hjorth, D. and C. Steyaert (eds) (2004), *Narrative and Discursive Approaches in Entrepreneurship*, Cheltenham, UK and Northampton, MA, USA: Edward Elgar Publishing.

Hmieleski, K.M. and R.A. Baron (2009), 'Entrepreneurs' optimism and new venture performance: A social cognitive perspective', *Academy of Management Journal*, **52** (3), 473–488.

Jones, T. and M. Ram (2015), 'Entrepreneurship as ethnic minority liberation', in T. Baker and F. Welter (eds), *The Routledge Companion to Entrepreneurship*, New York: Routledge, pp. 391–405.

Kohn, M.L. and C. Schooler (1969), 'Class, occupation, and orientation', *American Sociological Review*, **34**, 659–678.

Kohn, M.L. and C. Schooler (1978), 'The reciprocal effects of the substantive complexity of work and intellectual flexibility: A longitudinal assessment', *American Journal of Sociology*, **84**, 24–52.

Kohn, M.L. and C. Schooler (1983), *Work and Personality: An Inquiry into the Impact of Social Stratification*, Norwood, NJ: Ablex Publishing.

Kundnani, A. (2000), 'Stumbling on: Race, class and England', *Race and Class*, **43**, 105–110.

Lippmann, S., A. Davis and H.E. Aldrich (2005), 'Entrepreneurship and inequality', *Research in the Sociology of Work*, **15**, 3–31.

Lounsbury, M. and M. Glynn (2001), 'Cultural entrepreneurship: stories, legitimacy, and the acquisition of resources', *Strategic Management Journal*, **22**, 545–564.

Milanovic, B. (2015), 'Global inequality of opportunity: How much of our income is determined by where we live?', *The Review of Economics and Statistics*, **97** (2), 452–460.

Moller, S., A.S. Alderson and F. Nielsen (2009), 'Changing patterns of income inequality in US counties, 1970–2000', *American Journal of Sociology*, **114**, 1037–1101.

Piketty, T. (2014), *Capital in the Twenty-First Century*, translated by Arthur Goldhammer, Cambridge, MA: Harvard University Press.

Portes, A. and L. Jensen (1989), 'The enclave and the entrants: Patterns of ethnic enterprise in Miami before and after Mariel', *American Sociological Review*, **54**, 929–949.

Powell, E.E. and T. Baker (2014), 'It's what you make of it: Founder identity and enacting strategic responses to adversity', *Academy of Management Journal*, **57** (5), 1406–1433.

Powell, E.E. and T. Baker (2015), 'Come together? Identity processes and organizing in multi-founder nascent ventures', Paper presented at the 2015 Academy of Management Annual Conference, Vancouver, British Columbia.

Ram, M. and D. Smallbone (2003), 'Policies to support ethnic minority enterprise: the English experience', *Entrepreneurship and Regional Development*, **15**, 151–166.

Rindova, V., D. Barry and D.J. Ketchen (2009), 'Entrepreneuring as emancipation', *Academy of Management Review*, **34** (3), 477–491.

Robinson, J.A., S. Robinson and L. Blockson (2007), 'Exploring stratification and entrepreneurship: African American women entrepreneurs redefine success in growth ventures', *Annals of the American Academy of Political and Social Science*, **613** (1), 131–154.

Ruef, M. (2010), *The Entrepreneurial Group: Social Identities, Relations, and Collective Action*, Princeton, NJ: Princeton University Press.

Sarasvathy, S.D. (2008), *Effectuation: Elements of Entrepreneurial Expertise*, Cheltenham, UK and Northampton, MA, USA: Edward Elgar Publishing.

Shane, S. (2000), 'Prior knowledge and the discovery of entrepreneurial opportunities', *Organization Science*, **11** (4), 448–469.

Shane, S. and S. Venkataraman (2000), 'The promise of entrepreneurship as a field of research', *Academy of Management Review*, **25**, 217–226.

Smallbone, D. and F. Welter (2001), 'The distinctiveness of entrepreneurship in transition economies', *Small Business Economics*, **16**, 249–262.

Smith, Adam (1909–1914), *Wealth of Nations*, edited by C. J. Bullock, Vol. X. The Harvard Classics. New York: P.F. Collier & Son.

Stark, D.C. (1996), 'Recombinant property in East European capitalism', *American Journal of Sociology*, **101**, 993–1027.

Stevenson, H.H. and J.C. Jarillo (1990), 'A paradigm of entrepreneurship: Entrepreneurial management', *Strategic Management Journal*, **11** (5), 17–27.

Stiglitz, Joseph E. (2015), *The Price of Inequality: How Today's Divided Society Endangers our Future*, New York: W.W. Norton & Company.

Stille, Alexander (2011), *The Paradox of the New Elite*, New York Times, 23 October 2011, p.SR1, New York Edition.

Stryker, S. (1980), *Symbolic Interactionism: A Social Structural Version*, Menlo Park, CA: Benjamin/ Cummings Publishing Company.

Tajfel, H. (1978), *Differentiation between Social Groups: Studies in the Social Psychology of Intergroup Relations*, European Monographs in Social Psychology, Vol. 14, London: Academic Press.

Venkataraman, S. (1997), 'The distinctive domain of entrepreneurship research: An editor's perspective', in J. Katz and R. Brockhaus (eds), *Advances in Entrepreneurship, Firm Emergence and Growth*, Greenwich, CT: JAI Press, pp. 119–138.

Webb, J.W., L. Tihanyi, R.D. Ireland and D.G. Sirmon (2009), 'You say illegal, I say legitimate: Entrepreneurship in the informal economy', *Academy of Management Review*, **34**, 492–510.

Weber, M. (1947), *The Theory of Social and Economic Organization*, edited with an introduction by Talcott Parsons and translated by A. M. Henderson and Talcott Parsons, New York: Free Press.

Welter, F. (2011), 'Contextualizing entrepreneurship: Conceptual challenges and ways forward', *Entrepreneurship Theory and Practice*, **35** (1), 165–184.

Yang, T. and H.E. Aldrich (2014), 'Who's the boss? Explaining gender inequality in entrepreneurial teams', *American Sociological Review*, **79** (2), 303–327.

Zahra, S. and G.G. Dess (2001), 'Dialogue', *Academy of Management Review*, **26**, 8–10.

5 The temporal dimension of context[1]

Stephen Lippmann and Howard E. Aldrich

Time marches on: prevailing uses of time in entrepreneurship research

Time appears frequently in entrepreneurship research as a theoretical construct and as a variable indicating duration or the length of various processes. As a theoretical construct, time is often used as a proxy for other meaningful processes, including experience (Kim and Longest 2014), efficacy (Almandoz 2012), success (Kalnins and Williams 2014), or commitment (Uy, Foo and Ilies 2015). Often time is mentioned as an afterthought in an acknowledgment of processes that are difficult to observe or that defy obvious explanation. Authors describe entrepreneurs as 'needing time' to accomplish a variety of goals, and many entrepreneurial processes are simply described as unfolding or occurring 'over time'. Time also appears frequently as a dependent or control variable. Most commonly, time is measured as the number of days, months or years that elapse between important events, such as the time between entrepreneurial entry and exit (Kalnins and Williams 2014; Naldi and Davidsson 2014). Occasionally, investigators conceptualize time in more deeply contextualized ways (Kim, Longest and Lippmann 2015; Miller and Sardais 2015).

Most of these studies make two problematic assumptions about time: (1) that time is linear and unfolds in steady, predictable ways, and (2) that entrepreneurship is teleological, imbued with a sense of purpose and inevitability. Linear notions of time conform to the ways we measure it with calendars and clocks, and therefore provide a convenient accounting scheme for the temporal context of entrepreneurship. Teleological arguments are supported by implicit assumptions about entrepreneurs' intentionality and control of their time, resources, and environments. When used in this way, time is typically a proxy for the accumulation of experience and resources, or exposure to risk. However, these facile notions of time do not begin capture the vastness and complexity of time (Koselleck 1985). As Menger (2014, p.50) noted, 'the fact that the future is irreducibly ambivalent means it cannot be understood as a mere increment or continuous accumulation vector'.

What do we miss by glossing over time, or simply treating it as the number of days, months or years that elapse between two discrete events? Even in a basic sense, time is not what it seems. Entrepreneurial actions are imprinted with the present, which immediately becomes the past, becoming ever more distant the longer entrepreneurial creations last into the future. Nascent entrepreneurs must make assumptions about the future, as they must anticipate increasing future demand for their products and services, for otherwise they will be unable to sustain their new ventures. And of course, entrepreneurs draw on the past, as they use pre-existing networks, resources and codes to plot their actions as they move through time. They often create elaborate rhetorical devices to give their ventures legitimate links with the past and thus ensure a better future (Cornelissen and Clarke 2010).

In each of these cases, time does not unfold sequentially from one moment to the next, nor do entrepreneurs necessarily experience it as a linear movement through space. Instead, entrepreneurs often must bend time, infusing the present with times past or those yet to come. Processes such as these have been considered at length by historians of art and other 'structural objects' (Nagel and Wood 2010) and appear in some theoretical treatments of entrepreneurship and organizational dynamics (Aldrich and Yang 2012; Stinchcombe 1965). However, the bulk of entrepreneurship studies are not particularly concerned with how temporal processes work or why they matter. When we consider these issues alongside the fact that individuals, groups and cultures carry with them dramatically different experiences of and orientations to time, we must reconsider our approaches to the temporal contexts of entrepreneurship.

Not so fast

Despite the intuitive appeal of treating time simply as 'clock time', we must resist the temptation and, instead, acknowledge that time is socially constructed (Aldrich 2009; Elder 1981). Historically, as economic relations took precedence over all other kinds of activities and relationships, instrumental rationality came to dominate human consciousness in the West. Activities begin to be valued for their present value or their discounted future value. Under the conditions humans encounter in their daily lives, their ability to cope with market forces did not need to be informed by any grand narrative or nuanced interpretations of time. On a very large scale, people have accepted the passage of time in terms of the tools we have invented to measure it.

However, when time is considered in terms of lived experience, intriguing alternatives exist for thinking about how and where time 'flows', and its implications for social and economic process, including entrepreneurship (Husserl 1960). We now explore three alternative conceptions of time that appear in other disciplines that focus on creative activities and which have implications for research on entrepreneurship.

Against linearity: nonlinear conceptions of time

In many ways, time is a figment of our individual and collective imaginations. We exist from moment to moment, but a sense of time arises out of our (individual and collective) memories (Dilthey 2002). In many cases, the fact that one moment succeeds another creates a continuous, linear experience of time. Indeed, our empirical research tends to assume such a process, as 'time' typically begins with some event of interest to investigators, after which entrepreneurs are followed at regular intervals to track progress or changes (Kim, Longest and Lippmann 2015; Lichtenstein, Dooley and Lumpkin 2006). For example, the Panel Study of Entrepreneurial Dynamics (PSED) attempted to conduct follow up interviews with respondents every 12 to 18 months (Gartner et al. 2004), and the Kauffman Firm Study (KFS) attempted to obtain archival records from Dun & Bradstreet listings every 12 months (Coleman and Robb 2009). Longitudinal studies that re-interview entrepreneurs at regular intervals may reify linear conceptions of time and gloss over the nonlinear ways in which time can operate. In reality, entrepreneurship may operate in a temporal context dramatically different from that captured by calendars and clocks.

Even though clock time moves forward, people are constantly shifting their attention to various points in time. Entrepreneurs, for example, can simultaneously feel pessimistic about past failures and optimistic about future opportunities (Miller and Sardais 2015). This 'bifurcation' of time suggests that as a cognitive construct it can move forward or backward, and at different speeds, with important implications for a variety of topics relevant to organizational and management scholars, including goals-setting, motivation and strategic choice (Fried and Slowik 2004; Hernes 2014; Nuttin 1985). Although much of the work on the nonlinearity of time is highly abstract, Shipp, Edwards and Lambert (2009) described Bluedorn's (2002) concept of *temporal focus* as a useful and measurable construct for understanding how individuals allocate their attention to perceptions of the past, present and future. Dozens of research projects have used the concept of temporal focus and its related constructs (Shipp, Edwards and Lambert 2009), but entrepreneurship researchers have been slow to adopt it, with some exceptions (Gilbert 2014; Tumasjan, Welpe and Spörrle 2013). In what follows, we suggest several ways in which scholars might utilize temporal focus to better understand entrepreneurial processes and outcomes.

Investigations of temporal focus can treat it as an outcome, by considering how temporal focus may change depending on the nature of the activity in which entrepreneurs are engaged. Different temporal foci may be engaged during different stages or activities. In the earliest stages of nascency, for example, entrepreneurs may orient their actions to the distant future, when they imagine their organization will be established. In other stages, they may become bogged down in the present and lose sight of the lessons of the past, or ignore the importance of preparing for future events. The nature of temporal focus may change when entrepreneurs enter into contracts with banks and suppliers. These shifts in temporal focus have important implications for entrepreneurial action and effectiveness.

Furthermore, temporal focus can be examined among different entrepreneurs with different levels of experience. Those with prior entrepreneurial activity may be more likely to think in terms of past actions, or use their earlier experience to guide current action. In such cases, the past may loom large over current actions, and historical imprinting may be particularly deep. On the other hand, new entrepreneurs may look to the future and select current actions with a more blind sense of optimism. Indeed, learning by entrepreneurs appears to be significantly influenced by the nature of past experience and how it aligns with current activities (Toft-Kehler, Wennberg and Kim 2014). While much of this is due to the accumulation of various kinds of knowledge, related research suggests a possible mediating role of temporal focus in the relationship between past experiences and current outcomes (Shipp, Edwards and Lambert 2009). Entrepreneurs may also use periodization strategically by offering period-specific interpretations of previous firm activities in ways that lend legitimacy to managerial successors or provide acceptable excuses for past failures.

Assuming that there are important differences in temporal focus across circumstances and entrepreneurs, as there are in other work-related contexts, researchers could also explore the degree to which temporal focus can itself lead to certain outcomes. For instance, a tendency to focus on the past may result in slower movement through the entrepreneurial process or be associated with less risk-taking, as past-oriented entrepreneurs see little reason to alter their conservative behaviour. Present-focused entrepreneurs may have more difficulty learning from experience, or a more difficult time goal-setting or envisioning the long-term effects of their decisions. A future focus may lead to more risk-taking as entrepreneurs envision a more positive future, but it can also lead to a failure to apply the lessons of the past as entrepreneurs discount events no longer salient to them.

A particularly intriguing possibility with regard to the nonlinearity of time is the ways in which entrepreneurs can use time as a strategic resource, bending or shifting time to gain advantages. Uncertainty increases as powerful social, economic and historical forces impress upon entrepreneurs and teams from above and below and constrain their activities. It is unlikely that most entrepreneurs or entrepreneurial teams will gain much leverage against those forces. However, on those occasions when entrepreneurs successfully create groups engaged in collective action, they may actually bend time or shift time to their own ends. For example, entrepreneurs may slow down or speed up the pace of their founding activities at strategic points in the start-up process. Or, they may effectively coordinate the temporal foci of their team members, finding ways to differentiate the assignment of people to tasks such that their differing temporal foci complement each other. In what ways do entrepreneurs use periodization strategies or other temporal rhetoric to sway stakeholders, such as by reframing past narratives or convincing them to ignore past failures and focus more on the promise of a better future? Questions like these about the strategic use of time will help uncover how it may be an important resource in addition to those such as financial, social and human capital that scholars typically study.

Against synchronicity: multiple actors, multiple temporalities

Time is often considered monolithic, as some detached, supra-individual process that unfolds in a physical sphere separate from but constitutive of human beings (Husserl 1960). Such monochronic notions of time are prevalent in Western physical and social science, reminding us that time is culturally situated and our own notions of it are culturally-specific (Helman 2005). It is most meaningful to humans as part of their individual, lived experience. For these reasons, some philosophers and historians conceive of multiple temporalities that operate in tandem (Braudel 1982). While treatments of such *heterochrony* by historians argue that time operates differently in different places or in different eras (Moxey 2013), it is likely most useful to entrepreneurship scholars in terms of individual differences in temporal orientations and the effects these differences have on teams and teamwork. By 'temporal orientation' we mean whether an individual's cognitive involvement is primarily with the past, present or future (Holman and Silver 1998).

Orientations to and experiences of time can differ dramatically across individuals. Mohammed and Harrison (2013) identified four dimensions along which temporal orientation can differ, including time urgency (a preoccupation with the passage of time, deadlines, and speed), time perspective (similar to temporal focus, described above), polysynchronicity (engaging in more than one task concurrently), and pacing style (working steadily from start to finish, quickly finishing tasks well before a deadline, or waiting until the last minute). These orientations bear obvious relationships to individual work styles, but also have important effects on the functioning of teams. When team members fail to achieve 'temporal consensus' (how tasks should be managed over a set period of time), coordination becomes more difficult and satisfaction with performance declines (Gevers and Peeters 2009). Under some conditions, however, temporal diversity among team members can be beneficial, as different members' approaches to time can allow for the completion of complex tasks, or the nature of uncertain tasks may vary over time (Mohammed and Harrison 2013; Mohammed and Nadkarni 2011).

Scholars of entrepreneurship could study the temporal orientations of entrepreneurs, with particular focus on heterogeneity and its effect on team functioning. Many aspects of entrepreneurial processes require a simultaneous focus on the past, present and future. While some individuals may be able to simultaneously balance these foci, in many cases a focus on one occurs at the expense of the others (Koselleck 1985). How does temporal focus diversity in entrepreneurial teams allow for the simultaneous consideration of past, present and future? And how might heterochrony among team members work to the group's advantage? Alternatively, are there ways in which temporal focus diversity can harm group functioning, as shown in research by Gevers and Peeters (2009)? Observers may misattribute individual differences in time orientation to more visible individual differences, such as gender or functional background. Such misattributions complicate the process of properly managing a team with a high degree of temporal diversity and may undermine its effectiveness.

Another possibility for considering multiple temporalities would be from a more macro-comparative perspective (Aldrich 2009). Indeed, the recent focus in art history on non-Western art has uncovered ways in which time moves differently in different places. Old notions that divided the history of art (generally) into what happened before, during and after the Renaissance ignored parallel or 'anachronic' developments in the non-Western world that required different periodization strategies and fundamentally different notions about the universality of time and development across the globe (Moxey 2013; Nagel and Wood 2010). Building on this and related work in market contexts (Khaire and Wadhwani 2010), scholars of entrepreneurship could fruitfully explore whether time operates at the same speed in different regions, different economies or different industries. For example, in new industries with few precedents for entrepreneurial action, are entrepreneurs under the same time pressure that they are in mature, more competitive industries?

Against teleology: embracing uncertainty and its role in entrepreneurial processes

Much of the empirical research on entrepreneurship, especially that taking a 'life cycle' approach, assumes a relatively linear unfolding of the start-up process, from idea generation, to resource mobilization, to functional establishment (Aldrich and Ruef 2006). Entrepreneurs, it is assumed, move through time with a clear goal in mind and their ability to accomplish various milestones in a timely manner ultimately results in success or failure. We may think about the future based on past experiences, but such projective attitude does not necessarily translate into effective action that actually brings about a desired state (Dilthey 2002). Entrepreneurship, like other creative processes, is infused with uncertainty. In addition to the uncertainty associated with the start-up process, especially for first-time entrepreneurs, in most industries it is difficult to accurately predict market opportunities and consumer demand. And, as Menger (2014, p. 133) noted, 'the uncertainty of success and the unpredictability of demand render obsolete, more or less rapidly, the information that a success generates concerning consumer preferences'.

How can acknowledging or even embracing the uncertainty of entrepreneurial processes and outcomes change the way in which we consider the temporal context of entrepreneurship? Entrepreneurs operate under conditions of high uncertainty, wherein their best moves must be seen as experiments and planning for the future can only be thought of in hopeful rather than certain terms. Knight's (1921) distinction between 'risk', which is ultimately calculable and 'uncertainty', which is not, highlights the importance of differentiating entrepreneurship from economic activities that depend on having enough information about the past to allow calculated assessments of risk. Although entrepreneurs generally know how much capital they are risking, they cannot really calculate with confidence their odds of their success. They are bedevilled by uncertainty but stand to profit handsomely if their experiment pays off.

Therefore, a key aspect of entrepreneurship involves thriving in situations of uncertainty in which many or most people are going to lose. Entrepreneurs may even have a stake in heightening the uncertainty facing others. By definition, if it were possible for entrepreneurs to truly characterize the context in which they work with meaningful labels, it would mean that they were operating under conditions of interpretive stability. Such contexts are not favourable for entrepreneurs seeking high returns on their efforts. Looking at more macro-level trends, questions emerge about how uncertainty may mediate the relationship between macro-level conditions and entrepreneurial ambitions or outcomes, or the ways in which uncertainty of demand (high in cultural industries) influences entrepreneurial ambition and strategy. Alternatively, research into the ways in which entrepreneurs exploit uncertainties associated with temporal processes to either gain an advantage over their competitors or reach stakeholders might be fruitful.

Implications for research

Given the complicated nature of temporality and the ways it contextualizes entrepreneurial action, we must adjust our research strategies for those questions in which time plays an important role. Models in related management fields exist from which entrepreneurship scholars can build or borrow in order to think more effectively about the temporal context of entrepreneurship (Wadhwani and Jones 2014). In traditional survey-based quantitative studies, scholars should think carefully about the ways in which time is measured and consider which measurement strategies are best suited to their research questions and designs (Gartner and Shane 1995). In addition, including measures developed by others (Mohammed and Nadkarni 2011; Shipp, Edwards and Lambert 2009) covering important temporal constructs, such as temporal focus and temporal orientation, would allow an examination of temporal diversity among entrepreneurs and entrepreneurial teams.

Other aspects of temporal context are best captured through archival, historical and narrative analyses of entrepreneurs and entrepreneurship (see Chapters 6 and 11 by Wadhwani). Such methodologies are becoming more popular in organizational, management and entrepreneurship studies (Decker 2014; Rowlinson, Hassard and Decker 2014; Wadhwani and Jones 2014) and are, of course, central to historical and other humanist examinations of the social and cultural importance and embeddedness of time and temporal processes. These methods allow us to unpack time, and go beyond the linear measures that are often necessitated by survey-based approaches (Isaac 1997). Indeed, by studying entrepreneurial endeavours over a long period, we can observe how their pacing changes over time and also the real future resembles the assumed one that influenced past entrepreneurial actions.

Conclusion

Linear and teleological conceptions of time assume entrepreneurial processes move neatly through time, with some set of activities marking the beginning, middle and end of entrepreneurship (Ruef 2005). These assumptions may arise from our efforts to create generalizable frameworks for understanding what are, to some degree, time-bound and historically contingent processes (Lippmann and Aldrich 2014). They may also arise from the largely retrospective ways in which we study entrepreneurship. When we look back in our histories and our retrospective surveys, do we impose a notion of time that may or may not exist for entrepreneurs as they are actually undertaking entrepreneurial activities? When our scholarly interests start with organizational establishment or failure, we may impose meaning to the past and to the entrepreneurial process by suggesting that is has a teleological movement through time (Aldrich 2015). Also, the uncertainty with which entrepreneurs operate requires that they impose meaning and continuity on the random detritus of the past by identifying, locating, situating the themes that allow themselves and other stakeholders to understand what it is that they are doing and to create interpretations that explain why they are doing it.

Although it is easy to take the temporal context of entrepreneurship for granted, and rely on convenient and simple ways to conceptualize and measure it, temporality is a complex and multifaceted concept. In a world increasingly dominated by the relentless advance of the forces of rationalization – calculability, technological control, efficiency and predictability – we are in danger of taking for granted a conception of time as measured by clocks and calendars (Ritzer 2008). However, cross-national and historical investigation has revealed that time is not necessarily linear, universal or progressive. We urge greater attention to theorizing and measuring the ways in which nonlinear, heterochronic and uncertain temporal contexts may influence entrepreneurship, and further exploration of the possibilities we have identified in order to capture the complexity and diversity of this fundamental contextual factor.

NOTE
1 We thank Christina Lubinski for helpful comments on an earlier version of this chapter.

Suggested readings

Abbott, Andrew (2001), *Time Matters: On Theory and Method*, Chicago, IL: University of Chicago Press. Abbott criticizes mainstream social science theoretical models for ignoring time and the ways simple linear models of time are reified using standard statistical techniques. He argues for the value of narrative methodologies and sequence analysis that can capture the importance of sequencing, and the often nonlinear unfolding of time. According to Abbott, ordering and pacing matter, but our models often gloss over their importance and our models and explanations for many social processes suffer as a result.

Lippmann, Stephen and Howard E. Aldrich (2014), 'History and evolutionary theory', in Marcelo Bucheli and R. Daniel Wadhwani (eds), *Organizations in Time: History, Theory, Methods*, Oxford: Oxford University Press, pp. 124–146. The authors argue that the evolutionary mechanisms of variation, selection, and retention can provide a generalizable framework for understanding the seemingly unique nature of historical processes including context, important events and the nature of individual cases. While the nature and importance of time differs across all of these categories, an evolutionary perspective allows scholars to draw meaningful cross-case conclusions.

Shipp, Abbie J., Jeff R. Edwards and Lisa S. Lambert (2009), 'Conceptualization and measurement of temporal focus: The subjective experience of the past, present, and future', *Organizational Behavior and Human Decision Processes*, **110** (1), 1–22. The authors introduce the concept of *temporal focus*, which describes the way people perceive time and how it affects attitudes and behaviours. It is potentially very useful to entrepreneurship research because across individuals, variations in temporal foci can lead to different outcomes. Among groups of individuals, different combinations of temporal foci can lead to congruencies or conflicts that can have important implications for entrepreneurial effectiveness.

References

Aldrich, Howard E. (2009), 'Lost in space, out of time: How and why we should study organizations comparatively', in Brayden King, Teppo Felin and David A. Whetten (eds), *Studying Differences Between Organizations: Comparative Approaches to Organizational Research* (Vol. 26), Bingley, UK: Emerald Group pp. 21–44.

Aldrich, Howard E. (2015), 'Perpetually on the eve of destruction? Understanding exits in capitalist societies at multiple levels of analysis', in Dawn R. DeTienne and Karl Wennberg (eds), *Research Handbook of Entrepreneurial Exit*, Cheltenham, UK and Northampton, MA, USA: Edward Elgar Publishing, pp. 11–41.

Aldrich, Howard E. and Martin Ruef (2006), *Organizations Evolving*, 2nd edn, London: Sage Publications.

Aldrich, Howard E. and Tiantian Yang (2012), 'Lost in translation: Cultural codes are not blueprints', *Strategic Entrepreneurship Journal*, **6** (1), 1–17.

Almandoz, J. (2012), 'Arriving at the starting line: The impact of community and financial logics on new banking ventures', *Academy of Management Journal*, **55** (6), 1381–1406.

Bluedorn, Allen C. (2002), *The Human Organization of Time: Temporal Realities and Experience*, Stanford, CA: Stanford Business Books.

Braudel, Fernand (1982), *Civilization and Capitalism, 15th–18th Century: The Wheels of Commerce*, Berkeley, CA: University of California Press.

Coleman, Susan and Alicia Robb (2009), 'A comparison of new firm financing by gender: Evidence from the Kauffman firm survey data', *Small Business Economics*, **33**, 397–411.

Cornelissen, Joep P. and Jean S. Clarke (2010), 'Imagining and rationalizing opportunities: Inductive reasoning and the creation and justification of new ventures', *Academy of Management Review*, **35** (4), 539–557.

Decker, Stephanie (2014), 'Solid intentions: An archival ethnography of corporate architecture and organizational remembering', *Organization*, **21** (4), 514–542.

Dilthey, W. (2002), *The Formation of the Historical World in the Human Sciences*, Princeton, NJ: Princeton University Press.

Elder, Glen H., Jr. (1981), 'History and the family: The discovery of complexity', *Journal of Marriage and Family*, **43** (3), 489–519.

Fried, Yitzhak and Linda Haynes Slowik (2004), 'Enriching goal-setting theory with time: An integrated approach', *Academy of Management Review*, **29** (3), 404–422.

Gartner, William B. and Scott Shane (1995), 'Measuring entrepreneurship over time', *Journal of Business Venturing*, **10**, 283–301.

Gartner, William B., Kelly G. Shaver, Nancy M. Carter and Paul D. Reynolds (eds), (2004), *Handbook of Entrepreneurial Dynamics: The Process of Business Creation in Contemporary America*, Thousand Oaks, CA: Sage.

Gevers, Josette M.P. and Miranda A.G. Peeters (2009), 'A pleasure working together? The effects of dissimilarity in team member conscientiousness on team temporal processes and individual satisfaction', *Journal of Organizational Behavior*, **30** (3), 379–400.

Gilbert, Brett Anitra (2014), 'Conceptualizing time in entrepreneurship', in Abbie J. Shipp and Ytizak Fried (eds), *Time and Work. Vol 2: How Time Impacts Groups, Organizations and Methodological Choices*, New York: Psychology Press, pp. 97–114.

Helman, Cecil G. (2005), 'Cultural aspects of time and ageing', *EMBO reports*, **6** (S1), S54–S58.

Hernes, Tor (2014), *A Process Theory of Organization*, Oxford: Oxford University Press.

Holman, E. Alison and Roxane Cohen Silver (1998), 'Getting 'stuck' in the past: Temporal orientation and coping with trauma', *Journal of Personality and Social Psychology*, **74** (5), 1146–1163.

Husserl, Edmund (1960), *Cartesian Meditations: An Introduction to Phenomonology*, The Hague: Martinus Nijhoff.

Isaac, Larry W. (1997), 'Transforming localities: Reflections on time, causality, and narrative in contemporary historical sociology', *Historical Methods: A Journal of Quantitative and Interdisciplinary History*, **30** (1), 4–12.

Kalnins, A. and M. Williams (2014), 'When do female-owned businesses out-survive male-owned businesses? A disaggregated approach by industry and geography', *Journal of Business Venturing*, **29** (6), 822–835.

Khaire, Mukti and R. Daniel Wadhwani (2010), 'Changing landscapes: The construction of meaning and value in a new market category – modern Indian art', *Academy of Management Journal*, **53** (6), 1281–1304.

Kim, P.H. and K.C. Longest (2014), 'You can't leave your work behind: Employment experience and founding collaborations', *Journal of Business Venturing*, **29** (6), 785–806.

Kim, P.H., K.C. Longest and S. Lippmann (2015), 'The tortoise versus the hare: Progress and business viability differences between conventional and leisure-based founders', *Journal of Business Venturing*, **30** (2), 185–204.

Knight, Frank H. (1921), *Risk, Uncertainty, and Profit*, Boston, MA: Houghton Mifflin.

Koselleck, Reinhart (1985), *Futures Past: On the Semantics of Historical Time*, Cambridge, MA: MIT Press.

Lichtenstein, Benyamin B., Kevin J. Dooley and G.T. Lumpkin (2006), 'Measuring emergence in the dynamics of new venture creation', *Journal of Business Venturing*, **21** (2), 153–175.

Lippmann, Stephen and Howard E. Aldrich (2014), 'History and evolutionary theory', in Marcelo Bucheli and R. Daniel Wadhwani (eds), *Organizations in Time: History, Theory, Methods*, Oxford: Oxford University Press, pp. 124–146.

Menger, Pierre-Michel (2014), *The Economics of Creativity: Art and Achievement under Uncertainty*, Cambridge, MA: Harvard Univesrity Press.

Miller, Danny and Cyrille Sardais (2015), 'Bifurcating time: How entrepreneurs reconcile the paradoxical demands of the job', *Entrepreneurship Theory and Practice*, **39** (3), 489–512.

Mohammed, Susan and David A. Harrison (2013), 'The clocks that time us are not the same: A theory of temporal diversity, task characteristics, and performance in teams', *Organizational Behavior and Human Decision Processes*, **122** (2), 244–256.

Mohammed, Susan and Sucheta Nadkarni (2011), 'Temporal diversity and team performance: The moderating role of team temporal leadership', *Academy of Management Journal*, **54** (3), 489–508.

Moxey, Keith P.F. (2013), *Visual Time: The Image in History*, Durham, NC: Duke University Press.

Nagel, Alexander and Christopher Wood (2010), *Anachronic Renaissance*, New York: Zone Books.

Naldi, Lucia and Per Davidsson (2014), 'Entrepreneurial growth: The role of international knowledge acquisition as moderated by firm age', *Journal of Business Venturing*, **29** (5), 687–703.

Nuttin, J. (1985), *Future Time Perspective and Motivation*, Leuven, Belgium: Leuven University Press and Lawrence Erlbaum Associates.

Ritzer, George (2008), *The McDonaldization of Society 5*, Los Angeles: Pine Forge Press.

Rowlinson, Michael, John Hassard and Stephanie Decker (2014), 'Research strategies for organizational history: A dialogue between historical theory and organization theory', *Academy of Management Review*, **39** (3), 250–274.

Ruef, Martin (2005), 'Origins of organizations: The entrepreneurial process', in Lisa A. Keister (ed.), *Research in the Sociology of Work* (Vol. 15), Greenwich, CT: JAI Press, pp. 63–100.

Shipp, Abbie J., Jeffrey R. Edwards and Lisa Schurer Lambert (2009), 'Conceptualization and measurement of temporal focus: The subjective experience of the past, present, and future', *Organizational Behavior and Human Decision Processes*, **110** (1), 1–22.

Stinchcombe, Arthur L. (1965), 'Social structure and organizations', in James G. March (ed.), *Handbook of Organizations*, Chicago, IL: Rand McNally, pp. 142–193.

Toft-Kehler, Rasmus, Karl Wennberg and Phillip H. Kim (2014), 'Practice makes perfect: Entrepreneurial-experience curves and venture performance', *Journal of Business Venturing*, **29** (4), 453–470.

Tumasjan, Andranik, Isabell Welpe and Matthias Spörrle (2013), 'Easy now, desirable later: The moderating role of temporal distance in opportunity evaluation and exploitation', *Entrepreneurship Theory and Practice*, **37** (4), 859–888.

Uy, Marilyn A., Maw-Der Foo and Remus Ilies (2015), 'Perceived progress variability and entrepreneurial effort intensity: The moderating role of venture goal commitment', *Journal of Business Venturing*, **30** (3), 375–389.

Wadhwani, R. Daniel and Geoffrey Jones (2014), 'Schumpeter's plea: Historical reasoning in entrepreneurship theory and research', in Marcelo Bucheli and R. Daniel Wadhwani (eds), *Organizations in Time: History, Theory, Methods*, Oxford, UK: Oxford University Press, pp. 192–216.

6 Entrepreneurship in historical context: using history to develop theory and understand process

R. Daniel Wadhwani

Introduction

The growing interest in contextual approaches to entrepreneurship research (Welter 2011; Zahra and Wright 2011) has included calls for greater attention to history in the study of entrepreneurship (Landström and Lohrke 2010; Welter 2011; Zahra and Wright 2011). Yet, with few exceptions (Casson and Godley 2005; Lippmann and Aldrich 2014; Wadhwani and Jones 2014), there has been little exploration of what historical contextualization entails and how it might be relevant to entrepreneurship research. This chapter examines what it means to place entrepreneurship in historical context, considers why this might be valuable to entrepreneurship research, and discusses the application of historical contextualization to specific questions within the domain of entrepreneurship scholarship.

My focus throughout the chapter is on historical contextualization as a programme of research that can render novel insights into entrepreneurial processes and theory building. Understanding historical contextualization as an interpretive or analytical activity – rather than thinking of historical context as an aspect of the external 'environment' or a set of antecedent conditions – is crucial to unlocking the promise of historical reasoning in entrepreneurship research and theory development, and to establishing a path forward for historical scholarship. Toward that end, this chapter, along with Chapter 11 on historical methods, not only elaborates on the analytical and interpretive processes involved in historical contextualization and their relevance to entrepreneurship research, but also highlights the practical issues involved in designing and carrying out such research.

What is historical contextualization?

Welter (2011) distinguishes between two approaches to contextualizing entrepreneurship research: 'contextualizing theory' involves 'acknowledging situational and temporal boundaries for entrepreneurship', while 'theorizing context' involves considering how context 'influences the nature and extent of entrepreneurship'. The distinction is directly relevant to how history is treated in entrepreneurship research. If viewed as a way to 'contextualize theory', history would be seen as the set of antecedent conditions that constrain or enable entrepreneurship, and the task of historical contextualization would largely be limited to identifying the antecedent conditions or events that affect entrepreneurial action. In contrast, when viewed as a way of 'theorizing context', history would be seen as a form of interpretive or analytical activity that offers insights into the theory of entrepreneurship itself. The task of historical contextualization would not be limited to identifying 'boundary conditions', but would involve exploring central research questions about entrepreneurship using a unique lens – that of historical perspective. It is in this later sense that historical contextualization holds its greatest promise of contributing unique insights into entrepreneurship research, and is hence the focus of this chapter.

Historical contextualization, in this sense, can be defined as *the analysis or interpretation of past event(s), in relationship to their time and place, in ways that address a question or problem that arises in the present.* The definition points to several significant characteristics of the nature of historical contextualization as an analytical or interpretive activity. First, historical contextualization involves a retrospective point of view. It is an analytical or interpretive activity that leverages the perspective of the historicizing agent by allowing an event to be understood in the context of not only its antecedents but also in terms of its consequences. Second, historical contextualization arises out of a question or problem that needs to be addressed in the present; while the event being analysed or interpreted may lie in the past, the purpose of analysing or interpreting it emerges from the need to address an issue in the present. Third, as an interpretive or analytical activity, historical contextualization involves establishing the relationship between events and their time and place; it implies that entrepreneurship and entrepreneurial processes can be *uniquely* understood by relating them to this historical context. The rest of this section examines in more detail the nature of the interpretive or analytical activity involved in historical contextualization.

Who engages in historical contextualization?

Approaching historical contextualization as an interpretive action rather than a fixed condition inherently raises the question of who is doing the interpretation. While it may seem obvious that in a chapter focused on historical contextualization as a research programme that we are concerned with how the researcher does the historical contextualization, this section will highlight the fact that entrepreneurs, too, engage in historical contextualization as part of everyday sense-making. Both scholarly and everyday historical contextualization provides opportunities for entrepreneurship research.

Scholarly historical contextualization is typically deliberate and designed. It is meant to achieve some research goal or intention in mind. Scholars often use historical contextualization because of the unique retrospective viewpoint it provides or the timescales which that historical perspective can provide. Entrepreneurship scholars, for instance, are familiar with the way in which Baumol (1990, p. 895) uses historical contextualization to examine and theorize how institutions shaped the relative productivity of entrepreneurial activity. 'Since the rules of the game usually change very slowly', Baumol explains, 'a case study approach to investigation of my hypotheses drives me unavoidably to examples spanning considerable periods of history and encompassing widely different cultures and geographic locations'. Scholarly historical contextualization, in this case, allows the researcher to examine entrepreneurial interactions and process in unique ways because of the long time spans and variations in behaviour that historical research allows, and because of the ability to examine the broad consequences of entrepreneurial processes.

However, scholars are not the only ones who engage in historical contextualization. Everyone engages in historical contextualization as part of making sense and communicating in their daily lives. As the philosopher of history Wilhelm Dilthey (Carr 1986, p. 4; Dilthey 1988) put it, 'we are historical beings first, before we are observers of history, and only because we are the former do we become the latter'. History, in this second sense, is part of everyday sense-making and communication by individuals and communities, including entrepreneurs and entrepreneurial groups. History is an integral aspect of everyday sense-making and communicating because actors' interpretations and understandings of the past are inherently linked to how they experience the present and set expectations for the future.

The questions of when, how, and toward what ends entrepreneurs use historical contextualization in the entrepreneurial process represents a distinct and separate research opportunity from the question of how scholars may use historical contextualization to study entrepreneurial sense-making. If, following Koselleck (2004), the 'space of experience' (historical contextualization) shapes everyday experiences and expectations, then the study of how everyday historical sense-making shapes perceptions of entrepreneurial opportunities, the understanding of risks, and future outcomes by actors could represent a significant area for exploration for entrepreneurship researchers. Studying historical contextualization as an everyday process would also be methodologically different from using history as a form of scholarly contextualization, as is explained in Chapter 11.

The purpose of turning to the past

Actors, whether scholarly or everyday ones, interpret the past for a purpose. Scholars typically pursue historical research to achieve an epistemic goal (such as theory building) while everyday actors use history toward practical ends, such as communicating an idea. Thus, it is important to recognize that the process of historical contextualization actually begins with a need or problem in the present, and identifying those needs or problems is essential to understanding the motives involved in turning to the past (Danto 1965).

Scholarly contextualization often has one of a number of possible motivations, each of which pertains to specific kinds of epistemic goals. MacLean, Harvey, and Clegg (2015) create a useful typology of four different types of intellectual contributions that historical perspective and research can provide, depending on whether the researcher is taking a primarily social scientific or narrative stance *and* whether the goals of historical contextualization are primarily expository or interpretive. Social scientific approaches to historical contextualization may be designed to test or refine theory, as is the case with Baumol's (1990) use of historical contextualization to develop the theoretical distinction between productive, unproductive, and destructive entrepreneurship. But they can also be used to reveal the operation of transformative social processes, as Cole (1959) does in describing 'entrepreneurial streams', the sequences of entrepreneurial action through which he posits that historical change occurs. Narrative approaches to history, likewise, can have different epistemic ends depending on whether their intention is to generate new theoretical constructs or to explain the form and origins of contemporary phenomena. Popp and Holt's (2013) use of historical narrative to highlight the differences in perspectives on entrepreneurial action retrospectively versus prospectively provides an exemplar of the former, while Gompers' (1994) narrative history of the development of the venture capital industry provides an application of the latter. Thus, historical contextualization can be used in making different kinds of scholarly contributions, an issue to which this chapter returns later.

In contrast, everyday historical contextualization by entrepreneurs themselves often involves more practical motivations. Intentional uses of the past might include conceiving or communicating ideas, framing decisions, establishing legitimacy, shaping expectations or wielding power (Brunninge 2009; Schultz and Hernes 2013; Suddaby, Foster, and Quinn Trank 2010). Such conscious uses of history are typically designed to have an effect on choices and action in the present or expectations about the future, rather than to make epistemic claims about the past in and for itself or to build theory. Unintentional (non-strategic) historical contextualization also occurs, and is often part of normal communication of meaning among members of a community that share a common past. Actors in a particular firm or industry, for instance, might refer to historical antecedents to convey information about some present condition without seeking to intentionally or consciously 'use history' (Kirsch, Moeen, and Wadhwani 2014).

The intended or implicit purpose of historical contextualization is important to recognize because it establishes the relationship between the past and some question or concern of relevance in the present (or future) and because it shapes the interpretive process of how the past will be contextualized, as is described in the next section.

The process of historical contextualization: periodization and historical logics

The interpretation of historical context itself involves establishing the relationship between events in the past and their time and place. Both scholars and everyday actors determine the relevant contextual relationships based on their motivation in turning to the past and establish the contextual relationship through processes of periodization and the assignment of historical logics.

Periodization is the interpretive process by which developments in the past are organized into coherent periods, eras, or epochs (Rowlinson, Hassard, and Decker 2014). It is inherent to historical contextualization in that it essentially defines boundaries of the context in which event(s) in the past ought to be understood, and establishes their relationship to concerns in the present. 'Periods' or 'eras' are not fixed attributes of the events themselves but are a part of the interpretive processes of establishing context through retrospective interpretation that links or groups together some developments in the past while separating others (Danto 1965). Take, for instance, the designations of the 'dot.com era' and 'Web 2.0' as periods or phases of development. Such periodizations imply coherence to entrepreneurial opportunities and actions during one period that distinguishes them from another. Or, in contrast, consider the periodizations used by Baumol in the process of creating a historically contextualized interpretation of the role of institutions in shaping entrepreneurial behaviour. Although these two examples point to two very different sorts of actors doing the historical contextualization and to different motivations, the periodization performs similar types of interpretive work in establishing temporally delineated coherence to events in the past and in implying a relationship to a problem or concern in the present. In the case of the 'dot.com era' and 'Web 2.0', the periodizations were developed and used by actors in everyday life to establish the coherence of particular kinds of start-up strategies and practices that were considered legitimate and important for a particular period. Baumol (1990), in contrast, is an example of scholarly historical contextualization designed to achieve the particular epistemic goal of illustrating the impact of institutional incentives on entrepreneurial behaviour.

The interpretive act of periodization is based on establishing coherence between the epistemic intent of the historicizing agent in turning to the past and the evidence or 'facts' about the past that seem relevant. Hence historical periodization will inherently differ in length and descriptive characteristics depending on the historical intentions of the actor(s) performing it. So, for instance, both the 'dot. com era' and 'Web 2.0' could fit within a broader periodization that historians sometimes designate as the Third Industrial Revolution, a period when communications and information technology is transforming industries, to distinguish it from both the first and second industrial revolutions that came before it. It is not that one periodization is more correct than another, but rather that the dot.com/ Web 2.0 periodization seeks different kinds of contextual knowledge of the past than the three industrial revolutions' periodization. The effectiveness of the periodization as an interpretive or analytical activity hence depends on how well it serves to coherently categorize events in the past into periods or eras that are relevant for the epistemic goal that the historical interpreter is trying to achieve.

While periodization establishes coherence by linking certain events in the past and distinguishing others by period, it does not necessarily establish causal links or semantic meanings between events within a period or across different periods. Historical contextualization thus involves the interpretation and establishment of plausible causal or semantic relationships between developments over time, what can be called historical logics. Wadhwani and Jones (2014) propose a typology of three different kinds of historical logics – structural, sequential/contingent, constitutive – that may each be useful for particular kinds of research using historical contextualization.

What Wadhwani and Jones (2014) call historical structuralism is based on the premise that certain past events or developments constrain subsequent choices or actions and that one of the useful purposes of historical contextualization is to identify these constraints over time. Within organizational theory, such theoretical constructs as path dependence, imprinting, and institutionalism contain within them structural logics or reasoning. Baumol (1990) provides perhaps the clearest and most widely known example of this kind of historical structural logic.

Sequential or contingent historical logics, in contrast, focus on moments and processes of contingent or actual change, and consider the confluence of actions and developments that make such change possible (Sewell 2005). Sometimes the focus is on a particular moment that, in historical hindsight, was a watershed moment; for instance, moments of crisis or disruptive change raise questions of what confluences of factors led to the moment becoming an historical 'event' – an instant in time when things were transformed. Just as often, such reasoning focuses on a sequence of developments that created significant changes within the context itself. Sequential or contingent reasoning is particularly useful in entrepreneurship scholarship that seeks to examine not only how context shapes action, but also how action reshapes context (Welter 2011). Schumpeter (Schumpeter 1947; Wadhwani 2010) was a strong advocate for this form of historical reasoning in entrepreneurship research, and it has proven especially useful in fields such as business history, where the rise of big business and the creation of global economies have been explained through sequences of entrepreneurial actions.

Finally, what Wadhwani and Jones (2014) call a constitutive historical logic focuses on how actors themselves understood the past and how this understanding shaped their future-directed entrepreneurial efforts. Rather than positing that the past is inherently enabling or constraining, a constitutive logic is based on the contention that the contextualization that matters is how actors themselves understood and represented the past because it is their own understanding that shapes how they viewed plausible and desirable futures. Constitutive historical logics emphasize the creative agency involved in historical contextualization, as actors develop interpretations of the past as they seek solutions to new challenges and opportunities in the present (for a related discussion of entrepreneurs' temporal orientations, see Chapter 5 by Lippmann and Aldrich).

Applications to entrepreneurship research

How might historical contextualization, of the sort discussed above, contribute to the empirical examination of questions of concern to entrepreneurship scholars? In this section, I examine two applications of everyday historical contextualization and two applications of scholarly historical contextualization that offer unique insights into entrepreneurship research (see Table 6.1 for a summary).

Identifying opportunities and dealing with uncertainty

'How do entrepreneurs identify entrepreneurial opportunities and deal with the uncertainty of the future?' Entrepreneurship scholars recognize the situated nature of opportunity identification/creation (Zahra and Wright 2011). Entrepreneurs do not identify (Kirzner 1997; Shane and Venkataraman 2000) or create opportunities (Alvarez and Barney 2007; Sarasvathy 2001) in a context-free vacuum. Rather, their perceptions of the context in which they are embedded shape the nature of the opportunities they consider to be plausible and attractive.

Examining how entrepreneurs' understanding of their own historical context shapes the situated nature of the opportunities they identify as plausible and attractive constitutes one promising avenue for research. Such research could examine how entrepreneurs' own understandings of history – such as the analogies or lessons they draw from the past – shape their perceptions of possible futures. For instance, such research might examine how entrepreneurs draw 'lessons' from the

Table 6.1 Designing historical research to build entrepreneurship theory

		Selected Entrepreneurship Fields of Research			
		Entrep'l Sensemaking	Team/ Network Formation	Institutional Interactions	Proccesses of Industrial Change
Contextualizing Elements	Historicizing Agent	Everyday actors	Everyday actors	Scholars	Scholars
	Historical Intent	Identify/ create plausible futures	Coordinate actors & resources	Develop theory of institutional effects	Develop theory of entrep'l change
	Periodization	Varying by intention	Varying by intention	Typically long duration	Typically long duration
	Historical Logics	Constitutive	Constitutive	Structural	Sequential/ contingent

Source: Author.

past and apply these in judging the plausibility of opportunities to the future using analogies or stories. Likewise, it might examine how their interpretations of the attractiveness or unattractiveness of conditions in the past shape their judgments about futures that are worth pursuing. Such an approach would also inherently entail exploring how entrepreneurs' interpretations of the history are used to deal with the uncertainty of entrepreneurial futures (McMullen and Shepherd 2006).

As Table 6.1 denotes, the design of such research would involve approaching opportunity identification as a process of 'everyday historical contextualization'. Researchers could analyse data based on interviews, observations, business plans, or even autobiographical sources to analyse how entrepreneurs interpret the past in a way that addresses the identification of opportunities in the present and to deal with uncertainty about the future. Researchers might consider analysing the periodization used by entrepreneurial actors and in making history relevant in judging the plausibility and attractiveness of the opportunities they perceive. The historical logic involved would essentially be constitutive in that it would entail considering how perceptions of the past shape entrepreneurial actors' understanding of the future. Taking these contextualization processes into account, researchers could examine when and why entrepreneurs turn to the past and the purposes that history serves. Examining the processes by which entrepreneurs establish periodization and use historical logics, possibly in collaboration with psychologists and social psychologists, would allow researchers a new perspective into the entrepreneurial sense-making process.

Team and network formation

'How are entrepreneurial teams formed and networks activated to pursue common understandings of future goods, services, and markets?' (Ruef, Aldrich, and Carter 2003). Entrepreneurial team building and network activation are based on the premise that actors can form groups or be part of networks that have some common understanding of purposive action or outcome in mind. How this common vision develops and how it shapes motivation and coordination is, of course, an important area for entrepreneurship research. Because history can be seen as providing common reference points for actors that shape not only shared perceptions of the past but also expectations of the future, everyday historical contextualization may be considered as an aspect of the team formation process. The processes by which shared interpretations of the past develop and how these interpretations shape shared team identity, facilitate communication, socialize members into the team or network, or establish common goals for the future thus represent another promising application of historical contextualization to entrepreneurial research.

Within historical theory, the processes by which inter-subjective understandings of the past are used to establish group identities and assign meaning and intentionality to action in the present is often referred to as the formation of 'imagined communities' (Anderson 2006). Studies of imagined community development have been applied to organizations as well as to communities and ethnic groups and nations.

Extending such an approach to examine entrepreneurial team and network formation holds promise for providing unique perspectives into processes by which
common understandings develop and how resources begin to be devoted to purposive ends. The epistemic goal of research in this second case would be to use
historical contextualization as a lens for studying *coordinated* action and resource
deployment and their application to shared plausible futures.

Historical contextualization in this sense would be an integral part of examining culture and communicative action within entrepreneurial teams and networks
(Lounsbury and Glynn 2001) and how these contribute to establishment of the
legitimacy of entrepreneurial efforts (Aldrich and Fiol 1994). Such forms of historical contextualization might be observed in the discourse of teams and networks,
such as in pitching ideas to investors, building new organizations, or establishing trust and legitimacy among customers. Research topics could include analysis
of the cultural, social, and communicative purposes that history serves, and the
practices by which particular interpretations of the past are developed and shared.
It may, for instance, examine how particular periodizations or historical logics
within an industry develop and come to be shared and taken for granted within an
entrepreneurial team, a network, or even within an emerging market. Examining
processes by which groups establish common understandings of historical context
may thus provide a unique perspective on coordinated action toward entrepreneurial futures, and researchers could examine these processes by which everyday
historical contextualization plays a role in coordination within teams and networks.

Institutional effects

'How do institutions shape entrepreneurial cognition and action?' Whereas everyday historical contextualization can be useful for examining the kind of individual
and collective sense-making in which entrepreneurs engage, scholarly historical
contextualization can provide a way to examine social structures and entrepreneurial processes that would be difficult to study without the benefit of historical
perspective. One topic for which this is especially true is the relationship between
institutions and entrepreneurship.

Welter (2011) categorizes institutions under spatial contextualization, but institutions can also be understood by studying them historically. Prominent institutional
theorists, in fact, recognize the presumptive historical nature of institutions in
pointing out that institutionalization takes place over long periods of time, and in
suggesting that they are best understood in historical perspective (Suddaby, Foster,
and Mills 2014). Moreover, because institutions only change slowly it is often difficult to study their effects on entrepreneurship without taking a long historical
lens into account.

Baumol (1990) provides a clear example of the value of historical contextualization
in understanding institutions and their effects on entrepreneurship that is already

familiar to entrepreneurship scholars. But the relative productivity of entrepreneur-ial behaviour is only one possible area of inquiry where history can illustrate the impact of institutions on entrepreneurship. Wadhwani and Jones (2014) suggest that it would be useful for studying the social structuring of entrepreneurial risk taking and the types of organizational forms that entrepreneurs use to assemble resources into productive collectives. Wadhwani (2011) for instance shows how differences in the institutionalized understanding of appropriate risk-taking in the savings bank industry in Germany and the United States in the late nineteenth and early twenti-eth century shaped whether innovations were introduced by incumbent or start-up firms.

Historical perspective is also needed to study the formation of institutions them-selves that may have been important to entrepreneurial action. Understanding why bankruptcy law, for instance, is more conducive to entrepreneurial risk taking in some national environments rather than others, or why (in the case of informal institutions) some national cultures came to stigmatize failure more than others can only be understood from a historical perspective precisely because institutions often develop in complex processes over long periods of time, and it is only in his-torical hindsight that we can study those processes effectively.

Such an approach to historical contextualization focuses on structural historical logics and typically delineates longer historical periods in order to identify the origins and effects of institutions. Because institutions often change slowly, or are based in rules or practices that formed long ago, a long historical lens is often needed to identify the variations in institutional structures that affect entrepre-neurial behaviour (North 1990). Thus, such research requires attention to perio-dizations that reveal variations in institutions over time (Baumol 1990) and the processes by which such institutions change (North 1990).

Sequences and processes of change

'How does entrepreneurial action and context interact over time to create change in markets, economies, and societies?' One of the promises of contextualized approaches to entrepreneurship research is to be able to examine not only how context shapes entrepreneurship, but also how entrepreneurial action shapes and changes contexts over time (Welter 2011). Such reciprocal processes cannot be grasped through cross sectional research, nor by studying context over short peri-ods of time. Rather, they are best identified by studying sequences of entrepre-neurial actions and their relationship to contexts over longer time spans. In other words, historical perspective allows researchers to systematically study multi-level interactions between entrepreneurial action, context, and change. Scholarly his-torical perspective is useful in such a case because 'looking back' is necessary for seeing and contextualizing how entrepreneurial actions reshaped contexts and in taking into account the dynamic relationship between different levels of analysis (Schumpeter 1947; Wadhwani 2010).

Historical perspective is useful when used in this way because it treats the relationship between context and entrepreneurial action not as fixed and one directional, but rather examines sequences of interactions between context and entrepreneurial action over time that allows for complex interrelationships between variables. A good example of the promise of this line of research is Jones and Wale's (1998) study of the impact of entrepreneurial action on patterns of globalization in the decades before World War I. Globalization and entrepreneurial action represent very different levels of analysis and it would be impossible to make reasonable claims about the role of entrepreneurs in 'creating' globalization by studying it at a single moment in time. Jones and Wale are able to use historical perspective to untangle the sequence of entrepreneurial actions that changed contexts and subsequently led to new entrepreneurial actions that cumulatively integrated the global economy over decades. In their case, they showed how entrepreneurial ventures spun off from trading companies that had initially sought to trade with the Far East identified opportunities to create shipping and transportation infrastructure companies, such as steamboats and railroads. The effect that these entrepreneurial actions had on context, in terms of infrastructure and knowledge of commodity production and demand, led to the creation of opportunities for new production oriented companies, like plantations and mines. By studying sequences of action and context, such historical studies allow scholars to account for large-scale change in markets, economies and capitalism itself, and provides a multi-level perspective on entrepreneurship.

Such an approach to historical contextualization could examine a number of topics within the domain of entrepreneurship research, including the emergence and evolution of new industries (Forbes and Kirsch 2011; Kirsch, Moeen, and Wadhwani 2014), the effects of entrepreneurship on growth and structural change in economies (Baumol and Strom 2007), and processes of 'creative destruction' more broadly (Schumpeter 1976 [1943]). The design of such research would need to identify periods of change and use contingent historical reasoning to identify the combination and sequence of actions that caused the change.

Conclusion

This chapter has examined the promise of historical contextualization as an interpretive or analytical activity that can provide unique insights into entrepreneurial theory and process. It has explored a number of central issues for consideration in the design of historical research on entrepreneurship, including the identification of who is the historical agent, why actors turn to the past to establish context, and how historical contextualization works through periodization and the assignment of historical logics. It also illustrated the applicability of historical contextualization to research questions of concern to entrepreneurship scholars, showing how the design of historical research would vary based on the nature of the research question posed.

The focus of this chapter on the nature and design of historically contextualized approaches to entrepreneurship research raises a related set of questions on historical data sources and methods. Given the retrospective point of view that historical perspective applies and the often un-systematic nature of the data sources involved, how can entrepreneurship scholars develop and present valid historical interpretations? Chapter 11, on historical methods, addresses these questions and can be used as a companion to this chapter in designing and carrying out historical research on entrepreneurship.

Suggested readings

Baumol, William J. (1990), 'Entrepreneurship: Productive, unproductive, and destructive', *Journal of Political Economy*, **98** (5), 893–921. This article is a example of the use of scholarly historical contextualization to build theory. Baumol uses a long historical lens to explore how changes in institutions over historical time shaped entrepreneurial energies toward productive, unproductive, or destructive ends.

Bucheli, Marcelo and R. Daniel Wadhwani (eds) (2014), *Organizations in Time: History, Theory and Methods*, Oxford: Oxford University Press. This is an edited volume that examines the epistemic, theoretical, and methodological opportunities and challenges of historical research on entrepreneurship, management, and organization. The volume includes detailed chapters on using historical methods to address management research questions, including a chapter devoted to entrepreneurship research entited 'Schumpeter's plea: Historical reasoning in entrepreneurship theory and research'.

Popp, Andrew and Robin Holt (2013), 'The presence of entrepreneurial opportunity', *Business History*, **55** (1), 9–28. Popp and Holt use historical records to explore the perception of entrepreneurial opportunity and the nature of uncertainty. They show how opportunities look different prospectively, from the point of view of entrepreneurship pursuing them, than they do retrospectively, after they've been brought to fruition. The article is a good example of the value of examining 'everyday historical contextualization' by entrepreneurs.

References

Aldrich, Howard and Marlene Fiol (1994), 'Fools rush in? The institutional context of industry creation', *Academy of Management Review*, **19** (4), 645–670.

Alvarez, Sharon A. and Jay B. Barney (2007), 'Discovery and creation: Alternative theories of entrepreneurial action', *Strategic Entrepreneurship Journal*, **1** (1–2), 11–26.

Anderson, Benedict (2006), *Imagined Communities: Reflections on the Origin and Spread of Nationalism*, London and New York: Verso Books.

Baumol, William J. (1990), 'Entrepreneurship: Productive, unproductive, and destructive', *Journal of Political Economy*, **98** (5), 893–921.

Baumol, William J. and Robert J. Strom (2007), 'Entrepreneurship and economic growth', *Strategic Entrepreneurship Journal*, **1** (3–4), 233–237.

Brunninge, Olof (2009), 'Using history in organizations', *Journal of Organizational Change Management*, **22** (1), 8–26.

Carr, David (1986), *Time, Narrative, and History*, Cambridge: Cambridge University Press.

Casson, Mark and Andrew Godley (2005), 'Entrepreneurship and historical explanation', in Youssef Cassis and Ioanna Pepelasis Minoglou (eds), *Entrepreneurship in Theory and History*, Basingstoke: Palgrave Macmillan, pp. 25–60.

Cole, Arthur (1959), *Business Enterprise in its Social Setting*, Cambridge, MA: Harvard University Press.

Danto, Arthur Coleman (1965), *Analytical Philosophy of History*, Cambridge: Cambridge University Press.

Dilthey, Wilhelm (1988), *Introduction to the Human Sciences: An Attempt to Lay a Foundation for the Study of Society and History* (Translated with an Introductory Essay by Ramon J. Betanzos), Detroit: Wayne State University Press.

Forbes, Daniel and David Kirsch (2011), 'The study of emerging industries: Recognizing and responding to some central problems', *Journal of Business Venturing*, **26**, 589–602.

Gompers, Paul (1994), 'The rise and fall of venture capital', *Business and Economic History*, 1–26.

Jones, Geoffrey and Judith Wale (1998), 'Merchants as business groups. British trading companies in Asia before 1945', *Business History Review*, **72**, 367–408.

Kirsch, David, Mahka Moeen, and R. Daniel Wadhwani (2014), 'Historicism and industry emergence: Industry knowledge from pre-emergence to stylized fact', in Marcelo Bucheli and R. Daniel Wadhwani (eds), *Organizations in Time: History, Theory, Methods*, Oxford: Oxford University Press, pp. 217–240.

Kirzner, Israel M (1997), 'Entrepreneurial discovery and the competitive market process: An Austrian approach', *Journal of Economic Literature*, 60–85.

Koselleck, R. (2004), *Futures Past: On the Semantics of Historical Time*, New York: Columbia University Press.

Landström, Hans and Franz Lohrke (eds) (2010), *Historical Foundations of Entrepreneurship Research*, Cheltenham, UK and Northampton, MA, USA: Edward Elgar Publishing.

Lippmann, Stephen and Howard E. Aldrich (2014), 'History and evolutionary theory', in Marcelo Bucheli and R. Daniel Wadhwani (eds), *Organizations in Time: History, Theory, Methods*, Oxford: Oxford University Press, pp. 124–146.

Lounsbury, Michael and Mary Ann Glynn (2001), 'Cultural entrepreneurship: Stories, legitimacy, and the acquisition of resources', *Strategic Management Journal*, **22** (6), 545–564.

Maclean, Mairi, Charles Harvey, and Stewart Clegg (2015), 'Conceptualizing historical organization studies', *Academy of Management Review*, doi: 10.5465/amr.2014.0133.

McMullen, Jeffery S. and Dean A. Shepherd (2006), 'Entrepreneurial action and the role of uncertainty in the theory of the entrepreneur', *Academy of Management Review*, **31** (1), 132–152.

North, Douglass C. (1990), *Institutions, Institutional Change, and Economic Performance*, Cambridge, New York: Cambridge University Press.

Popp, Andrew and Robin Holt (2013), 'The presence of entrepreneurial opportunity', *Business History*, **55** (1), 9–28.

Rowlinson, Michael, John Hassard, and Stephanie Decker (2014), 'Research strategies for organizational history: A dialogue between historical theory and organization theory', *Academy of Management Review*, **39** (3), 250–274.

Ruef, Martin, Howard Aldrich, and Nancy Carter (2003), 'The structure of founding teams: Homophily, strong ties and isolation among US entrepreneurs', *American Sociological Review*, **68** (2), 195–222.

Sarasvathy, Saras D (2001), 'Causation and effectuation: Toward a theoretical shift from economic inevitability to entrepreneurial contingency', *Academy of Management Review*, **26** (2), 243–263.

Schultz, Majken and Tor Hernes (2013), 'A temporal perspective on organizational identity', *Organization Science*, **24** (1), 1–21.

Schumpeter, Joseph A. (1947), 'The creative response in economic history', *Journal of Economic History*, 7 (2), 149–159.

Schumpeter, Joseph A. (1976 [1943]), *Capitalism, Socialism and Democracy*, 5th edn, London: George Allen & Unwin.

Sewell, William H. (2005), *Logics of History: Social Theory and Social Transformation*, Chicago, IL: University of Chicago Press.

Shane, Scott and Sankaran Venkataraman (2000), 'The promise of entrepreneurship as a field of research', *Academy of Management Review*, **25** (1), 217–226.

Suddaby, Roy, William M. Foster, and Albert J. Mills (2014), 'Historical institutionalism', in Marcelo Bucheli and R. Daniel Wadhwani (eds), *Organizations in Time: History, Theory, Methods*, Oxford: Oxford University Press, pp. 100–123.

Suddaby, Roy, William M. Foster, and Chris Quinn Trank (2010), 'Rhetorical history as a source of competitive advantage', *Advances in Strategic Management*, **27**, 147–173.

Wadhwani, R. Daniel (2010), 'Historical reasoning and the development of entrepreneurship theory', in Hans Landström and Franz Lohrke (eds), *Historical Foundations of Entrepreneurship Research*, Cheltenham, UK and Northampton, MA, USA: Edward Elgar Publishing, pp. 343–362.

Wadhwani, R. Daniel (2011), 'The institutional foundations of personal finance: Innovation in US savings banks, 1880s–1920s', *Business History Review*, **85** (3), 499–528.

Wadhwani, R. Daniel and Geoffrey Jones (2014), 'Schumpeter's plea: Historical reasoning in entrepreneurship theory and research', in Marcelo Bucheli and R. Daniel Wadhwani (eds), *Organizations in Time: History, Theory, Methods*, Oxford: Oxford University Press, pp. 192–216.

Welter, Friederike (2011), 'Contextualizing entrepreneurship – conceptual challenges and ways forward', *Entrepreneurship Theory and Practice*, **35** (1), 165–184.

Zahra, Shaker A. and Mike Wright (2011), 'Entrepreneurship's next act', *Academy of Management Perspectives*, **25** (4), 67–83.

7 A relational conceptualization of context and the real-time emergence of entrepreneurship processes

Denise Fletcher and Paul Selden

Introduction

When entrepreneurship researchers take account of context, they often highlight social, organizational, industry, economic, political, ethical and institutional aspects of entrepreneurial phenomena as being of causal significance (Low and MacMillan 1988; Ucbasaran et al. 2001; Welter 2011; Zahra 2007; Zahra and Wright 2011). As pointed out by Welter (2011), contextual factors are useful for drawing attention to 'when', 'where' and 'how' circumstances, situations, conditions and environments constrain and enable entrepreneurial events. This takes us beyond the general contextualization of research findings to saying something more substantive about the meaning and function of context in entrepreneurship research (Chalmers and Shaw 2015; Fletcher 2011; Steyaert and Bouwen 1997; van Gelderen et al. 2012). However, issues around how to 'theorize context', in the sense of how to systematically differentiate, select and integrate multiple contexts in an explanation, remain largely implicit. As Bamberger (2008, p. 839) puts it: 'we need to accelerate the transition from the contextualization of research findings to the generation and testing of context theories'.

One challenge of theorizing context in entrepreneurship research concerns the issue of how to account for the 'heterogeneous aspects of contexts' in 'delineating the microfoundations of entrepreneurship' (Zahra and Wright 2011, p. 67). When developing an explanation, the entrepreneurship researcher is faced with multiple 'distal' contexts (Schegloff 1991) relating to social, organizational, business, economic, political, ethical, discursive and institutional contexts, as well as multiple 'proximal' contexts (Schegloff 1991) relating to localized practices, contingent events, social interactions, individual reflexivity and life histories. How then does the entrepreneurship researcher differentiate and select different forms of context when creating an explanation? We can bring to the fore certain contextual details in order to indicate spatial, ethical, social, historical and institutional dimensions of a phenomenon. Or, we can examine how contextual factors constitute or validate causal explanations. But as Schegloff (1997, pp. 166–167) puts it, 'on what grounds should some characterization of aspects of a socio-cultural event be preferred to another'. The issue of differentiating and selecting contexts is also complicated by the fact that entrepreneurs adjust their relationships with multiple contexts in real-time under conditions of genuine uncertainty. How then do we deal with the temporal dynamics of context? – 'how the context itself evolves, how that impacts on the actors involved, and how actors co-create their context' (van Gelderen et al. 2012, p. 7).

A second difficulty arises when being inclusive of multiple contexts. We might acknowledge the multiplicity of contexts and the different levels of context (micro, meso and macro levels), as well as seeing entrepreneurship itself as a context for studying other phenomena (van Gelderen et al. 2012, p. 9). The task of integrating multiple contexts, however, is complicated by the understanding that, 'context runs in ever-widening circles because every context has its own context' (van Gelderen et al. 2012, p. 5). The resolution of this 'infinite regress' (Bauman and Briggs 1990, p. 68) of 'nested contexts'[1] (van Gelderen et al. 2012, p. 9 referring to Mitchell 1987) is typically 'post hoc, descriptive and speculative' (Bamberger 2008, p. 840), resulting in the listing, rather than the conceptual integration, of contexts. Therefore, as Welter (2011) suggests, part of the challenge in theorizing context involves accounting for two-way and multi-layered relationships between context and entrepreneurship. In this respect, there is the two-way issue of how multiple contexts relate to moments of entrepreneurial action, as well as the issue of 'theorizing top-down and bottom-up links' that cut across different levels of analysis (Welter 2011, p. 177).

A third challenge is that, 'when studying context [we] can easily fall into the trap of becoming acontextual' (van Gelderen et al. 2012, p. 12). According to van Gelderen et al. (2012) there are two extremes to this – contextual determinism and contextual relativism. On the one hand, in our efforts to speak of context, or to contextualize and generalize our findings, we often revert to 'pointing out generalities with deterministic influences' (van Gelderen et al. 2012, p. 12). On the other hand, by taking an entirely relativistic view of situated, localized or particularized contextual issues, 'generalization is undermined altogether and we once again have contextual determinism, which renders context as a prison from which escape is impossible' (van Gelderen et al. 2012, p. 12 referring to Burke 2002). Either way, unless 'contextualization is itself theory-grounded, such [approaches] are, at best, only likely to converge into significant new integrative theoretical frameworks at a very slow pace' (Bamberger 2008, p. 840).

In making a contribution to addressing these issues, we focus on how context is related to practical entrepreneurial activity in the field and the real-time emergence of entrepreneurial processes (O'Driscoll and Rizzo 1996). The issue of real-time emergence concerns how change is causally effected by practical entrepreneurial activity in the 'momentary present' (Dainton 2014; Emirbayer and Mische 1998). The momentary present, sometimes referred to as the 'specious present' (James 1890/1950) or the 'lived present' (Husserl 1964), is the transient 'time of actuality in which things happen and consciousness exists' (Shackle 1961, p. 14). A conceptual understanding of how changing configurations of contexts are interrelated to the specific spatio-temporal characteristics of real-time entrepreneurial activity has important implications for the challenges of theorizing context. If we can conceptualize the mechanism by which the entrepreneur combines changing configurations of contexts in real-time, we can then use this mechanism, theoretically and methodologically, to identify the changing patterns of contexts associated with the empirical events of an emergent entrepreneurial journey. The mechanism used by the entrepreneur to manage the proximal and distal contexts of real-time activity is, therefore, the mechanism that can be used by the researcher to theorize the proximal and distal contexts of specific events. Conceptualizing context in this way enables us to address Bamberger's (2008, p. 841) proposal that theorizing context requires the researcher: 'to build situational and/or temporal conditions directly into theory and . . . to explicate the mechanisms . . . linking these situational and temporal conditions to embedded phenomena'.

In this chapter, we, therefore, ask the question, 'How should we conceptualize the multiplicity of contexts in the real-time emergence of entrepreneurial processes?' We propose that the answer to this question involves developing a relational conception of context. From a relational perspective (Dewey and Bentley 1949; Emirbayer 1997; Gottlieb and Halpern 2002; Hosking et al. 1995; Nardi 1996; Shotter 1993; van Oers 1998), real-time emergence is explained in terms of how multiple contexts, related to diverse spatio-temporal circumstances in the past, are interrelated with 'agency' in the present moment (Emirbayer and Mische 1998). The relational interdependence of context and agency in the momentary present is causally constitutive of the interpretive and social actions that effect cognitive and social events in real-time.

In what follows, we first discuss the dominant tendency in entrepreneurship research to objectify the notion of context and the limitations this engenders for theorizing context. In the second part of the chapter, we address these limitations through a relational conceptualization of context, which explains how the interrelationship of multiple contexts and agency is constitutive of action (interpretive and social) in real-time emergence. In the third part, we explain how multiple contexts are combined with agency in real-time through the 'structure of time consciousness' (Kortooms 2012). Finally, it is argued that this conceptualization has important implications for identifying, selecting and integrating contexts in entrepreneurial explanations because it enables the theorization of multiple contexts as specific spatio-temporal dimensions of the explained event.

Objectifying context

The dominant conception of context in entrepreneurship research is to objectify context as a causal entity distinct from the agentic power of the individual entrepreneur (Whetten 2009; Welter 2011). This means that context forms the 'circumstances, conditions, situations, or environments that are external to the respective phenomenon and enable or constrain it' (Welter 2011, p. 167). Put another way, context functions as a *boundary condition* of action, which the entrepreneur can experience as an obstacle or exploit as an opportunity. As Welter (2011, pp. 165–166) explains, 'context simultaneously provides individuals with entrepreneurial opportunities and sets boundaries for their actions'. From this perspective, context is objectified as extra-personal entities, such as the *market pre-conditions* of entrepreneurial opportunities (Drucker 1985; Shane 2003), and the *resources* for entrepreneurial action, such as market information, firm characteristics, social capital and networks (Haugh 2007).

In relation to theory development, an objectifying conception of context is advanced in different ways. We objectify context when we 'factor-in' exogenous variables or contextual factors in order to *validate* our research findings. We objectify context when we privilege 'context' and 'process variables' as a means of identifying which key variables in a causal chain are important, or when we highlight the 'stabilizing influences' of contextual factors to enable explanation and prediction (Zahra 2007). In addition, researchers might objectify a range of actions as signifying particular kinds of contexts which later become labeled as social, institutional or spatial context by the 'aware' researcher. It should also be noted that some objectifying research traditions, such as positivism, are '*anticontextual* in the sense that participants [are] concerned with forming laws of nature and society . . . that [are] valid whatever the circumstances of time, place or persons' (van Gelderen et al. 2012, pp. 2–3) [emphasis added].

The tendency to objectify context is understandable in the sense that during scientific work it seems logical to break down complex empirical social phenomena along the lines of the analytical distinction between subject and object, or the inner and outer dimensions of entrepreneurial action. Whatever the rationale for objectifying context, incorporating multiple contexts into the research record becomes an analytical challenge because the researcher is making choices not only about which contextual factors are important, but also about the relative importance of different contexts. This challenge, as already mentioned, requires the conceptual differentiation, selection and integration of multiple contexts. Objectifying context, however, detracts from the imperative to theorize context in this way, because it implies that all contexts 'sit out' there as discrete entities in the field waiting for the engaged researcher to come along and select them from a known and finite list. From this perspective, the researcher is 'the judge of what merits inclusion' (Bauman and Briggs 1990, p. 68) without having to explain how contexts are conceptually interrelated.

The conceptual problem of objectifying context (both ontologically and epistemologically) is that it separates context from actioned events, as an antecedent condition. The epistemological notion that context is an object of perception, and the ontological position that context is an independent entity, simply categorizes context as 'not action'. As a result, an objectifying perspective involves little explanation of how contexts are related to each other and to context-specific activity in the process of real-time emergence. In other words, there is an absence of criteria for differentiating and selecting contexts in relation to the specific spatio-temporal circumstances of an actioned event, as well as the absence of frameworks for conceptualizing the relative causal significance of different contexts (that is, examining their interrelatedness). In the following discussion, we address the issue of how multiple contexts are related to actioned events through a relational understanding of how context is related to agency in real-time.

'Weaving together' action and context

Our starting point, in developing a relational conception of how context is related to real-time entrepreneurial activity, is to re-connect to the etymological root of the word 'context' which, as noted by Welter (2011), comes from the Latin *contexere*, meaning 'to weave together'. The original meaning of context, therefore, emphasizes a 'relationship between individual parts and the whole' (van Gelderen et al. 2012, p. 2). This notion of context as part of a functionally interrelated system follows from the relational principle that 'whatever is being studied must be thought of as a constellation of relationships' (Bradbury and Lichtenstein 2000, p. 552). In order to address our research question, from a relational perspective, we, therefore, need to know the relational system of which context is a part in the real-time emergence of entrepreneurial activity. Entrepreneurial activity unfolds in real-time as a succession of interconnected momentary presents. In each momentary present, interpretive and social actions create the emergent outcomes of entrepreneurial activity, such as events and artifacts. The duration of the momentary present, therefore, demarcates the boundary of the relational system of which context is a part, during the process of real-time emergence.

Within the parameters of the momentary present as a relational system, context is relationally interdependent, or 'woven together', with *agency* – agency being the dimension of action that does the 'weaving' (Emirbayer and Mische 1998). We do not use the term 'agency' here to signify the instrumental and rational individualism of the modernist paradigm, but the pragmatic and reflexive capacity to combine contexts relative to changing spatio-temporal circumstances (Emirbayer and Mische 1998). Agency has no personal or social content without a relationship with context. It is the *weaving together* of context and agency in the 'here and now' that connects the past, present and future dimensions of an unfolding entrepreneurial activity and *causes* the emergence of entrepreneurial phenomena. This holistic understanding enables us to theorize context in terms of its relational interdependence with agency (cf. Emirbayer and Mische's, 1998, relational conception of the interrelationship between agency and 'structural environments').

In the next section, we further develop our relational conception of context and agency through an examination of the nature of *relational causality* in social processes.

Context and relational causality

Relational modes of analysis have become increasingly influential since Emirbayer's (1997) 'manifesto for a relational sociology' in which he encourages social theorists to react to what he refers to as a fundamental dilemma: 'whether to conceive of the social world as consisting primarily in substances or processes, in static "things" or in dynamic unfolding relations' (p. 281). Emirbayer (1997, p. 281) argues that traditional models for undertaking social analysis – such as rational actor, norm-based or statistical variable analyses – are 'beholden to the idea that it is entities that come first and relations among them only subsequently'. What is distinctive about the notion of relationality is that it takes relations, rather than individuals, groups, attributes or categories, 'as the fundamental unit of social analysis' (Mische 2011, quoting Wellman 1988, p. 20).

A *relation* in a unit of relational analysis is an interdependence between two or more relational entities. If one is talking about social interaction, then a relational entity is a socially interacting individual, and relationality is an interdependence between two or more individuals. The relationality of a social transaction primarily concerns the interdependence of transacting individuals through (1) the social practice of linguistic performance (a spoken or written artifact); and (2) the interpretation of the performance in relation to meaning systems, such as discourses, narratives, institutions and cultural practices (see Chapter 3 by Steyaert on texts and language as context). If one is talking about sense-making processes, then relational interdependence is the self-reflexive relationship between the acting self and an objectified historical self (also referred to as the 'I-self' and the 'Me-self', see James 1890/1950). The acting self acts through its interdependence with an emergent historical self. At higher levels of analysis, relational entities are aggregated supra-individual structures, such as firm departments, networks, organizations and markets, which interrelate through self-organizing dynamics (Selden and Fletcher 2015). Taken as a whole, the domain of entrepreneurship involves a hierarchy of relationalities in the sense that relational interdependence between system components at lower levels of analysis is relationally interdependent with relational systems at higher levels of analysis (Selden and Fletcher 2015).

What then is the causal nature of a relational interdependence? Relational interdependence (Gottlieb and Halpern 2002) involves a 'generative' (Harré 1972), 'circular' (Juarrero 2000), 'path-dependent' (Garud and Karnøe 2003) and 'recursive' (Chiles et al. 2010) causality in the sense that the *outcomes* of relational interdependence redefine that interdependence. A relational process is, therefore, self-organizing and self-creating through the internal dynamics between its relational components. The notion of context is central to this circular process because context is both the outcome of relationality, and constituting of relationality. Interdependence between relational entities involves the outcome of that relationality becoming *contextual to* that interdependence. New context is created when the emergent outcome of relationality, such as an event, artifact or dynamic state, lapses into the past and then recontextualizes unfolding activity in the present. Rather than an entity or static property of relationality, context is, therefore, in a constant state of becoming, as the present redefines the past and the past redefines the present.

For example, at the level of a social dialogue, a context for an interacting individual is a *prior* communication event (emergent outcome) enacted by the other party to the dialogue. When the individual acts in relation to this context, a new communication event is created that immediately becomes the new context for both parties to the dialogue and redefines the significance of the first context. In one time frame, a prior event, causally effected by the first individual, is the immediate context for both individuals, and in another time frame the event created by the second individual becomes the immediate context for both individuals. In the case of sense-making processes, a context for an act of sense-making might be the *prior* experience of a contingent event. When the sense-maker acts in relation to this context, the interrelationship of agency and context immediately redefines the context for the activity. For example, if the experience of a contingent event is interpreted as problematic, it is this interpretation that then redefines the context for the next agency–context interrelationship. In the circular process of relational causality, context is, therefore, a relativity of the past to the present that has a causal significance in the present.

What then *is* context? The emergent outcomes of relational causality that become new context take on a variety of ontological forms. These forms include spoken texts, written texts, material artifacts (such as technologies and consumer goods), relational systems (such as social practices, organizations, networks and markets), cognitive capabilities (relating to knowledge, practice and information), and psychological states that are retained in memory (such as perceptions, contingent experience, interpretations and decisions) (see Chapter 2 by Brännback and Carsrud). These ontological forms of context, however, are only *contextual to action* when they interrelate with agency in the circular process of relational causality. When we socially signify events, material artifacts and relational systems as contexts, we are objectifying and entifying context as if it is independent of action. But it is only when these emergent outcomes interrelate with agency through praxis, interpretation, practical evaluation, creativity, imagination, reflection and other forms of sense-making activity that they constitute context as a relational cause. A material technological artifact, for example, is only contextual to action if it is interpreted as a perceptual object, reflected upon as a retained psychological state or otherwise related to agency.

We can, therefore, say that context in relational processes is fundamentally a temporal phenomenon in the sense that relational causality involves a circular process in which the past is contextual to the present and the present recreates context through its relationship with the past. In the next section, we discuss how this temporal characteristic of context is central to the process by which multiple contexts are combined in real-time entrepreneurial activity.

Multiple contexts and the temporal dimensions of real-time entrepreneurial activity

The issue of how human activity unfolds in real-time is a focus for traditions of inquiry that include phenomenology (Heidegger 1962; Husserl 1964), pragmatism (Dewey 1929/1958; James 1890/1950; Mead 1934), radical subjectivism (Shackle 1961; Lachmann 1977) and cognitive constructivism (Kelly 1955/63), as well as agency-, action- and activity-focused forms of sociological inquiry (Emirbayer and Mische 1998; Nardi 1996; Vygotsky 1994). These traditions explain the possibility of purposeful activity in terms of the temporal structure of human consciousness (Husserl 1964) or how the past, present and future dimensions of an activity are interrelated in the present moment of doing.

An individual is able to connect the past, present and future dimensions of an activity in the momentary present because the temporal structure of human consciousness facilitates a 'three-fold present' (St Augustine 1961) – the 'continuously present field of past–present–future [that coexists] in the interaction of memory, perception, desire, and anticipation' (Jaques 1982, p. 87). The temporal structure of consciousness concerns the reflexive ability of agency to be aware of multiple contexts relating to the past in the present moment. This present-past dynamic constitutes the three-fold present by combining the temporal orientation of agency towards a dimension of the activity, with contexts that each have a particular temporal significance for the emerging activity (cf. Emirbayer and Mische 1998). In each momentary present, agency has a temporal orientation *towards* either what has happened, what is happening now or what is intended/anticipated/expected to happen in the future, while a context *contextualizes* agency in terms of what has happened, what should happen now or what is intended/anticipated/expected to happen in the future (cf. Emirbayer and Mische 1998).

Entrepreneurial acts of intention, imagination and creativity, for example, involve future-oriented agency towards envisioning outcomes, such as a future market; acts of perception, evaluation and interpretation involve present-oriented agency towards contingent events, such as interaction with stakeholders; while acts of reflection and recollection involve past-oriented agency towards historical events, such as prior business decisions (Emirbayer and Mische 1998). Multiple contexts are combined by temporally-oriented agency in two ways: (1) *retained contexts* – the cognitive retention of past events in psychological states as an object of, and contextual to, agentic attention (Arstila and Lloyd 2014; Husserl 1964), and (2) *instantiated contexts* – the agentic instantiation of past events in the form of personal skill-like knowledge, social practices and heuristic guidelines for entrepreneurial activity (Sarason et al. 2006).

The reflexivity of agency is, therefore, able to connect the temporal dimensions of an activity by assuming a temporal orientation towards the activity and then comparing, contrasting and connecting retained contexts through the practice of instantiating context. By way of illustration, consider a scenario in which an entrepreneur is enacting a business idea in the context of interaction with a stakeholder in order to develop a business model. The stakeholder communicates market information which potentially contradicts the business idea. In the series of moments that follows this communication event, the entrepreneur reflexively combines multiple contexts in order to evaluate this information. First, the agency of the entrepreneur will be present-oriented towards the contingent experience of the communication event, which has been retained as a context for making the practical evaluation. Second, the act of making a practical evaluation will involve contextualizing the contingent experience with prior knowledge/practice instantiated in agency. Third, the entrepreneur must evaluate the communication event against the original business idea, which is also retained in short-term memory as a context for the practical evaluation. Whether the entrepreneur interprets the contingent experience as problematic or not is explained by the dynamics between these contexts as well as further retained contexts that are relevant to the evaluation. These may include an awareness of decision-making criteria, firm strategy, relevant historical events, such as market experience, information about market practice and the history of firm development. In this way, a multiplicity of contexts are contemporaneously interrelated within the short time frame of each momentary present. It should be noted that the entrepreneur's awareness of these contexts can be conscious, unconscious or *tacit* (that is, subsidiary to one's focal awareness).

When retained and instantiated contexts are interrelated by agency, in the momentary present, new context is created in the circular process of relational causality. This process of contextualization is dynamically creative in the sense that it involves interrelating new configurations of contexts as the activity emerges. From the emergent dynamic tensions and connections between multiple contexts, problems are experienced, opportunities are identified, transformations are initiated and solutions are found. Moreover, newly created context can itself embody dynamic tensions, such as the retention of an unresolved problem or time pressure; the possibility of a creative connection or the opportunity of a means–end relationship. A business deadline, for example, can be objectified in language as a point in time in the future, but the reflexive awareness of the deadline as a retained context involves a dynamic relational tension between present and future actions. A business problem can be objectified as a situation that needs to be resolved, but as a retained context it is an unresolved relational contradiction between 'what is' and 'what should, could or might be'. Similarly, a business idea can be objectified as a functional relationship between means and ends, but as a retained context it is a dynamic tension between ends that have yet to be realized and the task of acquiring the means to realize those ends. The agentic combination of multiple contexts in the momentary present, therefore, creates an array of contemporaneous interrelationships within the momentary present. These interrelationships are the actuality of transforming, creating and resolving problems and opportunities, from moment to moment, in the real-time emergence of an entrepreneurial activity.

Implications and conclusions

A relational explanation of how multiple contexts are causally interdependent with agency provides us with a framework for integrating multiple contexts in the explanation of an event. We are not suggesting here the possibility, or even desirability, of a complete reconstruction of how every context is implicated in every momentary present in a real-time process. Rather, a relational conception of context and agency enables the researcher to identify contexts that are associated with a selected empirical event, and which are causally significant in the emergence of that event, as in the scenario outlined above. Multiple contexts can be identified, selected and integrated into an explanation of this event according to a basic distinction between three forms of context: (i) the immediate sensory experience (and retention) of contingent events; (ii) the reflexive awareness of retained prior decisions and other psychological states; and (iii) the cognitive frameworks and structures that are instantiated in agency.

In our illustrative example, the entrepreneur's practical evaluation of the stake-holder communication (as either problematic or non-problematic) is the event being explained. That event can be conceptualized *as if* it was emergent within a momentary present, even if, in real-time, it emerged over a succession of momentary presents. In other words, a conceptual understanding of how context and agency are interrelated in the momentary present can be used to theorize how multiple contexts are contemporaneously and dynamically related to a selected empirical event. This approach explains how 'distal' contexts associated with historical tracts of time and 'proximal' contexts associated with localized circumstances and recent events (Schegloff 1991) are related to a specific transformational moment in the unfolding of an entrepreneurial activity. For example, in our illustrative example, the retention of the communication event can be interpreted as the entrepreneur using a 'proximal context' to monitor what is happening in the present relative to prior decisions regarding what is expected, predicted or intended to happen. Within the same time frame, instantiated context, associated with the distal contexts of personal and social practices, enables the entrepreneur to act in the present in a similar way to actions under similar circumstances in the historical past.

The contemporaneous dynamics between multiple contexts in real-time emergence, involving tensions, contradictions, asymmetries, juxtapositions and connections, have important implications for explaining the sudden, spontaneous and unexpected events of entrepreneurial 'transformation' (Dew et al. 2010), 'creativity' (Dimov 2007) and 'becoming' (Hjorth and Steyaert 2004). In addition, the conceptual idea that context is created, and only causally significant, within the momentary present, has implications for what we understand as the process of 'contextualization'. The notion of contextualization usually refers to either the research practice of contextualizing research findings or to the transaction of 'cues' in social interactions (Gumperz 1982). From the perspective of relational causality in context–agency relationships, the process of contextualization is a process of creating new context for each subsequent moment in the real-time emergence of an activity. A cycle of agency–context causality is, therefore, a unit of analysis for conceptualizing, not just how multiple contexts relate to an event, but also how contexts evolve and are redefined in relation to the changing spatio-temporal circumstances of real-time activity.

In this chapter we have only begun to explore the implications of a relational conception of context and agency in terms of theorizing context. We have made some first tentative steps in the interests of stimulating further discussion about how to address problems of theorizing context. The reconceptualization of context in terms of context–agency relationality helps us to address the problems of context we outlined at the beginning of the article. In particular, this approach addresses the issue of how to account for the 'heterogeneous aspects of contexts' in 'delineating the microfoundations of entrepreneurship' (Zahra and Wright 2011, p.67) by enabling the researcher to conceptualize multiple contexts in relation to the unique spatio-temporal circumstances of the explained event. A relational approach also addresses the problem of the infinite regress of nested contexts because contexts are only selected and conceptually integrated in terms of their causal significance for the explained event. Lastly, a relational conception of context addresses the problem of contextual relativism and theoretical generalization because the principles and mechanisms of context–agency relationality can be used to theorize context in relation to *any* event. Theoretical generalizations can, therefore, be inferred from a comparison of context-specific situations.

NOTE

1 A metaphor for describing 'nested contexts' is that a sentence is the context for a word; a paragraph is the context for a sentence; a chapter is the context for the paragraph; a book is the context for a chapter; and an author is the context for a book (this is expressed by Lonegan (1972) in Burke (2002), p.175).

Suggested readings

Bamberger, Peter (2008), 'From the editors: Beyond contextualization: Using context theories to narrow the micro–macro gap in management research', *Academy of Management Journal*, **51** (5), 839–846. Bamberger's article (although oriented towards management research in general) is useful for encouraging us, as the title infers, to go beyond contextualizing our research findings to thinking about context theories and theorizing context.

Van Gelderen, Marco, Enno Masurel and Karen Verduyn (2012), 'Introduction to "entrepreneurship in context"', in Marco van Gelderen and Enno Masurel (eds), *Entrepreneurship in Context*, London: Routledge, pp. 1–22. This introduction raises many of the key challenges faced when addressing context in entrepreneurship research. For example, it discusses the notion of nested contexts which is useful for moving away from objectifying contexts. It also encourages reflection upon what is context.

References

Arstila, V. and D. Lloyd (2014), *Subjective Time: The Philosophy, Psychology and Neuroscience of Temporality*, Cambridge, MA: MIT Press.

Augustine of Hippo, Saint (1961), *Confessions*, Harmondsworth, Middlesex: Penguin.

Bamberger, Peter (2008), 'From the editors: Beyond contextualization: Using context theories to narrow the micro–macro gap in management research', *Academy of Management Journal*, **51** (5), 839–846.

Bauman, R. and S.L. Briggs (1990), 'Poetics and performance as critical perspectives on language and social life', *Annual Review of Anthropology*, **19**, 59–88.

Bradbury, H. and B. Lichtenstein (2000), 'Relationality in organizational research: Exploring the space between', *Organization Science*, **11** (5), 551–564.

Burke, P. (2002), 'Context in context', *Common Knowledge*, **8** (1), 152–177.

Chalmers, Dominic M. and Eleanor Shaw (2015), 'The endogenous construction of entrepreneurial contexts: A practice-based perspective', *International Small Business Journal*, published online before print 21 September 2015, doi: 10.1177/0266242615589768.

Chiles, T.H., C.S. Tuggle, J.S. McMullan, L. Bierman and D.W. Greening (2010), 'Dynamic creation: Extending the radical Austrian approach to entrepreneurship', *Organization Studies*, **31** (7), 7–46.

Dainton, B. (2014), 'The phenomenal continuum', in V. Arstila and D. Lloyd (eds), *Subjective Time: The Philosophy, Psychology and Neuroscience of Temporality*, Cambridge, MA: MIT Press, pp. 101–138.

Dew, N., S. Read, S.D. Sarasvathy and R. Wiltbank (2010), 'On the entrepreneurial genesis of new markets: Effectual transformation versus causal search and selection', *Journal of Evolutionary Economics*, **21**, 231–253.

Dewey, John (1929/1958), *Experience and Nature*, New York: Dover.

Dewey, J. and A.F. Bentley (1949), *Knowing and the Known*, Boston, MA: Beacon.

Dimov, Dimo (2007), 'Beyond the single-person, single-insight attribution in understanding entrepreneurial opportunities', *Entrepreneurship Theory & Practice*, **31** (5), 713–731.

Drucker, Peter (1985), *Innovation and Entrepreneurship*, New York: Harper and Row.

Emirbayer, M. (1997), 'Manifesto for a relational sociology', *American Journal of Sociology*, **103** (2), 281–317.

Emirbayer, M. and A. Mische (1998), 'What is agency?', *American Journal of Sociology*, **103** (4), 962–1023.

Fletcher, Denise E. (2011), 'A curiosity of contexts: entrepreneurship, enactive research and autoethnography', *Entrepreneurship and Regional Development*, **23** (1–2), 65–76.

Garud, R. and P. Karnøe (2003), 'Bricolage versus breakthrough: Distributed and embedded agency in technology entrepreneurship', *Research Policy*, **32** (2), 277–300.

Gottlieb, G. and C.T. Halpern (2002), 'A relational view of causality in normal and abnormal development', *Development and Psychopathology*, **14**, 421–435.

Gumperz, J.J. (1982), *Discourse Strategies*, Cambridge: Cambridge University Press.

Harré, R. (1972), *The Philosophies of Science*, Oxford: Oxford University Press.

Haugh, Helen (2007), 'New strategies for a sustainable society: The growing contribution of social entrepreneurship', *Business Ethics Quarterly*, **17** (4), 743–749.

Heidegger, Martin (1962), *Being and Time*, New York: Harper and Row.

Hjorth, Daniel and Chris Steyaert (eds) (2004), *Narrative and Discursive Approaches in Entrepreneurship: A Second Movements in Entrepreneurship Book*, Cheltenham, UK and Northampton, MA, USA: Edward Elgar Publishing.

Hosking, Dian Marie, Peter Dachler and Kenneth J. Gergen (1995), *Management and Organization: Relational Alternatives to Individualism*, Avebury: Ashgate Publishing.

Husserl, E. (1964), *The Phenomenology of Internal-Time Consciousness*, trans. by J.S. Churchill, Bloomington, IN: Indiana University Press.

James, W. (1890/1950), *The Principles of Psychology* I–II, New York: Dover.

Jaques, E. (1982), *The Form of Time*, New York: Crane Russak.

Juarrero, A. (2000), 'Dynamics in action: Intentional behavior as a complex system', *Emergence*, **2** (2), 24–57.

Kelly, George A. (1955/1963), *A Theory of Personality: The Psychology of Personal Constructs*, New York: Norton.

Kortooms, Toine (2012), *The Phenomenology of Time: Edmund Husserl's Analysis of Time Consciousness*, Dordrecht: Kluwer.

Lachmann, L. (1977), *Capital, Expectations and the Market Process*, Kansas City: Sheed Andrews and McMeel.

Lonegan, B. (1972), *Method in Theology*, London: Darton, Longman and Todd.

Low, Murray B. and Ian C. MacMillan (1988), 'Entrepreneurship: past research and future challenges', *Journal of Management*, **14** (2), 139–161.

Mead, George H. (1934), *Mind, Self and Society*, ed. and introduced by C. Morris, Chicago, IL: University of Chicago Press.

Mische, Anne (2011), 'Relational sociology, culture, and agency', in John Scott and Peter Carrington (eds), *Sage Handbook of Social Network Analysis*, London: Sage Publications, pp. 80–99.

Mitchell, J.C. (1987), 'The situational perspective', in J.C. Mitchell (ed.), *Cities, Society and Social Perception: A Central African Perspective*, Oxford: Clarendon Press, pp. 1–33.

Nardi, N.B. (ed.) (1996), *Context and Consciousness: Activity Theory and Human–Computer Interaction*, Cambridge, MA: The MIT Press.

O'Driscoll, G.P. and M.J. Rizzo (1996), *The Economics of Time and Ignorance*, London and New York: Routledge.

Sarason, Y., T. Dean and J.F. Dillard (2006), 'Entrepreneurship as the nexus of individual and opportunity: A structuration view', *Journal of Business Venturing*, **21**, 286–305.

Schegloff, E. (1991), 'In another context', in A. Duranti and C. Goodwin (eds), *Rethinking Context: Language as an Interpretive Phenomenon*, Cambridge: Cambridge University Press, pp. 191–227.

Selden, Paul D. and Denise E. Fletcher (2015), 'The entrepreneurial journey as an emergent hierarchical system of artifact-creating processes', *Journal of Business Venturing*, **30** (4), 603–615.

Shackle, George L.S. (1961), *Decision, Order and Time in Human Affairs*, London: Cambridge University Press.

Shane, Scott (2003), *A General Theory of Entrepreneurship: The Individual–Opportunity Nexus*, Cheltenham, UK and Northampton, MA, USA: Edward Elgar Publishing.

Shotter, John (1993), *Conversational Realities: Constructing Life through Language*, Thousand Oaks, CA: Sage.

Steyaert, Chris and René Bouwen (1997), 'Telling stories of entrepreneurship – Towards a contextual epistemology for entrepreneurial studies', in Rik Donckels and Asko Miettinen (eds), *Entrepreneurship and SME Research: On its way to the Next Millennium*, Aldershot: Ashgate, pp. 47–61.

Ucbasaran, Deniz, Paul Westhead and Mike Wright (2001), 'The focus of entrepreneurial research: Contextual and process issues', *Entrepreneurship: Theory & Practice*, **25**, 57–78.

van Gelderen, Marco, Enno Masurel and Karen Verduyn (2012), 'Introduction to "Entrepreneurship in Context"', in Marco van Gelderen and Enno Masurel (eds), *Entrepreneurship in Context*, London: Routledge, pp. 1–22.

van Oers, B. (1998), 'From context to contextualizing', in E. Forman and B. van Oers (eds), *Mathematics Learning in Socio-Cultural Contexts*, Special Issue of Learning and Instruction, **8** (6), 473–488.

Vygotsky, L.S. (1994), *Thought and Language*, Cambridge, MA: The MIT Press.

Wellman, Barry (1988), 'Structural analysis: From method and metaphor to theory and substance', in Barry Wellman and S.D. Berkowitz (eds), in *Social Structures: A Network Approach*, Cambridge UK: Cambridge University Press, pp. 19–61.

Welter, Friederike (2011), 'Contextualizing entrepreneurship – conceptual challenges and ways forward', *Entrepreneurship Theory and Practice*, **35** (1), 165–184.

Whetten, David A. (2009), 'An examination of the interface between context and theory applied to the study of Chinese organizations', *Management and Organization Review*, **5**, 29–55.

Zahra, Shaker A. (2007), 'Contextualising theory building in entrepreneurship research', *Journal of Business Venturing*, **22**, 443–452.

Zahra, Shaker A. and Mike Wright (2011), 'Entrepreneurship's next act', *Academy of Management Perspectives*, **25** (4), 67–83.

8 Theorizing entrepreneurship in context[1]

Erik Stam

Introduction

All entrepreneurial phenomena occur within contexts. By itself this observation is somewhat innocuous: each human being thinks and acts within certain social, linguistic, and material contexts, and human beings are not disembodied spirits, but consist of flesh and blood, living at certain concrete times and places. Contexts matter for entrepreneurial action (see Welter 2011; Zahra et al. 2014), and a contextual approach to entrepreneurship clearly leads us away from context independent forms of inquiry (such as the personality traits and human capital approaches to entrepreneurship). But we must tackle the more difficult and more interesting issues of how (much) distinct contexts, and under which circumstances contexts matter for entrepreneurship. The conceptualization of the context in which entrepreneurial processes take place is still in its infancy. The purpose of this chapter is to explore the foundations for theorizing entrepreneurship in context. We define entrepreneurship here as the process in which opportunities for new value creation are identified, evaluated and exploited by individuals (Bruyat and Julien 2000; Shane and Venkatamaran 2000; Stam et al. 2012). A process in which the ultimate creation of new value is highly unpredictable (Knight 1921). The key questions are: what is the context of entrepreneurship and how can we know about this context? These are ontological ('what is?') and epistemological ('how can we know?') questions, which are fundamental to theory and empirics. The chapter thus begins with an introduction of the meta-theoretical building blocks for a contextual approach to entrepreneurship, namely constructive realism and methodological interactionism or relationalism. Behavioural research is always based, either implicitly or explicitly, on assumptions about the thought and behaviour of the actors involved. These meta-theoretical building blocks provide a general framework for the analysis of thought and action of entrepreneurs.

Next, we explore three modes of analysis in current social science that are essential for the study of entrepreneurship in context: evolutionary analysis, institutional analysis, and time-geography. Each mode of analysis approaches the context of entrepreneurship from different but complementary perspectives.

Meta-theoretical foundations

Theorizing necessitates a meta-theoretical foundation. The foundations for inquiry into real world issues are epistemology and ontology. Here we start with the epistemology (the study of knowledge), that is, the cognitive basis of the contextual approach to entrepreneurship. The term cognition refers to the way people perceive (perception, awareness, sensitivity to stimulus), interpret (meaning creation, understanding, knowledge), and evaluate (goal congruence) the world (Nooteboom 2000, also see Chapter 2 by Brännback and Carsrud). Cognition is about both the quantity of relevant information and the ability of the actor to process information. Cognitive capabilities of human beings are limited, and thus they are also not able to process all the available information: bounded rationality (Simon 1959). Next to information stimulus and processing, cognition is also about the hermeneutical interpretation and evaluation of information, which ultimately result in personal knowledge or belief. The proposed cognitive basis here is based on the assumptions that the mind is inextricably interwoven with the body (embodied cognition), world (situated cognition), and action (situated action). Embodied cognition assumes that agents' cognition cannot be separated from the body, as experience is rooted in bodily structures. Knowledge has to be actively constructed by embodied agents in their environment. Situated cognition or situated action emphasizes that cognition is constructed in interaction with the surrounding (material and social) environment of the embodied agent. In former approaches cognition was regarded as something that can be modelled by computers, and these approaches proposed that action is based on a cognitive structure that is context independent. In the situated cognition/action view the converse holds true: cognitive structure is based (but not determined) on action in a certain context (material and social environment). The situated action view connects with pragmatism in philosophy, where it is argued that there is no 'absolute' answer to 'perspective-independent' questions, but only 'objective solutions to problems which are situated in a place, at a time' (Putnam 1990, p. 178; also cf. Barnes 2008; Sunley 1996).

Regarding the ontological aspects of the contextual approach to entrepreneurship we assume that there is a world that exists independent of our ideas about it and that there is certain correspondence between this reality and our perception. This means that people may agree on certain aspects of reality, especially by constructing this reality inter-subjectively, that is, sharing information of other peoples' vantage point. Interaction with other persons may lead to a construction or deconstruction of certain aspects of reality. Relationalism becomes a synonym for hermeneutics, as in hermeneutics it is proposed that people interpret according to perspectives built on the past (that is, prior knowledge; Shane 2000), and thus the context of interpretation is not objectively given but is itself already constructed (Ley 1998; Nooteboom 2000). This does not lead to extreme relativistic, subjective, particular local knowledge as people have constructed their categories in a (partly) common material and social environment. So there is an area of common understanding beyond the particularities of local knowledge (Ley 1998, p. 28). Here the hermeneutic endeavour begins with the inevitable collision between evidence from different vantage points and the researcher. If we take this interaction between the embodied agent and his or her environment as central, then the starting point for analysing behaviour is methodological interactionism. Methodological interactionism means that social theories must be grounded in the interaction between individuals, and not just in the attitudes and behaviour of individuals (methodological individualism) or in the behaviour of irreducible groups of individuals (methodological holism; Blaug 1992, p. 250). There is a growing consensus on the relevance of methodological interactionism in innovation studies and in the study of identity formation.[2] For the proper analysis of these and other topics in entrepreneurship studies, methodological interactionism is almost indispensable. People are seen to perceive, interpret, and evaluate the world according to forms or categories of thought that they have developed in interaction with their context.

Relationalism is the central issue, not relativism. The concept of relationalism makes the point that cognition or more specifically the interpretation of events, while relational to an observing subject, is not entirely the product of each person's subject position. There are aspects of reality, the 'objective world', about which observers from different vantage points may agree, which are not arbitrary. This objective world exists independently from our knowledge. So a social constructivist theory of knowledge is reconciled here with a realist ontology: constructive realism. The meta-theoretical foundations for a contextual approach to entrepreneurship can be summarized in the statement that knowledge arises from categories that people construct in interaction with their material and social environment.

Modes of analysis

Every scientific field has to develop procedures (modes of analysis, theory, research design and method) that are relevant for its own research purposes (Toulmin 2001). Here the research purpose is to improve insight into the context of entrepreneurial phenomena. In order to understand the role of context in the realization of entrepreneurial processes we need modes of analysis to conceptualize this context. These modes of analysis provide the lenses through which to conceptualize the world or the language that makes it possible to analyse specific empirical issues. They offer heuristic devices in order to grasp reality. Context has been defined in the former section as the surrounding environment of the agent. This context has time- and place-specific material and social aspects, which may be experienced as subjective and objective. In the next sections three specific modes of analysis from social science are presented that are helpful in analysing entrepreneurial phenomena in such a context: evolutionary analysis, institutional analysis, and time-geography. Each of these modes of analysis recognizes the time-specific material and social aspects of the context in its own specific, but also partly overlapping way. These modes of analysis are also congruent with the philosophical foundations of the contextual approach to entrepreneurship.

Evolutionary analysis

Evolutionary analysis is about the analysis of the dynamic process that is behind observed change in socioeconomic systems. The use of evolutionary analysis makes it possible to explain how particular forms of organization and behaviour come to exist and evolve in specific kinds of environments. Evolution is a concept that has become quite central in debates in social science in general, but also in entrepreneurship studies in particular (Breslin 2008; Stam 2010). Evolution results from the operation of three generic processes: variation, selection, and retention (Aldrich 1999; Van de Ven and Poole 1995).

Variation refers to change from current routines and competences and the change in organizational forms. Even though the strict Darwinian evolutionary analogy would not give space for human reflexivity and conscious goal-seeking activity (Sunley 1996, p. 346), evolutionary analysis does not at all demand the absence of purposiveness. Variation can be intentional, when people actively attempt to generate alternatives and seek solutions to problems (intentional adaptation, which implies learning), but it can also be blind, that is, independent of environmental or selection pressures. These blind variations result from accidents, chance, luck, creative exploration, or what is sometimes called serendipity. However, mere adaptation might not be sufficient for organizations in certain situations. In fact, a too-perfect adaptation to the environment might preclude adaptability in subsequent rounds of competition. In this case an ability to redefine and recombine assets is needed to retain flexibility. In contrast with economic and sociological theories that exclude the individuality of the entrepreneur, evolutionary analysis dealing with complex systems views individuals and local events as a critical source of diversity and change (Garnsey 1998; Fuller and Moran 2001). Collective processes of complex systems are made up of 'the microscopic reality of diversity and individual subjectivity, which in fact provides the basis for the adaptive responses of the system and its creativity' (Allen 1997, p. 2).

Selection refers to the differential elimination of certain types of variation. Variations that are more fit to meet the demands of their environment are more probable than others to acquire resources and are thus selected. Processes of selection operate by affecting the availability of resources. Selection forces operate at different levels: fitness to different, nested environments. Three types of selection forces at the environmental level can be distinguished: economic (for example, market forces, competitive pressures), institutional (conformity to institutionalized norms), and spatial (climate, transport infrastructure) (Lambooy 2002). Economic selection forces act through markets that are embedded in an institutional environment and situated in a spatial environment.

The third evolutionary process involves the operation of a retention mechanism for the selective retention of positively selected variations. This retention provides the constraints on variation, as selected variations are preserved, duplicated, or otherwise reproduced. Within organizations this can be observed by the stability in the structure and activities of the organizations (inertia): 'organizational memory' in routines, standardization and specialization of roles, material resources such as buildings and machines. Within society in general, retention mechanisms can be found in the form of institutionalization of practices in cultural beliefs and values. Selected variations might also diffuse through imitation (mimetic effects) and the mobility of people and organizations. Distance (related to transport and communication networks) might play a major role as a barrier for diffusion (see Hägerstrand 1967), as might other factors like unwillingness and incompetence to imitate.

The selection pressures and the search for effective variation are only relevant if resources are scarce. Economic actors compete to obtain scarce resources because their supply is limited. A specific subcategory of evolutionary analysis in social science is the complexity approach (Arthur et al. 1997). This approach has also been called the process-and-emergence perspective because it focuses on understanding the emergence of self-organizing structures that create complexity out of simplicity and order out of chaos through interaction between the basic elements at the origin of the process. The central argument of complexity is that 'interactions between parts of systems create novel, unpredictable patterns, and that while the history of the system is relevant in understanding its dynamic, the isolation of individual parts of the system (analysis) does not reveal the causal mechanisms in the system' (Fuller and Moran 2001, p. 53).

In economics this approach has led to new ways of thinking about economic problems: the economy is regarded as an evolving complex system (Arthur et al. 1997; Beinhocker 2007), and the enterprise as a complex adaptive system (Fuller and Moran 2001) or an entrepreneurial system (Bruyat and Julien 2000). Some even argue that the notion of entrepreneurial behaviour (entrepreneurs as agents of change that introduce novel behaviours into the economy) is an unavoidable component of any complexity-based approach to the economy (Metcalfe et al. 2000, p. 9).

Complex systems may behave in ways that are very difficult to predict, although they are sensitive to initial conditions. With evolutionary analysis alternative development paths are permitted to unfold from the same initial conditions. These paths cannot be predicted, but evolutionary analysis provides a framework for understanding the complex mechanisms that generate these different paths of systems. These complex systems are the outcome of a relentless process of deliberate actions (adaptation) and unique, serendipitous interactions (feedback from the environment).

Evolving organizations as complex adaptive systems have to be observed in light of tensions between agency and structure. These structures enable and constrain the interdependent agents, and may act as selection forces. Through adaptation organizations may influence their environments, and through feedback the environments in turn influence the organizations. By implication, change is not an outcome of adaptation or environmental selection alone, but rather the joint outcome of intentionality and environmental effects. This points at the concept of coevolution, that is, mutual adaptation between the evolving unit and its environment. In this interactional, feedback perspective, the unidirectional view of cause-and-effect relationships gives way to a recursive bidirectional view of mutual causality. This adaptation in a coevolutionary process is path-dependent. Path-dependent processes may lead to outcomes other than those implied by historical efficiency. Complex systems (economies, firms) are subject to path dependent trajectories of development. At a lower level we could also recognize cognitive path dependence – 'you can't get everywhere from anywhere, and where you are now strongly constrains your potential future intellectual trajectories' (Clark 1997, p. 205).

Path dependence enables and constrains adaptation. The concept of path dependence is useful, but problematic for explaining novelty created by entrepreneurship. Entrepreneurship is about path creation, mindful deviation from existing structures that are the outcomes of past adaptations. In this sense it involves real creativity and reflexivity, not just imitation (Garud et al. 2010). This path creation points at the entrepreneurial paradox in evolutionary analysis: entrepreneurs as agents are embedded and situated in social and material structures (path dependence) but also break out of these structures by virtue of acting 'entrepreneurially' (path creation).

Institutional analysis

Institutional analysis is about the comparative and historical analysis of human social institutions: social relations, structures, processes, or objects (Granovetter 1992; Sayer 2000). The task of institutional analysis is providing us 'with those conceptual tools required to penetrate the maze of social relationships in which the economy was embedded' (Polanyi et al. 1957, p. 242). In institutional analysis institutions are described as a kind of infrastructure that enables and constrains human coordination and allocation of resources. Institutional analysis is about static phenomena as well as dynamic phenomena. In its dynamic version, institutional analysis is a methodology that encompasses changing and historically specific objects of analysis. In this sense it is better to treat the concept of 'institution' both as a pre-given entity (structure) and as an activity of institutionalizing (process), that is, offering or imposing enabling constraints (Nooteboom 2000). Organizations and institutions are considered as being produced by an ongoing process of organizing and institutionalizing. This aligns with the views of entrepreneurship as agents creating and transforming organizations (Gartner 1990; Sharma and Chrisman 1999) and institutions (Battilana et al. 2009; Maguire et al. 2004), and institutional theory of entrepreneurship (Sine and David 2010). Institutionalization can also be seen as an investment process in organizational forms that, for example, lower uncertainty or provide legitimacy and ultimately lower transaction costs. This also means that the institutional environment is no longer a fixed class of entities, but has become a relative concept that has to be defined for a specific 'coordination problem' in a specific context. More encompassing structures form the institutional environment for less encompassing ones (Nooteboom 2000, p. 94). Institutional analysis can therefore be practised on multiple levels (and spatial scales), as long as the levels of analysis are explicitly distinguished. The levels of institutional analysis lie along a continuum that ranges from personal networks at one pole and society itself at the other end. These levels of analysis can be related to agency and structures, in which 'higher-level' institutions (structures) provide enabling constraints at 'lower-level' institutions (agents). A social structure forms the institutional environment for another (lower-level) structure if it affects the causality of the actions of this lower-level structure (Nooteboom 2000, p. 111). For example, an enterprise is an institutional arrangement in the context of a national business system or national innovation system (national institutional environment). But the enterprise can be an institutional environment for intra-organizational processes. When networks are regarded as organizing institutions, network analysis becomes a specific branch of institutional analysis. Network analysis is useful as an analytical device for studying behaviour in context. As Thrift and Olds (1996, p. 333) write: 'The network serves as an analytical compromise, in the best sense of the word, between the fixities of bounded region metaphor and the fluidities of the flow metaphor'. Network analysis offers tools to identify and measure the structure of relationships within a selected group of actors, that is, within particular social contexts (Johannisson et al. 1994; Johannisson 1995). Networks can be conceptualized as intervening variables between institutional structures and the behaviour of actors. The focus of network analysis is based on the assumption of the importance of relationships among interacting units, and is thus completely in line with methodological interactionism.

The lowest level of institution should be higher than human beings, as human beings cannot be regarded as institutions. Entrepreneurs are the human beings that creatively destroy existing institutions if they perceive such action as profitable (Battilana et al. 2009; Maguire et al. 2004), and the entrepreneur is seen as the only actor who is able to 'bear uncertainty' that is involved in this action (Knight 1921). In this regard the entrepreneur is opposed to the 'manager' who acts on the basis of routines, and responds to changes in the environment by adaptation (Beckert 1999, p. 789). In institutional analysis the entrepreneurial paradox concerns innovation and tradition: the entrepreneur takes a reflective stance towards established contexts (innovation), but is also dependent on the (enabling) established contexts.

Time-geography

Time-geography is

> a foundation for a general geographical perspective. It represents a new structure of thought under development, which attempts to consolidate the spatial and temporal perspectives of different disciplines on a more solid basis than has thus far taken place. Time-geography is not a subject area per se, or a theory in its narrow sense, but rather an attempt to construct a broad structure of thought which may form a framework capable of fulfilling two tasks. The first is to receive and bring into contact knowledge from highly distinct scientific areas and from everyday praxis. The second is to reveal relations, the

nature of which escape researchers as soon as the object of research is separated from its
given milieu in order to study it in isolation, experimentally or in some other way distilled.
(Hägerstrand, in Lenntorp 1999, p. 155)

Time-geography should be seen as a foundation for building contextual theory:
it is both a mode of analysis that integrates knowledge from disparate academic
fields and everyday experiences, and a mode of analysis that provides a fine-grained
perspective on analysing the context as an inseparable part of human behaviour,
including entrepreneurial action. It also provides a necessary complement to historical approaches to entrepreneurship (see also Chapter 6 by Wadhwani). The
basic point of departure in time-geography (or 'geo-historical analysis' as it is sometimes called) is that 'when, where, and in what order something happens affects
how it happens' (Tilly, in Pred 1990, p. xi). In other words, the central explanatory variables are time, place and space, and irreversible sequence. The approach
demonstrates the situatedness of human actions and their products in particular
(time–space) settings whose arrangement then constrains and enables subsequent
human actions (path dependence). Space and time are inextricably interwoven,
even inseparable (Thrift 1996). Phenomena can be studied in different timescales
ranging from biographies, epochs, and episodes to events and on different spatial
scales ranging from 'face-to-face' proximity, districts, localities, regions and nations
to continents. The spatio-temporal situation of people and resources, their presence and absence, even constitutes entrepreneurial phenomena.

This constitutive property of (time–)space may be in terms of material preconditions for actions, but also in the constitution of meanings (Sayer 2000). This latter
aspect can be found in the changing meaning of relationships between actors when
they become spatially separated, and more broadly in the change of the functioning
of institutions. Time-geography is a contextual approach in which human activity is
treated as a social event in its immediate spatial and temporal setting (Hägerstrand
1984; Thrift 1996): 'human action always has to enfold in real dioramas [metaphor
for situations] and whatever foreseen or unexpected consequences come about,
they depend upon what is present and what is absent and in what sort of relations
precisely where the actions happen' (Hägerstrand 1984, p. 376). This context is not
necessarily 'local', it is 'a performative social situation, a plural event which is more
or less spatially extensive and more or less temporally specific' (Thrift 1996, p. 41).
Human practices are always situated in time and space, and the contexts in which
activity is situated are the result of institutions which themselves reflect social
structure. These institutions can be seen as nodes in time and space around which
human activity is concentrated (Thrift 1996).

Time-geography is complementary to the other two modes of analysis as it claims
that 'conventional social science has given history privileges while dismissing geography as unworthy of attention' (Tilly, in Pred 1990, p. xii). In this sense it criticizes
the neglect of the spatial dimension in, for example, institutional and evolutionary
analysis. These two modes of analysis take space only implicitly into account: in
institutional analysis the nation-state is often treated as the 'natural' boundary of

certain institutions and in evolutionary analysis the selection environment is often implicitly territorially bounded.

Time-geography illustrates the way that people trace out paths in time and space, moving from one place to another in order to fulfil particular purposes. The central concepts of this time-geography are path, project, and situation. Continuity and corporeality are essential, as they set limits on how and at what pace one situation can evolve into a following one. People draw paths that are made up of projects. The concept of project refers to all events in evolving situations that an actor must secure in order to reach a goal, that is, the practical realizations of intentions (Hägerstrand 1982, p. 324). This relates to the somewhat narrower concept of project in economics and organization studies (Whitley 2006). Paths can have different timescales ranging from a lifetime (starting at the point of birth and ending at the point of death) to a daily path. For analysing the behaviour of actors these constraints and their interactions (in direct obvious ways and in indirect ways which are less easily discovered) have to be studied together with intentions of the actors.

The basic model of time geography (Hägerstrand 1970) emphasizes the constraints of space and time on behaviour of individuals. Three types of constraints are conceptualized. The first one – capability constraints – are 'those which limit the activities of the individual because of his biological construction and/or the tools he can command' (Hägerstrand 1970, p. 12).

Coupling constraints are the second type, which 'define where, when, and for how long, the individual [path] has to join other individuals, tools, and materials in order to produce, consume, and transact' (Hägerstrand 1970, p. 14). The necessary grouping of several paths can be referred to as a 'bundle'. An example of coupling constraints is the fact that enterprises – as bundles of (intangible and tangible) resources – have concentrated most of their activities and resources at one point in space. In contrast with the predictions of many futurologists, most enterprises are still not 'virtual' and most people work together in spatial proximity and not in 'virtual teams', to ensure the human moment, necessary for effective communication about complex issues (Hallowell 1999). Even when they do not belong to the same firm, for example, at co-working spaces, incubators, and accelerators. However, this bundle does not always have to occur within spatial proximity of the composing parts. Telecommunication allows people to form bundles without being spatially proximate (time–space distanciation). Place-to-place interactions are made possible by (computer-)mediated place-to-place contacts with Internet, telephone, and so on (Wellman 2001). This means that in electronic space distance and transportation do not matter, the only necessity is being connected in 'electronic spaces'. If logistics and the supply of material products are involved, however, time costs induced by distance seem less affected by new and flexible transportation technologies. On the contrary, in some flexible and highly specialized production systems 'just-in-time' and other spatial logistics are of major importance and have important locational implications. 'Time' still is a very critical factor in management, sometimes reinforcing the crucial role of spatial proximity.

Customers want to decide as fast as possible and also want to get new goods and services quicker and quicker, which means that firms have to focus upon more rapid product development. For firms this means that they have to mobilize all the available knowledge, not only to accelerate the availability of their goods and services, but also to develop new solutions much faster. This also means that the organizational structure of the firm has to be adapted, or even completely renewed. The search for evermore fluid and market-responsive organizational forms has led to a focus on network enterprises and projects as a form of economic organization. These projects operate in a specific societal context: 'networks, localities, and institutions feed essential sources of information, legitimation, and trust that provide the very preconditions for the "projectification" of economic organisation' (Grabher 2001, p. 1329).

The third type of constraints relate to authority. These authority constraints restrict the set of possible actions in specific domains. A domain refers to 'a time–space entity within which things and events are under control of a given individual or a given group' (Hägerstrand 1970, p. 16). Actions in these domains are restricted by power, informal, and formal institutions. Domains can be found with different durations and at different, nested (spatial) scales. For example the premises of a firm may be a domain that lies in the domain of a municipality, which in its turn lies in the domain of a nation. While nations have a rather long duration, the premises of a firm might have a rather short one. Decision-makers in different domains can influence each other, for example, by trading or by negotiation. Just like institutions enable and constrain, space and time also constrain and enable. In this sense one might also conceptualize capability, coupling, and authority opportunities, that is, opportunities that are created due to particular capabilities, bundles, and/or authoritative powers. However, it depends on the particular interaction of agents and their context whether these opportunities are identified and pursued.

With time-geography the dialogic between the entrepreneur and new value creation can be analysed, within an ongoing process and situated within a specific context. Entrepreneurs introduce ideas that are completely new, or new to certain contexts. New ways of organizing – or rebundling – resources and collaborators from different contexts are introduced to realize opportunities perceived by the entrepreneur. The new organization that is created by the entrepreneur can be seen as the creation of a new bundle, a project that serves the purpose of jointly realizing the intentions that the entrepreneur is unable to realize by herself alone (capability constraints).

Conclusions and implications

In this chapter we provided meta-theoretical foundations and modes of analysis for a contextual approach to entrepreneurship. Even though entrepreneurship is about individuals undertaking entrepreneurial actions, these individuals and their

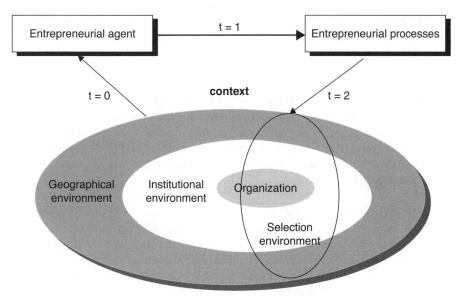

Source: Stam (2003, p. 22).

Figure 8.1   Entrepreneurship in interaction with its context

actions are enabled and constrained by their contexts. Entrepreneurial action is not only enabled and constrained by its contexts, but also affects contexts. We started with a discussion of the meta-theoretical foundations of the proposed contextual approach to entrepreneurship. We assume that cognition is constructed by embodied agents in interaction with their material and social environment. The world in which we live is to some extent socially constructed, but also exists independent of our knowledge about it. So on the one hand, everybody can perceive context in a way that is unique, due to personal experience and social affiliations. With respect to entrepreneurial action this means that people can imagine unique entrepreneurial opportunities, building on their unique biography including multiple contexts. But on the other hand, reality hits back in the sense that it is not a construction of individual and group perception only. Even if one imagines unique entrepreneurial opportunities, contextual conditions provide constraints in pursuing these. These positions lead to a constructive realism. As the interaction between the embodied agent and his or her environment is central, the starting point for analysing behaviour is a methodological interactionism: interactions between (groups of) human beings and their context.

Three different modes of analysis – evolutionary, institutional, and time-geography – each offer complementary insights for a contextual approach to entrepreneurship. For the explanation of entrepreneurial phenomena we need to take into account the interactions between entrepreneurial processes (by entrepreneurial agents) and their contexts (see Figure 8.1). Institutional analysis, evolutionary analysis, and time-geography are helpful starting points for theorizing entrepreneurial phenomena in context. Organizations can be regarded as the organizational context of entrepreneurship, while organizations are situated in a selection environment that is conditioned by an institutional and geographical environment.

For concrete research on entrepreneurial phenomena we may use more substantive theories that are congruent with this approach, or that can be made more contextual with this approach. Examples are the organizational capabilities approach (Teece et al. 2000), the resource dependence perspective (Pfeffer and Salancik 1978), the theory of planned behaviour (Ajzen 1991), and social action theory (Granovetter 1985).

One example of making the theory of planned behaviour more context sensitive is the way Stam et al. (2012) have added formal and informal institutions to the theory of planned behaviour, in order to provide a better understanding of how public policy might affect the prevalence of ambitious entrepreneurship. This links macro changes in the institutional environment to changes in both the intention and realization of venture growth.

Another example of how organizational capabilities and resource dependence theory can be used to understand how entrepreneurs shape their (geographically unfavourable) context, is the study by Vaessen (1993; see also Vaessen and Wever 1993; Vaessen and Keeble 1995). This study shows that geography is not destiny, and that entrepreneurs of high-growth firms have a choice in how to deal with geographically unfavourable (peripheral) contexts: they can manipulate it, adapt to it, make themselves immune to it, or utilize it. Even though they face a (geographically defined) selection environment, they can take action to either change this, or to circumvent particular elements of it.

Stam (2003, 2007) provides an example of how organizational capabilities and social action theory can be used to understand the way context constrains the behaviour of entrepreneurs and their (fast-growing) firms. This study shows that firms' locational behaviour is the outcome of a process of initiatives by entrepreneurs, enabled and constrained by resources, capabilities, and relations with stakeholders within and outside the firms: entrepreneurs decide whether to move their firms outside their spatial context (region of origin) for different reasons in distinct phases of the firms' life course. The spatial organization of entrepreneurial firms co-evolves with the accumulation of the firms' capabilities. The study provides a developmental approach (path) that incorporates evolutionary mechanisms and recognizes human agency.

The meta-theoretical foundations and mode of analysis presented and discussed in this chapter provide a basis for theory construction and concrete research on entrepreneurial phenomena. Only with more empirical research into these phenomena we can learn and unlearn, and possibly even make progress.

NOTES

1 This chapter is partly based on Stam (2003), Chapter 2.

2 In innovation studies there has been a shift from the linear model to the interactive model, in which technology is not regarded as 'manna from heaven' but as something that evolves in interaction between actors. For this interactive learning process the focus is not on pure scientific knowledge (episteme) but on the practical and tacit knowledge (techné) of the user (Nonaka and Takeuchi 1995; Polanyi 1962). See Giddens (1991) and Taylor (1989) for the relevance of methodological interactionism in identity studies.

Suggested readings

Three articles that explicitly theorize entrepreneurship in context, focussing on the geo-historical evolution of entrepreneurs, their firms, and other forms of governance:

Vaessen, P. and Wever, E. (1993), 'Spatial responsiveness of small firms', *Tijdschrift voor Economische en Sociale Geografie*, **84**, 119–131. This study shows that entrepreneurs have a choice in how to deal with geographically unfavourable (peripheral) contexts, taking action to either change this context, adapting to it, or to circumvent particular elements of it, making use of their own biographical resources.

Grabher, G. (2002), 'The project ecology of advertising: tasks, talents and teams', *Regional Studies*, **36** (3), 245–262. This study explores interdependencies between projects and firms as well as other more traditional 'permanent forms' of organization in one particular context, the London advertising industry. It shows how projects are interrelated with agencies, personal ties, localities and corporate networks, embedded in different organizational and social layers (that is, the project ecology).

Stam, E. (2007), 'Why butterflies don't leave: Locational behavior of entrepreneurial firms', *Economic Geography*, **83** (1), 27–50. This study shows how entrepreneurs' biographies and the evolution of their firms are intertwined and how this explains how spatial context affects the early life course of firms, but also how young firms can choose different spatial contexts to invest in.

References

Ajzen, I. (1991), 'The theory of planned behaviour', *Organizational Behavior and Human Decision Processes*, **50**, 179–211.

Aldrich, H.E. (1999), *Organizations Evolving*, London: Sage.

Allen, P. (1997), *Cities and Regions as Self-Organizing Systems; Models of Complexity*, London: Gordon and Breach.

Arthur, W.B., S. Durlauf, and D. Lane (1997), *The Economy as an Evolving Complex System II*, Reading, MA: Addison-Wesley.

Barnes, T.J. (2008), 'American pragmatism: Towards a geographical introduction', *Geoforum*, **39** (4), 1542–1554.

Battilana, J., B. Leca, and E. Boxenbaum (2009), 'How actors change institutions: Towards a theory of institutional entrepreneurship', *The Academy of Management Annals*, **3** (1), 65–107.

Beckert, J. (1999), 'Agency, entrepreneurs, and institutional change. The role of strategic choice and institutionalized practices in organizations', *Organization Studies*, **20**, 777–799.

Beinhocker, E.D. (2007), *The Origin of Wealth: The Radical Remaking of Economics and What it Means for Business and Society*, London: Random House.

Blaug, M. (1992), *The Methodology of Economics*, 2nd edn, Cambridge: Cambridge University Press.

Boschma, R. and R. Martin (eds) (2010), *The Handbook of Evolutionary Economic Geography*, Cheltenham, UK and Northampton, MA, USA: Edward Elgar Publishing.

Breslin, D. (2008), 'A review of the evolutionary approach to the study of entrepreneurship', *International Journal of Management Reviews*, **10** (4), 399–423.

Bruyat, C. and P.-A. Julien (2000), 'Defining the field of research in entrepreneurship', *Journal of Business Venturing*, **16**, 165–180.

Clark, A. (1997), *Being There: Putting Brain, Body, and World Together Again*, Boston, MA: MIT Press.

Fuller, T. and P. Moran (2001), 'Small enterprises as complex adaptive systems: A methodological question?', *Entrepreneurship & Regional Development*, **13**, 47–63.

Garnsey, E. (1998), 'The genesis of the high technology milieu: a study in complexity', *International Journal of Urban and Regional Research*, **22** (3), 361–377.

Gartner, W.B. (1990), 'What are we talking about when we talk about entrepreneurship?', *Journal of Business Venturing*, **5** (1), 15–28.

Garud, R., A. Kumaraswamy, and P. Karnøe (2010), 'Path dependence or path creation?', *Journal of Management Studies*, **47** (4), 760–774.

Giddens, A. (1991), *Modernity and Self-Identity*, Cambridge: Polity Press.

Grabher, G. (2001), 'Locating economic action: Projects, networks, localities, institutions', *Environment and Planning A*, **33** (8), 1329–1334.

Grabher, G. (2002), 'The project ecology of advertising: Tasks, talents and teams', *Regional Studies*, **36** (3), 245–262.

Granovetter, M. (1985), 'Economic action and social structure: The problem of embeddedness', *American Journal of Sociology*, 481–510.

Granovetter, M. (1992), 'Economic institutions as social constructions: A framework for analysis', *Acta Sociologica*, **35** (1), 3–11.

Hallowell, E.M. (1999), 'The human moment at work', *Harvard Business Review*, **77** (1), 58–66.

Hägerstrand, T. (1967), *Innovation Diffusion as a Spatial Process*, trans. by A. Pred, Chicago, IL: Chicago University Press.

Hägerstrand, T. (1970), 'What about people in regional science?', *Regional Science Association Papers*, **XXIV**, 7–21.

Hägerstrand, T. (1982), 'Diorama, path and project', *Tijdschrift voor Economische en Sociale Geografie*, **73**, 323–339.

Hägerstrand, T. (1984), 'Presence and absence: A look at conceptual choices and bodily necessities', *Regional Studies*, **18**, 373–380.

Johannisson, B. (1995), 'Paradigms and entrepreneurial networks – Some methodological challenges', *Entrepreneurship & Regional Development*, **7** (3), 215–232.

Johannisson, B., O. Alexanderson, K. Nowicki, and K. Senneseth (1994), 'Beyond anarchy and organization: Entrepreneurs in contextual networks', *Entrepreneurship & Regional Development*, **6** (4), 329–356.

Knight, F. (1921), *Risk, Uncertainty and Profit*, Boston, MA: Houghton Mifflin.

Lambooy, J.G. (2002), 'Knowledge and urban economic development: An evolutionary perspective', *Urban Studies*, **39** (5–6), 1019–1035.

Lenntorp, B. (1999), 'Time-geography – At the end of its beginning', *GeoJournal*, **48**, 155–158.

Ley, D. (1998), 'Postmodern epistemologies: Are we stuck with our relatives?', in H. Aay and S. Griffioen (eds), *Geography and Worldview: A Christian Reconnaissance*, Lanham, MD: University Press of America, pp. 19–36.

Maguire, S., C. Hardy, and T.B. Lawrence (2004), 'Institutional entrepreneurship in emerging fields: HIV/AIDS treatment advocacy in Canada', *Academy of Management Journal*, **47** (5), 657–679.

Metcalfe, J.S., M.R. Fonseca, and R. Ramlogan (2000), *Innovation, Growth and Competition: Evolving Complexity or Complex Evolution*, Manchester: CRIC, University of Manchester.

Nonaka, I. and H. Takeuchi (1995), *The Knowledge Creating Company*, Oxford: Oxford University Press.

Nooteboom, B. (2000), *Learning and Innovation in Organizations and Economies*, Oxford: Oxford University Press.

Pfeffer, J. and G.R. Salancik (1978), *The External Control of Organizations: A Resource Dependence Perspective*, New York: Harper and Row.

Polanyi, K., C.M. Arensberg, and H.W. Pearson (1957), *Trade and Market in the Early Empires. Economies in History and Theory*, New York: Free Press.

Polanyi, M. (1962), *Personal Knowledge*, London: Routledge.

Pred, A.R. (1990), *Making Histories and Constructing Human Geographies: The Local Transformation of Practice, Power Relations, and Consciousness*, Boulder, CO: Westview Press.

Putnam, H. (1990), *Realism with a Human Face*, Cambridge: Harvard University Press.

Sayer, A. (2000), *Realism and Social Science*, London: Sage.

Shane, S. (2000), 'Prior knowledge and the discovery of entrepreneurial opportunities', *Organization Science*, **11** (4), 448–469.

Shane, S. and S. Venkataraman (2000), 'The promise of entrepreneurship as a field of research', *Academy of Management Review*, **25** (1), 217–226.

Sharma, P. and S.J.J. Chrisman (1999), 'Toward a reconciliation of the definitional issues in the field of corporate entrepreneurship', *Entrepreneurship Theory and Practice*, **23** (3), 11–27.

Simon, H.A. (1959), 'Theories of decision making in economics and behavioral science', *American Economic Review*, **49**, 253–283.

Sine, W.D. and R.J. David (ed.) (2010), *Institutions and Entrepreneurship*, Research in the Sociology of Work, Vol. 21, London: Emerald Group Publishing Limited.

Stam, E. (2003), *Why Butterflies Don't Leave: Locational Evolution of Evolving Enterprises*, PhD thesis, Utrecht University.

Stam, E. (2007), 'Why butterflies don't leave: Locational behavior of entrepreneurial firms', *Economic Geography*, **83** (1), 27–50.

Stam, E. (2010), 'Entrepreneurship, evolution and geography', in R. Boschma and R.L. Martin (eds), *The Handbook of Evolutionary Economic Geography*, Cheltenham, UK and Northampton, MA, USA: Edward Elgar Publishing, pp. 307–348.

Stam, E., N. Bosma, A. Van Witteloostuijn, J. De Jong, S. Bogaert, N. Edwards, and F. Jaspers (2012), *Ambitious Entrepreneurship. A Review of the Academic Literature and New Directions for Public Policy*, AWT Report 41, The Hague: AWT.

Sunley, P. (1996), 'Context in economic geography: the relevance of pragmatism', *Progress in Human Geography*, **20**, 338–355.

Taylor, C. (1989), *The Sources of the Self: The Making of the Modern Identity*, Cambridge, MA: Harvard University Press.

Teece, D.J., G. Pisano, and A. Shuen (2000), 'Dynamic capabilities and strategic management', in G. Dosi, R. Nelson, and S.G. Winter (eds), *The Nature and Dynamics of Organizational Capabilities*, New York: Oxford University Press, pp. 334–362.

Thrift, N. (1996), *Spatial Formations*, London: Sage.

Thrift, N. and K. Olds (1996), 'Refiguring the economic in economic geography', *Progress in Human Geography*, **20**, 311–337.

Toulmin, S. (2001), *Return to Reason*, Cambridge, MA: Harvard University Press.

Vaessen, P. (1993), *Small business growth in contrasting environments*, PhD thesis Katholieke Universiteit Nijmegen.

Vaessen, P. and D. Keeble (1995), 'Growth-oriented SMEs in unfavourable regional environments', *Regional Studies*, **29** (6), 489–505.

Vaessen, P. and E. Wever (1993), 'Spatial responsiveness of small firms', *Tijdschrift voor Economische en Sociale Geografie*, **84**, 119–131.

Van de Ven, A.H. and M.S. Poole (1995), 'Explaining development and change in organizations', *Academy of Management Review*, **20**, 510–540.

Wellman, B. (2001), 'Physical place and cyberplace: The rise of personalized networking', *International Journal of Urban and Regional Research*, **25**, 227–252.

Welter, F. (2011), 'Contextualizing entrepreneurship – Conceptual challenges and ways forward', *Entrepreneurship Theory and Practice*, **35** (1), 165–184.

Whitley, R. (2006), 'Project-based firms: New organizational form or variations on a theme?', *Industrial and Corporate Change*, **15** (1), 77–99.

Zahra, S.A., M. Wright, and S.G. Abdelgawad (2014), 'Contextualization and the advancement of entrepreneurship research', *International Small Business Journal*, **32** (5), 479–500.

9 Methodological approaches towards context-sensitive entrepreneurship research

Simone Chlosta

Getting into methodological trouble

> Reading the literature, one can easily (but mistakenly) conclude that entrepreneurship is a one-time act that ends with the creation of a firm. (Zahra and Wright 2011, p. 70)

As an entrepreneur and entrepreneurship researcher at the same time, I learned that venture creation is far away from being linear and that there happens a lot inside and outside the founder or the venture which is neither predictable nor following a causal chain. Especially the beginning of the company's life cycle I experienced as weird and surprising. Actions taken in one situation had no direct influence on the founder and the venture but hit back indirectly much later. The context of the entrepreneur has so many different faces; it can be familiar and helpful, for example, when looking for advice in one's network, asking friends and family for support, but also hostile and unknown when not succeeding in the market. But, despite the many and varied facets of context, I am utterly convinced that context is in no way unimportant or controllable. We as entrepreneurs or entrepreneurship researchers are surrounded by and infused with our individual context, for example, in terms of cognitions, emotions, or perceptions of opportunities.

Since the 1980s the field of entrepreneurship has grown and became an autonomous and accepted discipline. Therefore, we as entrepreneurship researchers know that first of all, entrepreneurship is a process (Baron and Shane 2005) and not a one-time act and second, it does not take place in isolation like in a laboratory without interfering effects. Brännback and Carsrud (Chapter 2) looked through entrepreneurship papers and research designs and found that the majority of entrepreneurship researchers treated and still treat context as a control variable drawing a rather simplified picture of entrepreneurial reality. What we need is a truly fresh methodological look at our field. Context is part of our entrepreneurial reality and needs to be included in each step of our research process, from choosing the research team to interpreting and publishing the results. Like the entrepreneurs themselves their context also varies, changes over time or remains stable; it always depends. Only when we decide to ignore context so that it becomes an unobserved variable, we get into (methodological) trouble and run the risk of reducing the external validity of our findings.

In the following, I will give a résumé of the current discussion regarding the (de-) contextualized entrepreneurship research methodology. I will also try to extract criteria for context-sensitive entrepreneurship research and apply them to the different stages of the research process. The chapter closes with a selection of open questions and thoughts worth exploring which hopefully contribute to an ongoing and lively research conversation across disciplines.

The context-sensitivity of our current research methodology

When searching for context-sensitive entrepreneurship studies, our methodological approaches can be described as rather uncreative (Hjorth et al. 2008) and homogeneous. The majority of entrepreneurship studies are quantitative, cross-sectional, single country (mostly US-based) and single-source (Spedale and Watson 2013). Researchers rather seem to play it safe to get published, that is, they use 'accepted' theories and address narrow research questions to a small audience (Shepherd 2015). Although incremental research is important to the field it should not dominate our research designs because it 'fails to challenge, however, taken for granted assumptions about entrepreneurship and entrepreneurs' (Zahra and Wright 2011, p. 68).

During the last decades the common treatment of context, let it be the gender of the entrepreneur (social context) or the region where the venture is founded (spatial context) was to control for it. We as researchers were more interested in illuminating the effect of our independent variables on the dependent variable and tried to reduce the 'error variance' produced by contextual influences as much as we could (see also Chapter 2 by Brännback and Carsrud). This state can be described as a state of 'absolute decontextualization'. Unfortunately, too many entrepreneurship researchers still control for contextual influences to exclude them from their research design.

When you take any entrepreneurship journal and pick any empirical article, what does the research design look like? Where empirical studies include context they mostly include dimensions which are easy to measure, that is, the when (temporal) and where (spatial) dimension (Welter 2011; Zahra et al. 2014), despite a huge range of different dimensions (Whetten 1989). A typical empirical context paper is characterized by a comparative research design. Often two context dimensions (for example, spatial and institutional) are chosen. The spatial dimension is mostly 'operationalized' through stating the country where the study took place. The institutional one is, for example, measured with the help of the participants' self-perception of the cultural dimension. In the limitations section the authors usually state that the data is self-reported and single-source and that longitudinal research would yield better results. The majority of studies would have benefited from a more detailed operationalization of context or at least a description of context as a first step towards context-sensitivity. Another possible (and simple) path would be the addition of an additional data source, for example official data offering details about the chosen country (more detailed spatial or institutional information) and the measurement of culture at two levels (person and country-level). The use of multiple sources supports the researcher to examine the phenomenon from different perspectives and the interpretation of interactions between them (see also Chapter 11 by Wadhwani). This short example demonstrates that a greater awareness of context in our research design does not have to go hand-in-hand with a huge amount of time and resources. It would already help when all of us pose this extra question: how can I integrate context?

At the moment it seems that we have a broader acceptance of contextualization from a conceptual perspective (for example, Welter 2011) in contrast to empirical studies (Zahra and Wright 2011). In the latter case, we still find a stronger tendency towards the generalization of findings instead of their contextualization. But when we treat context as a part of the entrepreneurial story this should not be opposed to the generalization of our findings (see Chapter 1 by Welter, Gartner and Wright). Acknowledging that contextual phenomena are more than 'error variance' (Bamberger 2008) can help us to better explain counterintuitive findings and reversal causal directions (Johns 2006).

Spedale and Watson (2013, p.4) also criticize that context is too often seen as 'merely background' within our research methodology. Despite many calls since the mid-1980s, that 'entrepreneurship is embedded in its social context' (Aldrich and Zimmer 1986, p.3) only a few papers provide information about their research setting and surroundings (Spedale and Watson 2013; Welter 2011). Spedale and Watson's (2013, p.11) own field study showed 'a muddled and fuzzy chain of activities rather than the linear, rational plan described in mainstream entrepreneurship models'. Therefore the authors (Spedale and Watson 2013, p.13) suggest to move away from linearity and calculative logic ('causation model of mainstream entrepreneurship studies') when studying entrepreneurship in context.

It is time that our community begins to envision the advantages of context-sensitive entrepreneurship research (Bamberger 2008). To contextualize our research can help us to terminate many questionable methodological dichotomies which still exist: qualitative versus quantitative, micro versus macro, individual versus context and so on. The long-lasting dichotomy of qualitative and quantitative studies seems to have created a 'dual-class society' regarding our research methodology. Johns describes this dichotomy by stating that 'some qualitative researchers get so immersed in context that they fail to recognize universal phenomena' while some quantitative researchers seem 'almost desperate to ensure that reviewers and readers see their results as generalizable' (Johns 2006, p.404).

Unfortunately, in entrepreneurship research quantitative studies are oftentimes regarded as 'more scientific' because they collect big data and use the latest statistical analyses (Aldrich 2014). Qualitative studies are still considered producing rather vague results which are not really 'countable'. Aldrich (2014) already clarified that this way of labelling our research is not only imprecise and confounds data analysis with data collection but also distracts us from the question we should care about: which method of data collection and analysis fits the research question we want to answer. And, that's where context comes into play: the researcher's understanding of the interaction between context and research methods is crucial for the interpretation of the data later on.

When we want to become more context-sensitive in our research we should stop hiding behind analytical methods and software issues. Abandoning the above-mentioned dichotomies can help us to understand that context-sensitive research needs 'thick, detailed descriptions of actual actions in real-life contexts that recover and preserve the actual meaning that actors ascribe to these actions and settings' (Gephart 2004, p. 455). When we open up to contextual influences in our studies as described above this includes also that we open up to more creativity and imagination in our research methodology. Controlling for contextual influences restricts our view of what the entrepreneurial phenomenon is like (what we wanted to see and not how it really is). Including contextual influences will produce unexpected findings, varying and changing directions of effects. This requires that we open our mind and pursue new ideas regardless of whether they are consistent with what is currently known and considered acceptable in terms of methodology, and so on.

Context-sensitive research not only includes the different dimensions but also the underlying mechanisms (for example, sources of dynamism and variety) which link entrepreneurial phenomena with context (Bamberger 2008). To get an idea of what these mechanisms look like we need to analyse different points in time so that phenomena can unfold. The majority of entrepreneurship studies focus on content-related phenomena. They are far easier to measure than process-variables that change and cross levels or units of analysis. Additionally, the context surrounding these process-oriented phenomena is also subject to change, which again affects the relevance and duration of the process variables (Zahra 2007). Despite the challenge, process studies can help clarify which variables are important and why they influence the outcomes researchers seek to explain. The interplay between content and process can sharpen the researcher's focus on studying important contextual variables that explain the variance found in their variables of interest.

Researching processes and context includes different directions: top-down as well as bottom-up processes (Kozlowski and Klein 2000). The majority of studies solely include top-down processes (Welter 2011) which describe the downward influence of upper-level variables such as institutional contexts on lower-level variables like the rate or survival of new ventures (for example, governmental programmes supporting new ventures). However, reality-based contextual research should also integrate the reverse influence: when the number of start-ups applying for support programmes decreases the governmental programmes will be stopped in the long run. This example clarifies that we need to measure dynamic relationships of variables that unfold over time (Bamberger 2008). Doing more process research implies giving up on the dominance of mail surveys, cross-sectional studies, and the dichotomy between research methodologies.

As our field has achieved legitimacy this is not only a threat (for example, by playing it safe) but also an opportunity for empirical developments. For our methodological advancement we need to explore our units of analysis. Is it the single entrepreneurial action or a sequence of activities to 'build a theory of micro-foundations of entrepreneurial action' (Shepherd 2015, p. 490)? According to Shepherd (2015, p. 494) 'activity is the key unit of analysis'. With this understanding we get a picture of the entrepreneurial process that is 'more dynamic, fine-grained and immersed' (instead of linear, detached from everyday entrepreneurship, and with little insight into practice). But, how should we start changing our research orientation? This leads us to the next section where I will go into more detail.

Giving context-sensitive research a chance

Talking about the operationalization of context, we need to admit that a context-sensitive approach is important at any stage of the research process: from research design, data collection, analysis, to the final article (Bortz and Döring 2006; Cesinger 2013). To begin, we should question ourselves at each stage whether and how we can act more context-sensitively. In the following, I present an exemplary reflection of the different stages of the research process. However, before we get to the first step of the research process, let's highlight our own role as researcher and its interaction with context (see Table 9.1 for an illustration).

Table 9.1   Exemplary illustration of context-sensitive research

Role	Tasks	Current research practices	Future research practices	Exemplary measures
Researcher	Choosing the entire research design and conducting the survey (within her/his context).	No description of the role, rather distant. No description of the effect of the researcher on context and vice versa (interaction).	Describe the context the researcher works in, pay attention to the role the researcher plays (active, engaged in the setting), how she/he designs and conducts the survey, and what effect it might have on the results and the interpretation.	Gender, field of study/discipline of researcher or team, decision-making/sequence of activities: motivation for method and scales, approach towards sample, point in time of study and economic situation, publication strategies.

Source: Author, based upon Zahra and Wright (2011).

Research design

When framing our research design in a context-sensitive way this includes the application of an overall context-sensitive lens *and* discrete context perspectives (Welter 2011). We have to pay attention to entrepreneurial phenomena taking place within certain context dimensions, for example within situational or temporal boundaries (Welter 2011). In doing so we have to consider the different sides of context which can exist simultaneously (dark and bright side, enhancing and restraining effects), the different levels as well as different perspectives (for example, of the entrepreneur, the venture) which can be interlinked, impact each other, vary, and unfold over time (Cesinger 2013).

Designing our studies context-sensitively means that we have to leave our methodological comfort zone. This includes abandoning what I call the 'laboratory perspective': we as researchers are not able to control for context, because (a) in general, we do not conduct lab research, and (b) we won't be able to picture entrepreneurial reality by hiding an important part of reality. As Welter (2016) already suggested, we conduct more context-sensitive research when we are unfamiliar with a certain context. So, the first step in our research process might be the compilation of a multidisciplinary research team. Different disciplines come along with different lenses on the phenomenon. This multi-lens research design can facilitate the dialogue across disciplines and help us to cross our man-made methodological (and theoretical) boundaries.

Data collection

When deciding about our method of data collection the most important question is: how does it fit our research question (Aldrich 2014). This should be the key question and not whether we prefer to do a 'qualitative' or 'quantitative' study. Basically, in order to collect context-sensitive data a combination of methods and data sources is recommended. Qualitative research is more sensitive to the full range and depth of discrete contextual aspects. It offers the chance to discover new contextual influences. For example, with the help of interviews with or observations of entrepreneurs, we as researchers become more engaged with our study subjects compared to online surveys. Quantitative methods can provide additional sources (for example, official data about the venture) and thus an additional perspective on the phenomenon. Wadhwani (Chapter 11) also recommends applying heterogeneous sources as they present the perspectives of different actors within a certain context and might enhance the meaningfulness and relevance of our data.

When deciding about our measures, we need to reflect whether we know how our well-known constructs are developed (for example, with what kind of sample, at what point in time?) and whether they fit our context-sensitive research approach. Probably the question accompanying this decision is which units of analysis adequately represent contextualized entrepreneurship (Shepherd 2015; Welter 2011). First of all, instead of applying a single (and rather static) construct which we measure only once we might favour a sequence of activities to examine the phenomenon over time. This processual approach would allow the units of analysis to vary over time and interact with different context dimensions. So, instead of using 'prefabricated' constructs we choose small and descriptive steps as measures.

However, the decision about the units of analysis also comes with difficulties: sometimes it might not be unambiguous which unit of analysis is adequate. When making a consumption decision is our unit of analysis the individual or the household or the individual within the household? Which effect does the unit of analysis-perspective (like household) have on the strategies of the venture? Does it include all facets or does it emphasize the household (Welter 2011)? This example shows that the appropriate unit of analysis always depends on the research question and cannot be decided independently.

Data analysis

When analysing our data, we again need to distinguish between aspects of contexts. This not only includes the naming of context dimensions, for example spatial or social contexts (Welter 2011). A further approach might be to classify the different contexts according to their 'measurability', for example, their stability over time, their situation-specificity, their origin and so on. For example, in trait research some traits are considered as rather stable and slowly changing over time while others are situation-specific and varying across situations (McCrae and Costa 1997). When we borrow this distinction for our context-sensitive data analysis we might reconsider the household example mentioned above. While attempting to analyse the social context, in this case the household, we realize that, on the one side, the household can be seen as a rather stable and slowly changing context (such as the number of people within the household) which is easy to measure. On the other side, it can be considered a cognitive construct which is rather fluid, dynamic and varying. Why is that? Because the household context not only exists as surrounding of the entrepreneur but is also perceived by her/him and thus a cognitive construct which might vary according to the entrepreneur's cognition or emotions (for example, how supportive is the household perceived?). This aspect of context is rather difficult to measure as it interacts with the entrepreneur and can be seen as being 'inside' of the entrepreneur. Thus, context can have different aspects, stable and varying ones. This brings us back to the previous discussion about different sources of data. With the help of 'subjective' or self-reported data we get an insight into the endogenous aspect of context, the 'inside' of the entrepreneur (also see Chapter 1 by Welter, Gartner and Wright and Chapter 2 by Brännback and Carsrud). Combining different sources of data can help us to detect several aspects of context.

Data interpretation and publication

The interpretation of our data depends not only on the context which surrounded the data collection process but also on the researcher's understanding of the context around her/him (Aldrich 2014). The final step of the context-sensitive research process includes detailed information about each step in our research. We need to inform our audience about our motivation for why certain decisions were made, why we chose this particular sample, where and when our study took place, and so on. Our audience can better assess the applicability of our findings as soon as we provide some form of 'situational linking' (Bamberger 2008, p. 840). When interpreting our results, our context-sensitive approach will help us to explain why results found in Silicon Valley will not fit in Berlin. Due to the inclusion of context we provide a better explanation of the variety, depths and richness of entrepreneurship (Welter 2011).

Again, we will benefit from our multidisciplinary approach. As I already stated at the beginning of this section, our role as researcher is not context-free but embedded in our individual context and that in turn is influenced by our research community. With the help of multidisciplinary research teams we also address the heterogeneity and multiplicity of contexts in which entrepreneurship (research) takes place (Zahra and Wright 2011). Bringing together different research communities encourages their dialogue. When discussing the results together with researchers from different disciplines with different perspectives, methods, approaches, this might enhance the quality and accuracy of our interpretations. Probably at the beginning the different perspectives resemble a huge jigsaw puzzle where a single part has only little meaning but taking all parts together forms a complete picture in the end: 'the whole is different from the sum of its parts' (Köhler 1969, p. 10).

For the final interpretation, discussion and publication of our research results we need to be aware that differences in general and differences in findings are 'normal' and not something we should try to avoid. The entrepreneurial world is about differences because entrepreneurs, contexts and ventures are not alike – something which is also explored in Chapter 1 of this book. So, we might have to revise our own 'publication culture'. This takes us back to the beginning where we highlighted our role as researchers within the research process. Context-sensitive research starts and ends with us.

Looking ahead: what are open questions and thoughts worth exploring?

First of all, we have to question our role as researchers. Has context in former studies just been forgotten, consciously ignored or regarded as unimportant? Was it too complex, time-consuming or not obligatory for us to integrate context in the research framework?

In the previous section I described a feasible course of action for context-sensitive research. But, why not be open for more creativity and imagination? What would be the ideal route of contextualized research? As we have so many calls for process studies in entrepreneurship (in almost 100 per cent of the limitation sections of entrepreneurship papers) why not do something like the movie *Boyhood* (2014) which was filmed over 12 years? The design of the movie sounds a lot like a context-sensitive research study: experimental design, interaction with real people/practitioners, process view, observation, including different and varying dimensions and levels where effects unfold over time.

Another weakness refers to the measures we use in our day-to-day research. How context-sensitive are they (scales, constructs)? Entrepreneurship is quite complex but many popular measures in entrepreneurship were developed without sufficiently considering the process perspective or the match with their study subjects (for example, the usage of student samples instead of real entrepreneur samples). We need to leave 'snap-shot' research behind and approach process research (Shepherd 2015). This immediately leads to the question how to conduct it? Should we try and map the 'big picture' by including diverse (and varying) dimensions, levels of context and directions of effects? Or should we operationalize and categorize context step-by-step with some sort of a modular system (construction kit principle)?

Summing up, context needs to become part of the story instead of being a mere control variable. We need to learn from and interact with our study subject, that is, with 'real entrepreneurs' and become engaged in the setting. We need to tear down the existing boundaries and dichotomies and be open to other perspectives, disciplines, and paths. We need a bigger variety of research tools as each measure has its limitations. And, we have to keep in mind that we as researchers do research on context within our own contexts. When we, for example approach the entrepreneurial reality with a camera (or video camera), we will only see and understand the entrepreneurial world through the lens of the camera. It depends on us how narrow or wide our perspective is. All decisions will influence our final picture (or film).

To cut a long story short, we need to create an awareness of the responsibility we have as researchers. Our results depend not only on the methods we use but also how we use them. This again is influenced by our individual perspectives, experiences and cognitions. After all, we are in a situation similar to our study subjects. When we take two researchers, give them the same research question, let them describe how they approach and conduct the research task, we might not get the same results. Why is that? Because of context effects! In almost the same manner as two entrepreneurs starting with the same idea might differ regarding their resulting ventures. When we finally realize the necessity to include context in our study designs, future context-sensitive entrepreneurship research might consist of a 4 (or more) D design providing real cause-and-effect models.

Conclusion

Acting more context-sensitively within the research process implies that we are aware of the role we play as researchers. When choosing our research methodology we need to be concerned about 'the crowding out effect' (Shepherd 2015, p. 501): that is, 'crowding out of the more exploratory by the more exploitive' (novel questions versus incremental research). And we need to be engaged in our research: thinking entrepreneurially (open minded versus sticking to traditions); thinking in terms of interactions and changes instead of linearity, causality and direct effects; thinking of a series of activities instead of single actions and most important, remaining passionate about what we do and using this energy to make real contributions to the field (Shepherd 2015). This approach is risky as it differs from the familiar (methodological) paths and might complicate our understanding of entrepreneurial phenomena at first (Spedale and Watson 2013).

However, it is the entrepreneurial reality we want to picture. Therefore, we need to get in touch with the real entrepreneurial world, its parts and players involved. This includes besides the entrepreneur and the venture also the context of the past, the present and the future, that is, being 'sensitive to time and place, to language and bodies, to event and contingencies' (Hjorth et al. 2008, p. 82). It is time for our research methodology to undergo a 'contextual treatment' to better mirror the contextualized entrepreneurial reality instead of longing for statistical certainty which we translate into generalized models of behaviour.

Suggested readings

Shepherd, Dean (2015), 'Party on! A call for entrepreneurship research that is more interactive, activity based, cognitively hot, compassionate, and prosocial', *Journal of Business Venturing*, **30** (4), 489–507. Dean Shepherd suggests a completely new thinking which is very inspiring. He offers new methodological pathways towards contextualized entrepreneurship.

Welter, Friederike (2011), 'Contextualizing entrepreneurship – Conceptual challenges and ways forward', *Entrepreneurship Theory and Practice*, **35** (1), 165–184. It is already a classic and must-read for all entrepreneurship researchers. And contrary to what Spedale and Watson (2013) state, it does not complicate matters but goes beyond the call (of many researchers) that context matters.

Bamberger, Peter (2008), 'From the editors: Beyond contextualization: Using context theories to narrow the micro–macro gap in management research', *Academy of Management Journal*, **51** (5), 839–846. This is an eye-opener. It goes beyond mere criticism and does not remain hypothetical, but gives precise suggestions for a better empirical, theory-based, methodological approach.

References

Aldrich, Howard E. (2014), 'Stand up and be counted: Why social science should stop using the qualitative/quantitative dichotomy', Blog of the American Sociological Association, Section on Organization,

Occupations, and Work, 27 November, accessed 11 December 2015 at http://workinprogress. oowsection.org/2014/11/27/stand-up-and-be-counted-why-social-science-should-stop-using-the-qualitativequantitative-dichotomy-2/.

Aldrich, Howard E. and Catherine Zimmer (1986), 'Entrepreneurship through social networks', in Donald Sexton and Raymond Smilor (eds), *The Art and Science of Entrepreneurship*, New York: Ballinger, pp. 3–23.

Bamberger, Peter (2008), 'From the editors: Beyond contextualization: Using context theories to narrow the micro–macro gap in management research', *Academy of Management Journal*, **51** (5), 839–846.

Baron, Robert A. and Scott A. Shane (2005), *Entrepreneurship: A Process Perspective*, Ohio: South Western, Thomson.

Bortz, Jürgen and Nicole Döring (2006), *Forschungsmethoden und Evaluation für Human- und Sozialwissenschaftler*, Berlin: Springer Verlag.

Cesinger, Beate (2013), *Context and Complexity of International Entrepreneurship as a Field of Research*, Dissertation, Utrecht: Utrecht University Repository.

Gephart, Robert P. (2004), 'Qualitative research and the Academy of Management Journal', *Academy of Management Journal*, **47** (4), 454–462.

Hjorth, Daniel, Campbell Jones and William B. Gartner (2008), 'Introduction for "recreating/ recontextualising entrepreneurship"', *Scandinavian Journal of Management*, **24** (2), 81–84.

Johns, Gary (2006), 'The essential impact of context on organizational behavior', *Academy of Management Review*, **31** (2), 386–408.

Köhler, Wolfgang (1969), *The Task of Gestalt Psychology*, Princeton, NJ: Princeton University Press.

Kozlowski, Steve J. and Katherine J. Klein (2000), 'A multilevel approach to theory and research in organizations: Contextual, temporal and emergent processes' in Katherine J. Klein and Steve J. Kozlowski (eds), *Multilevel Theory, Research, and Methods in Organizations: Foundations, Extensions and New Directions*, San Francisco: Jossey-Bass, pp. 3–90.

McCrae, Robert R. and Paul T. Costa Jr. (1997), 'Personality trait structure as a human universal', *American Psychologist*, **52** (5), 509–516.

Shepherd, Dean (2015), 'Party on! A call for entrepreneurship research that is more interactive, activity based, cognitively hot, compassionate, and prosocial', *Journal of Business Venturing*, **30** (4), 489–507.

Spedale, Simona and Tony J. Watson (2013), 'The emergence of entrepreneurial action: At the cross-roads between institutional logics and individual life-orientation', *International Small Business Journal*, **32** (7), 759–776.

Welter, Friederike (2011), 'Contextualizing entrepreneurship – Conceptual challenges and ways forward', *Entrepreneurship Theory and Practice*, **35** (1), 165–184.

Welter, Friederike (2016), 'Wandering between contexts', in David Audretsch and Erik Lehmann (eds), *The Routledge Companion to Makers of Modern Entrepreneurship*, London: Routledge, forthcoming.

Whetten, David A. (1989), 'What constitutes a theoretical contribution?', *Academy of Management Review*, **14** (4), 490–495.

Zahra, Shaker A. (2007), 'Contextualizing theory building in entrepreneurship research', *Journal of Business Venturing*, **22** (3), 443–452.

Zahra, Shaker A. and Mike Wright (2011), 'Entrepreneurship's next act', *Academy of Management Perspectives*, **25** (4), 67–83.

Zahra, Shaker A., Mike Wright and Sondos G. Abdelgawad (2014), 'Contextualization and the advancement of entrepreneurship research', *International Small Business Journal*, **32** (5), 479–500.

10 Advancing understanding of entrepreneurial embeddedness: forms of capital, social contexts and time

Sarah Drakopoulou Dodd, Tobias Pret and Eleanor Shaw

Context and embeddedness

Recent years have seen ongoing support for a more critical, contextualized, inclusive scholarship that focuses on the inter-subjective, relational, mutable, embedded nature of entrepreneurial phenomena, studied through richer methodologies (Jones and Spicer 2005; Ogbor 2000; Steyaert 2011; see also Chapter 2 by Brännback and Carsrud). Anderson, Drakopoulou Dodd, and Jack (2012, p. 964) summarize this position as 'the recognition that entrepreneurship is not purely an economic, individualised act, but one that is embedded in, and draws from society . . . and the appreciation that entrepreneurship is a process . . . that changes over time'. Our task in this chapter is to build on these advances to explore: (1) how we can move still further away from perceptions of economic individualism; (2) how we might better explore networked social contexts of entrepreneurs; and (3) how we might go about considering the issue of time more deeply.

To provide a frame for this exploration, we draw on Bourdieu's (1977, 1984, 1986) theory of practice. Bourdieu's work has, as we shall show below, already proved both useful and influential within entrepreneurship and the wider management and organizational disciplines (Özbilgin and Tatli 2005; Patel and Conklin 2009; Terjesen and Elam 2009). As an indicator of his influence, it is worth noting that Google Scholar reports over 425 000 citations of Bourdieu's work – many more than those of other great sociologists, such as Weber (192 000), Durkheim (111 000), or Talcott Parsons (106 000).[1]

Bourdieu defines contexts as *fields*, which are bounded social spaces comprising individual agents and the relationships that link them (Lockett et al. 2014). Field theory can thus be applied as a lens through which a wide range of entrepreneurial contexts can be viewed, from a geographically bounded locality (Light and Dana 2013), to an industrial sector or subsector (Umney and Kretsos 2014), an entrepreneurial network (Anderson, Drakopoulou Dodd, and Jack 2010) or a digital community of practice. Bourdieu (1986) proposes that agents perform strategic actions to accumulate economic, cultural, social, and symbolic *capital* in order to improve their relative positions within fields (Pret, Shaw, and Drakopoulou Dodd

2015). Each field has its own 'rules of the game' (*habitus*) and stakes under contestation (*illusio*), which are understood, agreed, learnt, and co-developed by its agents (Bourdieu 1984). Also shared are the fundamental beliefs and viewpoints (*doxa*), which the powerful typically enact to maintain their dominant positions within a field (Drakopoulou Dodd et al. 2014). Although actions and interactions are influenced by *habitus*, *illusio*, and *doxa*, individual *practice* may still challenge these prevailing norms and beliefs (De Clercq and Voronov 2009a).[2]

A plethora of work from other disciplines and perspectives has made exciting use of Bourdieu's ideas, opening us up to a diverse and stimulating range of scholarly inspiration (see, for example, Eikhof and Haunschild 2007; Emirbayer and Johnson 2008; Friedland 2009; Wilson et al. 2016). The proximity of Bourdieu's approaches to other forms of social site ontology extends this reach still further. In related work, for example, Chia and Holt (2006) argue that practical actions and relationships precede individual identity and strategic intent. From this foundation, they develop a Heideggerian approach to strategy-as-practice in which the actor is construed as a 'non-deliberate, relationally-constituted nexus of social activities' (Chia and Holt 2006, p. 644). The relationality of strategic praxis, and the unreflective but patterned nature of emergent practice are strongly present in the work of both Bourdieu and Heidegger, signalling a firm connection. Pursuing these theoretical overlaps further highlights the epistemological benefits of these cognate approaches. Following Heidegger (1962), the complexities of entrepreneurship embedded in context can be understood as processual, engaged, ongoing, and meaning-saturated interactions, which are enacted within a nexus of relationships and projects. Theoretical reasons, choices, and justifications that are uncovered through immersion within such embedded contexts can be 'simultaneously plausible (general), accessible (simple), and consensually valid (accurate)' (Weick 1999, p. 136). Conversely, reflecting on organizational phenomena employing abstract and context-free approaches *may* provide retrospective explanations that are both general and simple. However, as such explanations are 'stripped of context, situation, configuration, relational meaning, and particulars' (Weick 1999, p. 136), they ultimately lack accuracy. Even more importantly, such explanatory theories rarely manage to move us, as they are not representative of the world in which individuals are embedded.

Similar to Heidegger's (1962) approach, Bourdieu's (1977, 1984) work provides an opportunity for considering, within the ambit of one interconnected theoretical frame, the many aspects of context, incorporating its structures, agents and their connections (*field*); social norms, beliefs, and motivations (*habitus*); and the resources accumulated and exchanged between agents (*capital*). Epistemological schisms have often been perceived to structure past and current entrepreneurship scholarship into opposing 'camps' (Coviello and Jones 2004; Grant and Perren 2002; McDonald et al. 2015). Taking a Bourdieusian approach to studying entrepreneurship as relationality allows scholars to overcome dichotomies between agency and structure, positivism and social constructionism, and qualitative and quantitative research approaches (Özbilgin and Tatli 2005). Tatli et al. (2014, p. 628) perceive

Bourdieu's 'relational perspective as an improved alternative to fragmented and often hostile methodological traditions and paradigmatic divisions in entrepreneurship research'.

The various dimensions of Bourdieu's work provide us with conceptual tools for considering a diverse range of entrepreneurial phenomena, from behavioural norms to strategic power plays (Karataş-Özkan and Chell 2015); from winning legitimacy to wider considerations of employing various forms of capital (De Clercq and Voronov 2009b); from the interrelations of specific individuals to the structure and dynamics of context (McKeever, Anderson, and Jack 2014). Indeed, much of the scholarship on context has enacted Bourdieusian thinking, whether explicitly or implicitly. Drakopoulou Dodd et al. (2014) review entrepreneurship research which makes use of Bourdieu, arguing that distinct, but interrelated, streams of this work have tackled several main areas.

First, studies of entrepreneurial networking and relationships have long drawn upon Bourdieusian concepts, notably social capital and *habitus*, to explain the nature, processes, and structures of embedded, contextualized, patterned interactions (see for example Anderson, Drakopoulou Dodd, and Jack 2010; Batjargal 2003; Patel and Terjesen 2011). Studies of transnational entrepreneurship have made extensive use of these concepts to further understanding of entrepreneurs who are differently embedded within both a home and a host context, and the bifocal capital enactment strategies this demands (Drori, Honig, and Ginsberg 2010; Patel and Conklin 2009; Terjesen and Elam 2009). Second, studies of entrepreneurial learning have employed Bourdieu's theories to analyse the individual, micro-level capital of nascent entrepreneurs and to connect this to the meso-level *habitus*, which affects their behaviours while it is simultaneously being built by them (Karataş-Özkan 2011; Karataş-Özkan and Chell 2010). Third, highlighting the importance of symbolic capital, studies of entrepreneurial legitimation have taken a detailed Bourdieusian approach to explain how entrepreneurs simultaneously fit in to their existing contexts (by following *habitus*-specific behaviours), whilst also standing out through innovation (De Clercq and Voronov 2009a, 2009b; Stringfellow, Shaw, and Maclean 2014). De Clercq and Voronov (2009b) argue that to become favourably embedded within a desired context, entrepreneurs are required to conform to extant norms, modus operandi, and power structures. Although their entrepreneurial status licenses a degree of product or market innovation, their legitimation depends on this *not* being disruptive enough to threaten the status quo of dominant incumbents within the field. Entrepreneurs become legitimated within their contexts, according to this view, when they 'somehow stir up yet also validate the current field order' (De Clercq and Voronov 2009a, p. 804). Importantly, Bourdieu's approach reminds us of the significance of domination, and the concentration of capitals in the hands of institutional power structures.

Tatli et al. (2014) provided a comprehensive and inspiring vision for research questions and directions that can be explored with a Bourdieusian frame. We seek to add to their ideas by highlighting some specific Bourdieu-inspired topics and methods we judge to be of particular relevance for extending our knowledge of entrepreneurial embeddedness. These 'dreams' are driven largely by our own recent research experiences. We will argue that, by more fully considering interactions between Bourdieu's different forms of capital, advances can be made away from the strait jacket of economic individualism, especially for 'missing' entrepreneurial contexts. Next, we will consider how and why we might better explore the net-worked social contexts of entrepreneurs by engaging more fully with the *field* level of analysis and recognizing our own embeddedness within these fields. Finally, we will turn to temporal embeddedness and propose theoretical and empirical tools for extending our work in this direction, so as to deepen our understandings of *habitus, practice,* and *illusio.* We note that, although it is a complex and lengthy analytic process to apply the full complement of Bourdieu's concepts within spe-cific empirical studies, cherry-picking individual elements of the theory of practice risks ignoring its inner logic and failing to unlock its full potential (Emirbayer and Johnson 2008).

Advancing beyond economic individualism

It has become ever clearer that making sense of capital accumulation and expendi-ture cannot simply be limited to considerations of finance, funding, intellectual property, and tangible assets. Crucial though economic capital is, the entrepre-neurial process invests, creates, shares, and exchanges a far wider range of resources (Pret, Shaw, and Drakopoulou Dodd 2015; Scott 2012). Even the most neoclassi-cal of economists would recognize that cultural capital, which includes but is not limited to human capital (Jayawarna, Jones, and Macpherson 2014; Vershinina, Barrett, and Meyer 2011), is also of essence in entrepreneurship. Many studies have drawn attention to and explored crucial facets of entrepreneurial social capital (Light and Dana 2013; McKeever, Anderson, and Jack 2014; Stam, Arzlanian, and Elfring 2014). Furthermore, scholarship on entrepreneurial legitimation and phi-lanthropy has highlighted the significance of symbolic capital (Harvey et al. 2011; Shaw et al. 2013).

While strong stand-alone knowledge has been developed, particularly for social capital, much work remains to be done to further our understanding of capital conversions and the interplay between and enactment of alternative capitals within embedded entrepreneurial fields. Nevertheless, our own interactions with entrepre-neurs, reading, and research all lead us to an ever stronger view that the multifaceted and intertwined creation and conversion of various forms of capital – especially cultural, social, and symbolic capital – is at the heart of the entrepreneurial pro-cess. For example, in our study of capital conversions amongst craft entrepre-neurs (Pret, Shaw, and Drakopoulou Dodd 2015), we found that co-creation of novel cultural capital among crafters was particularly important. Indeed, much of the cultural capital, including craft skills, dispositions, and knowledge, was per-ceived to be a resource held at community level. Symbolic capital, achieved through awards, publicity, and prestigious international exhibitions, was often converted into higher order social capital through its provision of access to new and highly productive relational ties. Combinations of capital – 'bundles' of resources – were also deployed to spark further creative entrepreneurship, as when social capital was combined with cultural capital through relational learning. Overall, participants described almost no barriers or inhibitors to capital conversion, instead emphasizing 'an ease, a naturalness, a speed and flexibility to capital conversion' (Pret, Shaw, and Drakopoulou Dodd 2015, p. 15). Importantly, this phenomenological study uncovered strong evidence against the dominance of economic capital, showing

> that craft entrepreneurs seem to give no primacy to economic capital when converting the various types of resources they possess. Instead, we find that economic capital conversions are part of a larger process of capital conversion. . . . It is the proficiency in performing these other conversions that affects the abilities of craft entrepreneurs to accumulate economic capital. (Pret, Shaw, and Drakopoulou Dodd 2015, p. 16)

Johnstone and Lionais (2004) argue that, in locations where capitalistic relations are less robust, such as depleted communities, the entrepreneurial process may adapt and manifest itself differently. Areas without capital power will demand, provoke, and create novel entrepreneurial responses to this condition (see also Chapter 4 by Baker and Powell). Recent scholarship exploring entrepreneurship in a variety of marginal contexts has highlighted the discourses, structures, and practices of liberation that disenfranchised entrepreneurs enact. For example, Drakopoulou Dodd (2014) explores a case study of punk rock entrepreneurship and concludes that 'powerlessness has thus been turned into a tool for resistance, which is expressed directly in discourse, and enacted through the building of alternative interlocking entrepreneurial structures. . . .. By staying largely outside the ambit of industry power structures – by remaining marginalized – freedom from mainstream dominance is achieved' (Drakopoulou Dodd 2014, pp. 192–193). Georgiou et al. (2013) also find an entrepreneurship of resistance in their study of post-colonialism and entrepreneurial networks, where cultural hybrids emerge that both mimic and resist dominant forces. Entrepreneurship, then, can act as a vehicle for the disenfranchised to enact 'the creativity involved in moving among various cultural frameworks and in resisting the colonizer by disrupting its imposed knowledge and practices' (Frenkel 2008, p. 927). Marginality, the position of powerlessness, can thus be deployed as a resource, permitting a special kind of liberated entrepreneurship.

Recognizing the barriers around established fields (with their norms and structures of dominance), entrepreneurship of resistance turns being beyond the barriers into a space of freedom, a space of play. The means available beyond mainstream field barriers are not typically economic, but they are perhaps all the more influential for that. In the hands of the disenfranchised, cultural, social, and symbolic resources can become creative tools of entrepreneurial resistance. This is not an easy path: acute shortage of resources and exclusion from mainstream fields of the powerful combine to create a very difficult context for entrepreneurship. Nevertheless, a key strength of marginal entrepreneurs, who are shut out of or deliberately resist the orthodox *habitus*, is that they can provide an alternative social construction of entrepreneurship to challenge the overly-familiar and often unquestioned meme that entrepreneurship has become (culturally, economically, politically, and intellectually). Along with many of our fellow scholars, then, we propose that a still greater variety of entrepreneurial fields, particularly those 'hidden' beyond the mainstream, should be studied to better understand embeddedness. However, caution is clearly required against an over-romanticization of marginality, or tacit implications that entrepreneurship is a path to self-liberation for all who find themselves in poverty, requiring only ingenuity and hard work.

If we are to extend our studies to include contexts and entrepreneurs who are financially impoverished and, typically, socially marginalized, then a de-emphasis on economic capital is surely also in order. Bourdieu (1984) himself cautioned against accepting the primacy of economic capital, proposing that commitment to the logic of the economic 'game' is a culturally grounded social construction. When entrepreneurs are embedded in contexts that are particularly limited in economic resources or rich in other forms of capital, their venture creation and growth is creatively pursued through interactions of non-economic forms of capital (Pret, Shaw, and Drakopoulou Dodd 2015; see also Baker and Nelson 2005; Powell and Baker 2014).

We believe there is a clear imperative for deeper and more sustained attention to be paid to the complex creation and conversion of capitals. How is one form of capital – or a combination of forms – converted into another by entrepreneurs? What processes does this involve? How does the nature and process of conversion vary by context? What stakes (*illusio*) are being pursued through these conversions? What generative grammars (*habitus*) shape these practices? There is significant evidence that specific fields – be they local geographic contexts, sectorial structures, or specific sub-cultures – engage differently in capital conversion. What are the drivers of these differences? And can processual patterns be identified that sustain across (at least some of these) diverse fields? Whilst we have focused here on marginal and alternative contexts, it is worth recalling that Bourdieu's original work concentrated on socioeconomic elites and their acquisition and retention of power. Elites, entrepreneurial or otherwise, are particularly skilled at enacting and reinforcing strategies that enhance and maintain their accumulations of capital and positions within fields. Marginal entrepreneurs, we suggest, require quite different strategies to achieve their objectives, some of which we have suggested here, and further study of which is particularly welcomed (see also Powell and Baker 2014).

Networked social context

In line with wider understandings of the open sharing economy, extant research indicates that, for many contexts, considerable capital is co-created, held at the network level, and shared freely between entrepreneurial network members (Scott 2012). In Pret, Shaw, and Drakopoulou Dodd's (2015) study of rural craft entrepreneurs, for example, we found myriad examples of knowledge, skills, and information (cultural capital) being readily shared throughout networks. In recent empirical work exploring an urban craft beer community, the field was characterized by the open sharing of equipment, raw materials, and even the sale of the final product throughout the networks of head brewers.[3] We found that high-growth brewers helped smaller, newer entrants to the field, because they received similar support from established brewers when they were starting out. The help they offered included access to production lines and resulted in the co-creation of new, collaborative beer. Specific field norms (*habitus*) shape these complex co-creations and conversions of capital; while economic capital, in the form of increased sales, was indeed achieved, this was far from the most valued aspect of these interactions.

We believe that there are clear messages from these studies, our related theorizing, and wider related work from entrepreneurship and beyond. First, it may be time to review the understanding of all fields as being in a de facto state of ongoing struggles over *individualized economic* power and position, largely enacted through the individual exchange of capitals. Trends towards the sharing, collaborative economy include open innovation, peer-to-peer business models, and crowd funding platforms (Umney and Kretsos 2014). Thus, it is perhaps to be anticipated that modern entrepreneurial resource utilization, both at start-up and throughout growth phases, will also be characterized by greater sharing and collaboration than has been postulated by economics-inspired theories.

As well as horizontal sharing of capital, vertical co-creation and deployment of capitals is also ever more evident. Suppliers, distributors, and consumers are engaged in the co-creation of entrepreneurship, as studies, particularly on social capital, have shown (Anderson, Drakopoulou Dodd, and Jack 2010). Again, the network, field, or community level of these interactions has been a prominent feature emerging from our recent empirical work. Although our empirical inspiration has come from entrepreneurs in marginal and counter-cultural contexts, it is also likely that some of the same practices are enacted by power elites, a topic which merits further research. Notwithstanding, we believe that assumptions of economically-focused power struggles, competition, and the pursuit of individual capital accumulation may be masking more nuanced, interesting, and important models of community creation, ownership, and usage of various forms of capital.

To further our understandings of the various forms of capital and their conversions, explorations are required into the 'modus operandi' (*habitus*) and practices through which diverse network-level forms of capital are enacted by entrepreneurs and their varied ties. This will necessitate studies at the level of field, network (whether local, sectorial, digital or a combination of all these), and the 'ego' and 'alters' of a specific entrepreneur. To be effective, such studies should include engagement with community members (by attending meetings, events, trade shows, social receptions, and accessing digital sites of communication), as well as with network members (Jack et al. 2010; McKeever, Jack, and Anderson 2015).

Temporal embeddedness

To what extent can an embeddedness approach assist in addressing the demands that time be taken more seriously and investigated more critically (both empirically and theoretically; see also Chapter 5 by Lippmann and Aldrich)? Drakopoulou Dodd, Anderson, and Jack (2013) deploy a Heideggerian philosophy of time, consistent with Bourdieu's approach, to study the role of time in family firms. They find that day-to-day entrepreneurial 'performative interactions . . . are contextualized within the everyday practical time of habitus-specific cultural conventions. When challenged, internally or externally, family firm managers have shown a clear ability to switch into a more rational, calculative and conscious temporal frame' (Drakopoulou Dodd, Anderson, and Jack 2013, p. 44). They also find that the family firm's past is constantly relationally re-created and re-thought as a sense-making resource to shape shared understandings of the present moment's meaning. Similarly, futures are ever re-imagined in the present as a way of building shared moments of vision in the here-and-now: 'The present moment of the family firm is always experienced as both thrown (from its past) and projecting (into its future) in a peculiarly rich manner' (Drakopoulou Dodd, Anderson, and Jack 2013, p. 45).

Can our empirical work take up the challenge of developing more temporally embedded empirical methods? If we are to develop deeper insights into how time is woven into the co-construction of context, then it seems clear that our methods must adapt to take account of this (see also Chapter 11 by Wadhwani). Longitudinal studies and panel data provide opportunities for gathering time-focused data and are much welcomed. However, we contend that it is possible to go further than either of these methods towards gaining privileged access to the subtleties and complexities of temporal context. Our dream here is to see more of us invest in embedding ourselves within entrepreneurial contexts in ways that resonate with the processes and structures of these fields themselves, on their own terms and in their own times (Jack and Anderson 2002). Opportunities, for example, are offered by a personal commitment to quasi-ethnographic approaches, to being *within* entrepreneurial contexts over time (McKeever, Jack, and Anderson 2015), although this is indeed a considerable challenge to the modern academic. The time involved is substantial and the analytic skills required are demanding.

Equally, if we recognize that reality is co-constructed and that interrelationships and interactions are the fabric through which our worlds are made real to us, then this also entails a recognition that it is disingenuous to consider ourselves as distanced, disembodied, external observers of entrepreneurship. Arguing that entrepreneurs inter-subjectively co-create realities – 'Being in a world' in Heidegger's (1962, p. 33) terms – is surely only legitimate if we also accept that our own interventions in these worlds are also necessarily inter-subjective. Which epistemologies are consistent and fruitful, given such an acceptance (see also Chapter 8 by Stam)? What methods can be most honestly, rigorously, and relevantly deployed to embrace this stance, while also permitting us to study contexts unfolding through process over time (see also Chapter 7 by Fletcher and Selden)?

The view of semi-structured interviews most consistent with the arguments developed here would construe these as co-constructed narratives developed by researchers and inter-subjects. They re-create – at the specific place and time of their enactment – a narrative of an entrepreneurial past, present, and future. They give us a 'truth', a 'reality', but it is a reality bound to the contextual moment – temporal, social, and geographic – at which the interview is constructed by researcher and entrepreneur. Such realities present a current re-telling of past processes and there is value in this. However, it is questionable whether they can show us processes in motion. This is a thorny methodological issue: how can we and our entrepreneurial inter-subjects study process as it happens?

Relational practice is an important aspect of Bourdieu's approach: it enacts and exposes *habitus*, it encompasses the processes of capital (co-)creation, sharing, and conversion, and it is the way in which entrepreneurs move through time. So, figuring out how to better study practice is a matter of considerable concern to those interested in embeddedness (see also Chapter 3 by Steyaert). Again, we propose that more diverse methods be considered and that the role of both researcher and inter-subject in co-creating this knowledge be recognized, perhaps even celebrated. Relevant methods would seem to include immersive participant observation, shadowing, entrepreneurial diaries (perhaps in blog, audio, or video blog form), ethnographies, and action research. Particularly promising is experience sampling methodology (ESM), which Maw-Der Foo and his colleagues have introduced to entrepreneurship scholarship (Foo, Uy, and Baron 2009; Uy, Foo, and Aguinis 2010). Experimentation with mobile applications and wearables, through which we can engage entrepreneurs in recording or creating their own data, also seems overdue. So, too, is the use of social media data as a means for investigating online communities and their interactions (Fischer and Reuber 2014). Entrepreneurs interact with their networks online, often in public forums, and we are missing a large part of their interrelationships if we fail to also engage with these aspects of their ecosystems.

In our role as editors and reviewers of journals, as supervisors and examiners of PhDs, as conference and workshop leaders, as readers and writers, we can and should actively encourage greater diversity of methods. Articles, conference papers, and book chapters that present and discuss methodological experimentation are also needed to build shared knowledge and move the field forward. This, of course, includes honest and frank discussion of methods that proved intractable or unsuccessful: learning from failure is considered a hallmark of entrepreneurship itself, after all (Shepherd 2003).

There is a teleological issue to unpick here, too. Studying entrepreneurial *illusio* – the diverse stakes for which entrepreneurs strive in various fields and contexts – surely requires us to question what our own *illusio* might be. For what is our research undertaken? What are our stakes? For whom do we conduct research? Bengt Johanisson argued strongly for transformative, enactive research, using 'the Aristotelian notion of phronesis or practical wisdom, as the way to blur, entwine and hook up theory and practice, and to update his life-long vision that entrepreneurship is a matter of (inter)activity' (Steyaert and Landström 2011, p. 131). We would echo the assertion that the most engaged, relational mode of studying entrepreneurial embeddedness is just such an approach, where we see 'entrepreneurship and entrepreneurship research as a practice of creative organizing' (Steyaert 2011, p. 80). This means moving beyond even the demands of action research to creatively organize research projects which not only fully involve entrepreneurs – widely understood as inter-subjects – but which also aim to impact in a positive way upon their lives. For UK scholars, this imperative is now formally linked to state research funding through assessment of research impact. Here, certainly, is an opportunity to emphasize interaction, transformation, and our own embeddedness in entrepreneurial ecosystems as a scholarly essential.

Conclusion

This chapter has set out what is, for us, part of the current agenda for extending and deepening our understanding of embeddedness in context. We agree with Tatli et al. (2014) that Bourdieu's work has much to offer as a conceptual framework for furthering our knowledge of entrepreneurial embeddedness. We argue that it is time to de-stabilize the primacy of economic capital and to consider instead, in more detail and nuance, the complex interplays of cultural, social, and symbolic capital. We also believe that explorations into the processes and norms of capital co-creation and conversion should include a wider range of network and field level studies, not least to challenge assumptions about the inherently competitive nature of field interactions. We propose that a wider range of non-mainstream contexts be explored, especially those lacking significant endowments of economic capital. To make better sense of temporal embeddedness through a relational lens, we advocate adopting methodologies which allow us to embed ourselves within entrepreneurial contexts in ways that resonate with the processes and structures of these fields on their own terms and in their own times. Finally, we believe that recognizing the inter-subjectivity of entrepreneurial embeddedness should be extended into our epistemology and enacted through our methods. We look forward to sharing this journey with you.

NOTES

1 We thank our reviewers Ted Baker and Erin Powell for pointing out that Bourdieu's citations total more than those of these other three leading sociologists combined (Source: www.scholar.google.com; accessed on 15 December 2015).

2 For a more detailed overview of Bourdieu's theoretical frame, see Drakopoulou Dodd et al.'s (2014) review of his work, in their study of qualitative authorship in entrepreneurship research.

3 The research team for this ongoing study comprises Sarah Drakopoulou Dodd, Angelo Bisignano, Ciaràn Mac an Bhaird, and Juliette Wilson.

Suggested readings

De Clercq, Dirk and Maxim Voronov (2009b), 'Toward a practice perspective of entrepreneurship: Entrepreneurial legitimacy as habitus', *International Small Business Journal*, **27** (4), 395–419. This article is an excellent example of the deployment of Bourdieu's work in an entrepreneurial research setting, highlighting the relevance and reach of this theory in deepening our understanding of context.

Drakopoulou Dodd, Sarah, Seonaidh McDonald, Gerard McElwee, and Robert Smith (2014), 'A Bourdieuan analysis of qualitative authorship in entrepreneurship scholarship', *Journal of Small Business Management*, **52** (4), 633–654. In this article, the Bourdieusian lens is turned onto our own context, to reflect on the field of entrepreneurship. This study exposes key processes, structures, and relationships within qualitative entrepreneurship scholarship.

Tatli, Ahu, Joana Vassilopoulou, Mustafa Özbilgin, Cynthia Forson, and Natasha Slutskaya (2014), 'A Bourdieuan relational perspective for entrepreneurship research', *Journal of Small Business Management*, **52** (4), 615–632. This article sets out very clearly the agenda for deploying Bourdieu's approach within entrepreneurship research. As such, it provides an excellent conceptual grounding for considering context, whilst also providing a portfolio of relevant research questions.

References

Anderson, Alistair R., Sarah Drakopoulou Dodd, and Sarah L. Jack (2010), 'Network practices and entrepreneurial growth', *Scandinavian Journal of Management*, **26** (2), 121–133.

Anderson, Alistair R., Sarah Drakopoulou Dodd, and Sarah L. Jack (2012), 'Entrepreneurship as connecting: Some implications for theorising and practice', *Management Decision*, **50** (5), 958–971.

Baker, Ted and Reed E. Nelson (2005), 'Creating something from nothing: Resource construction through entrepreneurial bricolage', *Administrative Science Quarterly*, **50** (3), 329–366.

Batjargal, Bat (2003), 'Social capital and entrepreneurial performance in Russia: A longitudinal study', *Organization Studies*, **24** (4), 535–556.

Bourdieu, Pierre (1977), *Outline of a Theory of Practice*, Cambridge, MA: Cambridge University Press.

Bourdieu, Pierre (1984), *Distinction: A Social Critique of the Judgement of Taste*, Cambridge, MA: Harvard University Press.

Bourdieu, Pierre (1986), 'The forms of capital', in John G. Richardson (ed.), *The Handbook of Theory and Research for the Sociology of Education*, New York: Greenwood Press, pp. 241–258.

Chia, Robert and Robin Holt (2006), 'Strategy as practical coping: A Heideggerian perspective', *Organization Studies*, **27** (5), 635–655.

Coviello, Nicole E. and Marian V. Jones (2004), 'Methodological issues in international entrepreneurship research', *Journal of Business Venturing*, **19** (4), 485–508.

De Clercq, Dirk and Maxim Voronov (2009a), 'The role of domination in newcomers' legitimation as entrepreneurs', *Organization*, **16** (6), 799–827.

De Clercq, Dirk and Maxim Voronov (2009b), 'Toward a practice perspective of entrepreneurship: Entrepreneurial legitimacy as habitus', *International Small Business Journal*, **27** (4), 395–419.

Drakopoulou Dodd, Sarah (2014), 'Roots radical – Place, power and practice in punk entrepreneurship', *Entrepreneurship & Regional Development*, **26** (1–2), 165–205.

Drakopoulou Dodd, Sarah, Alistair R. Anderson, and Sarah L. Jack (2013), 'Being in time and the family owned firm', *Scandinavian Journal of Management*, **29** (1), 35–47.

Drakopoulou Dodd, Sarah, Seonaidh McDonald, Gerard McElwee, and Robert Smith (2014), 'A Bourdieuan analysis of qualitative authorship in entrepreneurship scholarship', *Journal of Small Business Management*, **52** (4), 633–654.

Drori, Israel, Benson Honig, and Ari Ginsberg (2010), 'Researching transnational entrepreneurship: An approach based on the theory of practice', in Benson Honig, Israel Drori, and Barbara Carmichael (eds), *Transnational and Immigrant Entrepreneurship in a Globalized World*, Toronto: University of Toronto Press, pp. 1–30.

Eikhof, Doris R. and Axel Haunschild (2007), 'For art's sake! Artistic and economic logics in creative production', *Journal of Organizational Behavior*, **28** (5), 523–538.

Emirbayer, Mustafa and Victoria Johnson (2008), 'Bourdieu and organizational analysis', *Theory and Society*, **37** (1), 1–44.

Fischer, Eileen and A. Rebecca Reuber (2014), 'Online entrepreneurial communication: Mitigating uncertainty and increasing differentiation via Twitter', *Journal of Business Venturing*, **29** (4), 565–583.

Foo, Maw-Der, Marilyn A. Uy, and Robert A. Baron (2009), 'How do feelings influence effort? An empirical study of entrepreneurs' affect and venture effort', *Journal of Applied Psychology*, **94** (4), 1086–1094.

Frenkel, Michal (2008), 'The multinational corporation as a third space: Rethinking international management discourse on knowledge transfer through Homi Bhabha', *Academy of Management Review*, **33** (4), 924–942.

Friedland, Roger (2009), 'The endless fields of Pierre Bourdieu', *Organization*, **16** (6), 887–917.

Georgiou, Catherine, Sarah Drakopoulou Dodd, Constantine Andriopoulos, and Manto Gotsi (2013), 'Colonialism's influence on national patterns of entrepreneurial networking', *International Small Business Journal*, **31** (2), 217–224.

Grant, Paul and Lew Perren (2002), 'Small business and entrepreneurial research: Meta-theories, paradigms and prejudices', *International Small Business Journal*, **20** (2), 185–211.

Harvey, Charles, Mairi Maclean, Jillian Gordon, and Eleanor Shaw (2011), 'Andrew Carnegie and the foundations of contemporary entrepreneurial philanthropy', *Business History*, **53** (3), 425–450.

Heidegger, Martin (1962), *Being and Time*, Oxford, UK: Blackwell.

Jack, Sarah L. and Alistair R. Anderson (2002), 'The effects of embeddedness on the entrepreneurial process', *Journal of Business Venturing*, **17** (5), 467–487.

Jack, Sarah L., Susan Moult, Alistair R. Anderson, and Sarah Drakopoulou Dodd (2010), 'An entrepreneurial network evolving: Patterns of change', *International Small Business Journal*, **28** (4), 315–337.

Jayawarna, Dilani, Oswald Jones, and Allan Macpherson (2014), 'Entrepreneurial potential: The role of human and cultural capitals', *International Small Business Journal*, **32** (8), 918–943.

Johnstone, Harvey and Doug Lionais (2004), 'Depleted communities and community business entrepreneurship: revaluing space through place', *Entrepreneurship & Regional Development*, **16** (3), 217–233.

Jones, Campbell and André Spicer (2005), 'The sublime object of entrepreneurship', *Organization*, **12** (2), 223–246.

Karataş-Özkan, Mine (2011), 'Understanding relational qualities of entrepreneurial learning: Towards a multi-layered approach', *Entrepreneurship & Regional Development*, **23** (9–10), 877–906.

Karataş-Özkan, Mine and Elizabeth Chell (2010), *Nascent Entrepreneurship and Learning*, Cheltenham, UK and Northampton, MA, USA: Edward Elgar Publishing.

Karataş-Özkan, Mine and Elizabeth Chell (2015), 'Gender inequalities in academic innovation and enterprise: A Bourdieuian analysis', *British Journal of Management*, **26** (1), 109–125.

Light, Ivan and Léo-Paul Dana (2013), 'Boundaries of social capital in entrepreneurship', *Entrepreneurship Theory and Practice*, **37** (3), 603–624.

Lockett, Andy, Graeme Currie, Rachael Finn, Graham Martin, and Justin Waring (2014), 'The influence of social position on sensemaking about organizational change', *Academy of Management Journal*, **57** (4), 1102–1129.

McDonald, Seonaidh, Bee C. Gan, Simon S. Fraser, Adekunie Oke, and Alistair R. Anderson (2015), 'A review of research methods in entrepreneurship 1985–2013', *International Journal of Entrepreneurial Behavior & Research*, **21** (3), 291–315.

McKeever, Edward, Alistair R. Anderson, and Sarah L. Jack (2014), 'Entrepreneurship and mutuality: Social capital in processes and practices', *Entrepreneurship & Regional Development*, **26** (5–6), 453–477.

McKeever, Edward, Sarah L. Jack, and Alistair R. Anderson (2015), 'Embedded entrepreneurship in the creative re-construction of place', *Journal of Business Venturing*, **30** (1), 50–65.

Ogbor, John O. (2000), 'Mythicizing and reification in entrepreneurial discourse: Ideology-critique of entrepreneurial studies', *Journal of Management Studies*, **37** (5), 605–635.

Özbilgin, Mustafa and Ahu Tatli (2005), 'Book review essay: Understanding Bourdieu's contribution to organization and management studies', *Academy of Management Review*, **30** (4), 855–869.

Patel, Pankaj C. and Betty Conklin (2009), 'The balancing act: The role of transnational habitus and social networks in balancing transnational entrepreneurial activities', *Entrepreneurship Theory and Practice*, **33** (5), 1045–1078.

Patel, Pankaj C. and Siri Terjesen (2011), 'Complementary effects of network range and tie strength in enhancing transnational venture performance', *Strategic Entrepreneurship Journal*, **5** (1), 58–80.

Powell, E. Erin and Ted Baker (2014), 'It's what you make of it: Founder identity and enacting strategic responses to adversity', *Academy of Management Journal*, **57** (5), 1406–1433.

Pret, Tobias, Eleanor Shaw, and Sarah Drakopoulou Dodd (2015), 'Painting the full picture: The conversion of economic, cultural, social and symbolic capital', *International Small Business Journal*. Epub ahead of print 27 July, doi: 10.1177/0266242615595450.

Scott, Michael (2012), 'Cultural entrepreneurs, cultural entrepreneurship: Music producers mobilising and converting Bourdieu's alternative capitals', *Poetics*, **40** (3), 237–255.

Shaw, Eleanor, Jillian Gordon, Charles Harvey, and Mairi Maclean (2013), 'Exploring contemporary entrepreneurial philanthropy', *International Small Business Journal*, **31** (5), 580–599.

Shepherd, Dean A. (2003), 'Learning from business failure: Propositions of grief recovery for the self-employed', *Academy of Management Review*, **28** (2), 318–328.

Stam, Wouter, Souren Arzlanian, and Tom Elfring (2014), 'Social capital of entrepreneurs and small firm performance: A meta-analysis of contextual and methodological moderators', *Journal of Business Venturing*, **29** (1), 152–173.

Steyaert, Chris (2011), 'Entrepreneurship as in(ter)vention: Reconsidering the conceptual politics of method in entrepreneurship studies', *Entrepreneurship & Regional Development*, **23** (1–2), 77–88.

Steyaert, Chris and Hans Landström (2011), 'Enacting entrepreneurship research in a pioneering, provocative and participative way: On the work of Bengt Johannisson', *Small Business Economics*, **36** (2), 123–134.

Stringfellow, Lindsay, Eleanor Shaw, and Mairi Maclean (2014), 'Apostasy versus legitimacy: Relational dynamics and routes to resource acquisition in entrepreneurial ventures', *International Small Business Journal*, **32** (5), 571–592.

Tatli, Ahu, Joana Vassilopoulou, Mustafa Özbilgin, Cynthia Forson, and Natasha Slutskaya (2014), 'A Bourdieuan relational perspective for entrepreneurship research', *Journal of Small Business Management*, **52** (4), 615–632.

Terjesen, Siri and Amanda B. Elam (2009), 'Transnational entrepreneurs' venture internationalization strategies: A practice theory approach', *Entrepreneurship Theory and Practice*, **33** (5), 1093–1120.

Umney, Charles and Lefteris Kretsos (2014), 'Creative labour and collective interaction: The working lives of young jazz musicians in London', *Work, Employment & Society*, **28** (4), 571–588.

Uy, Marilyn A., Maw-Der Foo, and Herman Aguinis (2010), 'Using experience sampling methodology to advance entrepreneurship theory and research', *Organizational Research Methods*, **13** (1), 31–54.

Vershinina, Natalia, Rowena Barrett, and Michael Meyer (2011), 'Forms of capital, intra-ethnic variation and Polish entrepreneurs in Leicester', *Work, Employment & Society*, **25** (1), 101–117.

Weick, Karl E. (1999), 'That's moving: Theories that matter', *Journal of Management Inquiry*, **8** (2), 134–142.

Wilson, Juliette, Norin Arshed, Eleanor Shaw, and Tobias Pret (2016), 'Expanding the domain of festival research: A review and research agenda', *International Journal of Management Reviews*, Epub ahead of print 15 February, doi: 10.1111/ijmr.12093.

11 Historical methods for contextualizing entrepreneurship research[1]

R. Daniel Wadhwani

Introduction

Management scholars have become increasingly aware of the value of historical approaches in entrepreneurship research (Forbes and Kirsch 2011; Landström and Lohrke 2010; Wadhwani and Jones 2014). Calls for historical contextualization form part of the broader agenda of fostering more deeply contextualized research on entrepreneurship (Welter 2011; Zahra and Wright 2011).

In Chapter 6, I outlined what historical contextualization means and why it could be valuable to entrepreneurship scholarship. I defined historical contextualization as *the analysis or interpretation of past event(s), in relationship to their time and place, in ways that address a question or problem that arises in the present,* and I highlighted the value of historical perspective in addressing a number of crucial questions in the domain of entrepreneurship research. These included questions of how entrepreneurs and entrepreneurial teams understood their own historical context, as well as how researchers could use historical contextualization to examine topics that require historical perspective, such as the effects of institutions on entrepreneurship and the processes of entrepreneurial change.

But the retrospective nature of historical contextualization also raises a set of methodological opportunities and challenges. Precisely because of the unique perspective that historical contextualization allows, researchers employing historical contextualization must contend with the particular character of historical evidence, its analysis/interpretation, and the presentation of findings. Unlike in the case of ethnographic methods, for instance, which are based on direct observation of events under examination, historical perspective does not allow for the observation of events of interest by the researcher; the behaviour, action, thought, and communication under study have to be reconstructed through the evidence that remains from the past. These challenges are compounded by the need to take into account the very different historical situations in which the event(s) took place. Historical methods can be understood as *the set of research practices designed to address the opportunities and challenges involved in the retrospective analysis or interpretation of evidence about events that occurred in the past* (Kipping, Wadhwani, and Bucheli 2014).

This chapter introduces readers to these methodological practices and discusses their relevance to entrepreneurship research. It examines historical sources, techniques of interpretation and analysis, and the forms in which findings are presented, with attention to how these differ depending on the particular kinds of goals and approaches considered in the research. The chapter concludes with a brief discussion of the need for entrepreneurship researchers and reviewers to better understand and appreciate historical methods in order to unlock the potential of historical contextualization in entrepreneurship research.

Clio's toolkit[2]

Historical methods have been designed to capitalize on the unique analytical and interpretive opportunities historical perspective provides while addressing the challenges of making valid claims about event(s) in the past given its distance from the present. These tools do not take the form of a clear-cut recipe book with step by step instructions to be blindly followed regardless of research outcomes or circumstances, but rather forms a set of established 'practices' and 'precedents' that guide the process of analysing and interpreting historical evidence.

There are a number of reasons why historical methods are based on practices or precedents rather than on methodological formulae. First, the specific tools used or the ways in which they are used depend on the nature of the knowledge of the past that the researcher seeks. Because of the 'pluralistic' nature of historical knowledge (Maclean, Harvey, and Clegg 2015), researchers need to adjust their choice and use of tools to address the specific kind of knowledge that is sought. And second, historical methods continue to be an arena of ongoing experimentation and change, as researchers confront the specific challenges and opportunities of the particular projects in which they are engaged (Howell and Prevenier 2001). Thus, like the adjudicatory methods used in common law countries, historical methods have evolved a number of practices or precedents that researchers should consider in using historical evidence to address entrepreneurship theory.

Sources and source criticism

Source criticism refers to the process by which traces or material from the past are transformed by the researcher into evidence or data that pertain to the research question of interest. Because historical researchers cannot engage in direct observation, evidence on the event of interest needs to be (re)constructed from the documentary sources that remain. It is for this reason that historical researchers typically refer to 'sources' rather than 'data' when discussing evidence, because of the need to critically evaluate such sources in judging what they can or cannot reveal to a researcher about the topic of interest. Evidence or traces from the past become a 'source of information' when the researcher establishes its relevance to the research question that has been posed (Lipartito 2013; Rowlinson, Hassard, and Decker 2014).

Historical methods also distinguish between primary and secondary sources, with primary sources given preference as evidence over secondary ones as a type of evidence in addressing the research question. The distinction between primary and secondary sources can be formulated in a number of different ways. Often historical researchers refer to primary sources as those produced at the time of the events under investigation, while secondary sources are documents or scholarship produced later, which recount the events from a greater distance. An arguably better way to think about the distinction is that the '*primacy*' of a source is a relative construct and is based on a source's centrality as evidence in relationship to the research question under consideration (Kipping, Wadhwani, and Bucheli 2014). Thus, magazine and newspaper articles recounting the origins of the Small Business Administration (SBA) in the United States might be a secondary source if the research question under consideration pertained to why the SBA was established, but might serve as a primary source if the research question pertained to the changing ways in which government support for small business was portrayed in the media over the course of the second half of the twentieth century.

Academic historians often give preference to archival sources, documents, and other primary source material held in special repositories. Archival sources can be particularly valuable for researchers because they may include quantitative and qualitative sources that were held privately by individuals or companies, and hence may contain unique and private information about thought processes, communications, or strategy that are difficult to attain from public sources. Forbes and Kirsch (2011) for instance point out that archival sources can be a particularly rich source of studying the emergence of new industries. But archival sources can also have significant drawbacks. In some contexts, archival records have not been kept or are incomplete or inaccessible to researchers (Decker 2013). Even when they are available, researchers need to understand that they may be organized or kept in a way that may convey certain types of information and not others. Moreover, archival research can be very time consuming. Thus, entrepreneurship researchers need to use critical judgment in considering why and how archival research is being employment vis-à-vis a research question, and whether other primary and secondary sources might better address a question at hand.

In addition to taking into account the primacy of a source, historical research practices include evaluating the *validity* and *credibility* of sources in addressing the research question. Validity pertains to 'establishing its authenticity and pertinence for the research question at hand', including '(a) the provenance of a source; (b) its intended audience and purpose; and (c) the context under which it was written' (Donnelly and Norton 2011, cited in Kipping, Wadhwani, and Bucheli 2014, p. 313). Establishing validity involves the process of transforming a documentary trace or fragment from the past into a source that is considered pertinent in some way to analysing or interpreting the event(s) of interest. But not all valid sources are treated equally in historical interpretation and analysis, and the process of determining source *credibility* involves 'assessing a source's trustworthiness or reliability in addressing the researcher's question' (Kipping, Wadhwani, and Bucheli

2014, p. 314). The original author of a source may have had a particular intention in producing it or may have been in a good or poor position from which to convey information about the event, and so assessing credibility is important in determining the author's intention and position with regard to the event under consideration. Moreover, all sources (including archival ones) needed to be organized and preserved from the time they were produced until the moment the researcher encountered them. Thus, assessing credibility involves taking into consideration the interests of those who preserved the sources and the organization and form in which the sources are presented in order to assess what has been preserved and what was not, and how the organization of what was preserved shapes its interpretation (Lipartito 2014).

Finally, in part because of the importance of these considerations of the nature and type of sources used in understanding the past, historical research typically involves expectations about transparency about the sources, so that specific claims can be linked back to the sources and documents. The purpose of source transparency is not so much to allow for replication, in the scientific sense, but to allow critical readers and reviewers to judge how the interpretation or analysis was conducted.

Triangulation

Triangulation refers to the use of multiple sources, and multiple *types* of sources, to examine a research question. As Howell and Prevenier (2001, p. 69) point out, 'Typically, historians do not rely on just one source to study an event or a historical process, but on many, and they construct their own interpretations about the past by means of comparison among sources'. Triangulation serves a number of purposes. Sometimes, it is used to validate or confirm evidence about an event from multiple sources, in order to address credibility concerns that source criticism has raised about any one source. Even more importantly, however, triangulation allows a researcher to interpret or analyse an event in novel and productive ways. For instance, given that the perspective and intent of authors might differ, it allows a researcher to examine the same event from different perspectives. Or, in triangulating between primary and secondary sources, a researcher may be able to place the event in a broader context in a way that a single source may be incapable of doing. Moreover, triangulating between sources may allow a researcher to track an event or development over a longer period of time than any single source may be capable of doing (Kipping, Wadhwani, and Bucheli 2014).

The relative value of consistency or heterogeneity in sources that are being triangulated depends on the purposes for which the sources are being used. Consistency among sources – for example, in quantitative data on an event or series of events over a long period – can facilitate the use of a source to test or elaborate on theoretical claims. For instance, research that seeks to track business start-up activity in a particular ecosystem over a long period of time might need to triangulate between sources from city directories, census statistics, patent filings, and tax records, with the intent of examining consistency between these sources in reporting entrepreneurial activity (Lamoreaux, Levenstein, and Sokoloff 2006). On the other hand, heterogeneity among sources often introduces new perspectives or contexts that allow for novel interpretations that can contribute to theory building or the exploration of complex social processes. Heterogeneity of sources, representing the voices of different actors (entrepreneurs, investors, policymakers, university officials, labour) in the same ecosystem mentioned above would allow researchers to examine start-up activity from different perspectives and incorporate analysis and interpretation of the dialogue and interaction between them.

Hermeneutic interpretation

The challenge of interpreting and analysing fragmented and incomplete sources from the past is compounded by the fact that the social and cultural context in which these sources were produced was often quite different from that of the researcher. Thus, in cases where historical contextualization requires the establishment of meaning or that takes into account motives as part of its examination of an event, researchers face the additional challenge of interpreting meaning within the setting in which it was produced.

Hermeneutics, a body of theory pertaining to how meaning arises out of texts, is useful in interpreting sources in a way that takes into account the contexts in which they were produced. Hermeneutic theory posits that an interpreter can draw meaning from a text by moving back and forth between texts and the broader contexts in which they were created, around what is referred to as a 'hermeneutic circle'. In practice, this is done by examining a particular source in relationship to the other sources that surround it and to which it refers, taking into account broader and broader related texts as one moves through interpretive iterations around the hermeneutic circle. Such an interpretive process could include not only the immediate primary sources to which a focal source refers but also the secondary sources that establish the context for the event or action to which the source refers. The researcher continues to question and interrogate the source in broader contexts until a stable and robust interpretation is found that addresses the research question, or until this interpretation raises doubts about the way in which the research question is itself formulated, in which case the question should be reformulated and the interpretive processes started again. Khaire and Wadhwani (2010), for instance, use historical hermeneutic interpretation in order to understand how fine art auction houses interpreted twentieth-century Indian art, and to track how shifts in this interpretation of Indian art allowed for the creation of a new market category and the entrance of new auction houses. Likewise, Popp and Holt (2013) use a form of hermeneutic interpretation to try to distinguish how the entrepreneurs they studied saw a future opportunity prospectively from how we as researchers view it retrospectively.

Critical hermeneutic theory adds the lens of power to the hermeneutic interpretation process. It seeks to not just interpret meaning from particular sources, but to also incorporate how the authors of particular sources sought to produce interpretations or meanings that would triumph over competing meanings of an event, or to consider how one particular interpretation or history 'won out' over competing interpretations. Phillips and Brown (1993, p. 1547), for instance, used critical hermeneutics to examine how corporate advertising campaigns 'create and disseminate cultural forms that support preferred patterns of power and dominance'. Historical research that critiques the expansion of entrepreneurial rhetoric into non-commercial realms of social life, such as 'cultural entrepreneurship', 'social entrepreneurship', and 'academic entrepreneurship', for instance, may use such an approach to hermeneutic interpretation.

Other techniques: structural history, microhistory, conceptual history, and beyond

The analytical and interpretive techniques I have described above form the basic tools in the historical toolkit. Much can be accomplished in entrepreneurship research with these alone. But there are numerous other historical techniques that can be used and applied in conjunction with source criticism, triangulation, and hermeneutic interpretation to address a range of more specific kinds of research questions. Though limitations on space prohibit an extensive discussion of other techniques, I will simply mention three and note their potential relevance to contextualization in entrepreneurship research.

Braudelian or *Annales* School structural history is a variety of historical interpretation that seeks to take into account multiple temporal perspectives in the interpretation or analysis of events, and particularly to incorporate 'long' temporal spans into research. Braudel (1958) distinguished between the short time spans that define the history of events from the longer temporal spans that characterize processes of change in social and economic conditions and that very long spans involved in processes of geographic and biological developments; he suggested that one way to understand continuity and change was to consider how these temporal processes co-occur and even intersect at particular moments in time. In fact, he suggested, that by taking into account these multiple layers of time, historical interpretation could incorporate other social sciences into research in a more synthetic way. Braudelian interpretations could be effectively used in understanding how persistent structural factors shape entrepreneurial behaviours as well as how 'conjunctures' – that is moments of structural change when near term events reconstitute long-term structures – lead to change in industries, economies, and capitalism itself. For instance, an interpretation of the rise of entrepreneurship in the last 30 years in relationship to the longer temporal span of changes in capitalism could lend itself to such structural examination of entrepreneurship.

Microhistory, in contrast to structural history, seeks to address large historical questions by looking in fine-grained detail at particular instances – such as the patterns of a life, a community, or organization (Ginzburg 1993). Also known as 'ethno-history', micro-history techniques apply an ethnographic sensibility to the interpretation of sources, and incorporate the historical perspective of the actors being studied. It is a technique that could be productively used in the careful study of particular entrepreneurial start-ups or entrepreneurial lives in conjunction with the much broader historical developments in which they are embedded. For instance, a micro-history of the development of a particular entrepreneurial eco-system from a historical perspective could shed light on how members of a community understood entrepreneurship and innovation and channelled resources to develop it in a way that could reveal broader processes of entrepreneurial ecosystem development at particular moments of time.

Whereas structural and micro-history change the scale at which historical interpretation and analysis is conducted, conceptual history shifts the focus from actions to ideas, language, and meaning as the events being analysed. Specifically, conceptual history traces the shifting ways in which key terms are developed and used as an essential and independent factor in historical processes and in how contextualization occurs (Koselleck 2002). Conceptual history holds particular promise in entrepreneurship studies, which still awaits research on how the term entrepreneurship and its various hyphenated cousins (social entrepreneurship, academic entrepreneurship, cultural entrepreneurship) have evolved in daily usage over time, and how the usage of the term has shaped expectations and behaviours.

Methods for scholarly versus everyday historical contextualization

The specific mix of interpretive and analytical tools one uses depends on the purposes of the research and the way history is being engaged. In Chapter 6, I distinguished between two types of historical contextualization. Scholarly historical contextualization is the explicit and conscious process of interpreting or analysing events in the past for theoretical or historiographical purposes in the present. By its nature, scholarly historical contextualization involves conscious intention to turn to and 'study' the past. In contrast, everyday historical contextualization is what human actors do as part of sense-making and communication; they interpret the past for purposes of understanding the present or establishing expectations about the future. It is sometimes intentional or instrumental, but may also be 'preconscious' or 'pre-theoretical' in that past experiences inherently shape our future expectations, whether they do so intentionally or not. History in this sense is the *object of research*, and can be useful for studying questions about sensemaking and communication, such as processes of opportunity recognition and team formation.

The interpretive tools used will inherently vary depending on whether one is using history as a scholarly method or studying history as a process of sense making and communication in everyday life. Because the use of history as a method involves a conscious and deliberate process of examining the past for theoretical or historiographical ends, it requires the use of interpretive and analytical tools that address the problems created by the temporal distance between the event under consideration and the evidence available in the present for reconstructing the past. Thus, all three basic tools discussed above – source criticism, triangulation, and hermeneutic interpretation – are useful methods for achieving the epistemic end.

In contrast, when studying history as a process of sense-making and communication by actors in everyday life, establishing the validity and credibility of their historical interpretation is not itself the purpose of the study. Rather, it is to grasp how their understanding of history shapes their experience in the present and expectation for the future. Hence, source criticism and triangulation are not pertinent methods for such a study. Instead the focus is on the hermeneutic interpretation of the texts such actors produce and analysis of how these interpretations shape their actions in the present.

The importance of form: tests versus narratives

An important matter for entrepreneurship researchers to consider in pursuing historical research pertains to the *form* in which analysis and interpretation is conveyed. Maclean, Harvey, and Clegg (2015) distinguish between social scientific forms and narrative forms of history. Whereas management researchers are familiar with the social scientific forms of findings presented as tests or revisions of theory or as articulations of social process, they may be less familiar with narrative forms of presentation, which are very common in historical research. Hence, understanding the differences between these forms of historical presentation of findings, how they work to make particular kinds of intellectual contributions and the kinds of expectations they set vis-à-vis sources and their analysis or interpretation is essential to the overall process of designing, pursuing, and evaluating historical research.

Certain varieties of historical research – particularly economic history and most social scientific history – use analytical tests of particular historical claims or seek to identify social processes. Such studies use historical sources and evidence to test or revise theoretical claims or to analyse sequences of events that describe a social process at work. The findings often appear in a form that is similar to or compatible with the kinds of findings found in mainstream management journals, in that they may set up a historically contextualized hypothesis that is tested with evidence, may use historical events as cases from which to build or revise theory, or may conform to the expectations of process research. Within the domain of entrepreneurship research, Lamoreaux, Levenstein, and Sokoloff (2006), Baumol (1990), and Cole (1959) provide exemplars respectively of uses of historical evidence as tests of hypotheses, development of theory, and articulation of entrepreneurial processes.

The presentation of findings in the form of historical narratives, in contrast, is much less common in management research, but is an accepted standard in academic historical research. Historical narratives, it is important to preface, are not 'cases' in the conventional sense of being a set of qualitative evidence about a particular situation that can be used to build a general theory. Rather, historical narratives are syntheses that fit together analysed evidence into 'representations' of events in the past from the perspective of the present in the form of a narrative arc, with a beginning, a middle, and an end (Ricoeur 1984, 2004).

One way to understand the interpretive process of creating and presenting a historical narrative is by distinguishing it from a simple historical chronicle. A chronicle entails plotting all pertinent events on a timeline. Historical narratives, in contrast, synthesize evidence that has been analysed into a representation with a beginning, middle, and end in a way that addresses a research question (White 1987). In doing so a historical narrative 'grasps together' or 'fits together' the pieces of evidence on the origins of the events under consideration, the key motives, meanings, causes, and consequences pertaining to the events themselves, and their eventual (contingent or conflicted) resolution. By 'fitting together' events into a coherent synthesis, historical narratives typically assign: (a) causes and effects; (b) meanings; and (c) alternative paths of development. They do this by engaging in the contextualizing activities – establishing the purposes of the turn to history, periodizing evidence, and establishing causal or semantic links across time – discussed in Chapter 6.

The process of creating a historical narrative thus involves interpretive judgments about particular pieces of evidence and where and how they fit into a coherent narrative. The interpretation process involves foregrounding, back-grounding and the elision of particular events, grouping together events or actors into classes, establishing relationships and sequences of events and consequences, and the assembly of all into a coherent narrative arc. The process of fitting together evidence into narrative explanation entails judgments not only about the relative importance of particular evidence but also whether the evidence cumulatively warrants a revision of the historical narrative itself. The revision of historical narratives is hence an integral aspect of the nature of historical narrative accounts, as new historical narratives of events are developed to incorporate new evidence, new research questions or perspectives, and even new perspectives onto the past as events in the present continue to unfold (Ricoeur 2004).

As representations of social action, historical narratives allow us to see events in new ways, to suggest new understandings and new visions of cause and effect, of patterns of meaning, and of processes of change. Whereas historical research that takes the form of 'tests' or 'processes' allow for assessment of the validity of particular claims about an event in historical context, historical narratives can be used for a number of different kinds of purposes. Commonly they are used to produce or revise historical accounts of an event of special importance to a research community, such as Gompers' (1994) historical narrative of the rise of the venture capital financing in the United States, or for providing conceptual and categorical insights based on historical perspective, as Popp and Holt's (2013) perspective on entrepreneurial opportunities does.

Conclusion

The development of historically contextualized research on entrepreneurship hinges on the acceptance of historical methods as a set of valid and valuable approaches to research, one that is recognized and understood by both individual researchers and the community as a whole. But recognition and acceptance of historical methods depends on a clear understanding of historical interpretive and analytical practices, and their purpose and validity as a way of establishing historical context.

This chapter has sought to facilitate the adoption of historical methods in entrepreneurship research by describing the purpose and nature of these historical practices. It has explained: (a) the particularities of historical evidence/data; (b) the techniques for analysing or interpreting evidence; and (c) the forms that findings can take, and related these to the nature of historical contextualization. It has also indicated the need for judgment on the part of researchers and reviewers in considering how evidence, analytical/interpretive techniques, and form are combined in the process of seeking historically contextualized answers to research questions in entrepreneurship. Because historical contextualization can make different kinds of intellectual contributions to entrepreneurship scholarship, the chapter has emphasized the ways in which the particular mix of evidence, methods, and forms should differ depending on the intellectual contribution that a researcher seeks to make.

Historical contextualization holds great promise as an emerging approach to entrepreneurship research. Researchers have the opportunity to examine important research questions anew by using historical perspective. And in drawing on the academic historical research practices described here, they also have a set of well-established scholarly tools and techniques for unlocking the past.

NOTES
1 I would like to thank Friederike Welter and Christina Lubinski for comments on earlier versions of the chapter.
2 Clio is the 'muse' of history.

Suggested readings

Kipping, Matthias, R. Daniel Wadhwani, and Marcelo Bucheli (2014), 'Analyzing and interpreting historical sources: A basic methodology', in Marcelo Bucheli and R. Daniel Wadhwani (eds), *Organizations in Time: History, Theory, Methods*, Oxford: Oxford University Press, pp. 305–329. This chapter provides a more in-depth introduction to the analysis of historical sources, and especially to source criticism, triangulation, and hermeneutics. It also provides examples of papers that employ historical methods.

Lipartito, Kenneth J. (2014), 'Historical sources and data', in Marcelo Bucheli and R. Daniel Wadhwani (eds), *Organizations in Time: History, Theory, Methods*, Oxford: Oxford University Press, pp. 284–304. This chapter provides an introduction to business sources and archives for conducting historical research, and explains the major issues involved in using and analysing these sources.

Maclean, Mairi, Charles Harvey, and Stewart Clegg (2015), 'Conceptualizing historical organization studies', *Academy of Management Review*, published online before print 13 July 2015, doi: 10.5465/amr.2014.0133. This paper provides a useful typology of different kinds of historical research on organizations.

Rowlinson, Michael, John Hassard, and Stephanie Decker (2014), 'Research strategies for organizational history: A dialogue between historical theory and organization theory', *Academy of Management Review*, **39** (3), 250–274. This paper lays out some of the key differences between historical and social scientifc research in the treatment of evidence, in the treatment of time, and in the presentation of findings.

References

Baumol, William J. (1990), 'Entrepreneurship: Productive, unproductive, and destructive', *Journal of Political Economy*, **98** (5), 893–921.

Braudel, Fernand (1958), 'Histoire et sciences sociales: la longue durée'. Paper presented at the Annales. Histoire, Sciences Sociales.

Cole, Arthur (1959), *Business Enterprise in its Social Setting*, Cambridge, MA: Harvard University Press.

Decker, Stephanie (2013), 'The silence of the archives: Business history, post-colonialism and archival ethnography', *Management and Organizational History*, **8** (2), 155–173.

Donnelly, Mark and Claire Norton (2011), *Doing History*, New York: Routledge.

Forbes, Daniel and David Kirsch (2011), 'The study of emerging industries: Recognizing and responding to some central problems', *Journal of Business Venturing*, **26**, 589–602.

Ginzburg, Carlo (1993), 'Microhistory', *Critical Inquiry*, **20**, 10–35.

Gompers, Paul (1994), 'The rise and fall of venture capital', *Business and Economic History*, **3** (2), 1–26.

Howell, Walter and Matha Prevenier (2001), *From Reliable Sources: An Introduction to Historical Methods*, Ithaca: Cornell University Press.

Khaire, Mukti and R. Daniel Wadhwani (2010), 'Changing landscapes: The construction of meaning and value in a new market category – Modern Indian art', *Academy of Management Journal*, **53** (6), 1281–1304.

Kipping, Matthias, R. Daniel Wadhwani, and Marcelo Bucheli (2014), 'Analyzing and interpreting historical sources: A basic methodology', in Marcelo Bucheli and R. Daniel Wadhwani (eds), *Organizations in Time: History, Theory, Methods*, Oxford: Oxford University Press, pp. 305–329.

Koselleck, Reinhart (2002), *The Practice of Conceptual History: Timing History, Spacing Concepts*, Palo Alto, CA: Stanford University Press.

Lamoreaux, Naomi R., Margaret Levenstein, and Kenneth Sokoloff (2006), 'Mobilizing venture capital during the second Industrial Revolution: Cleveland, Ohio, 1870–1920', *Capitalism and Society*, **1** (3), 1–61.

Landström, Hans and Franz Lohrke (eds) (2010), *Historical Foundations of Entrepreneurship Research*, Cheltenham, UK and Northampton, MA, USA: Edward Elgar Publishing.

Lipartito, Kenneth (2013), 'Connecting the cultural and the material in business history', *Enterprise and Society*, **14** (4), 686–704.

Lipartito, Kenneth J. (2014), 'Historical sources and data', in Marcelo Bucheli and R. Daniel Wadhwani (eds), *Organizations in Time: History, Theory, Methods*, Oxford: Oxford University Press, pp. 284–304.

Maclean, Mairi, Charles Harvey, and Stewart Clegg (2015), 'Conceptualizing historical organization studies', *Academy of Management Review*, published online before print 13 July 2015, doi: 10.5465/amr.2014.0133.

Phillips, Nelson and J.L. Brown (1993), 'Analyzing communication in and around organizations: A critical hermeneutic approach', *Academy of Management Journal*, **36** (6), 1547–1576.

Popp, Andrew and Robin Holt (2013), 'The presence of entrepreneurial opportunity', *Business History*, **55** (1), 9–28.

Ricoeur, Paul (1984), *Time and Narrative*, Chicago, IL: University of Chicago Press.

Ricoeur, Paul (2004), *Memory, History, Forgetting*, Chicago, IL: University of Chicago Press.

Rowlinson, Michael, John Hassard, and Stephanie Decker (2014), 'Research strategies for organizational history: A dialogue between historical theory and organization theory', *Academy of Management Review*, **39** (3), 250–274.

Wadhwani, R. Daniel and Geoffrey Jones (2014), 'Schumpeter's plea: Historical reasoning in entrepreneurship theory and research', in Marcelo Bucheli and R. Daniel Wadhwani (eds), *Organizations in Time: History, Theory, Methods*, Oxford: Oxford University Press, pp. 192–216.

Welter, Friederike (2011), 'Contextualizing entrepreneurship – Conceptual challenges and ways forward', *Entrepreneurship Theory and Practice*, **35** (1), 165–184.

White, Hayden (1987), *The Content of the Form: Narrative Discourse and Historical Representation*, Baltimore, MD: Johns Hopkins University Press.

Zahra, Shaker A. and Mike Wright (2011), 'Entrepreneurship's next act', *Academy of Management Perspectives*, **25** (4), 67–83.

12 Narrating context

William B. Gartner

Reader

Who are you? Who I am writing to? Are you an entrepreneurship scholar? Are you a doctoral student studying entrepreneurship? Are you someone 'else' that is not either of those types of readers? I write 'else' because, as a writer (more on that in the next section) I assume that my readers are scholars (for example, individuals with jobs in universities or research institutions) and doctoral students, and, maybe, a reader from the public policy area, or maybe, rarely, a reader who is a 'practitioner', that is, someone who isn't doing research on entrepreneurship, or isn't interested in the policy implications of entrepreneurship scholarship, but, who might be 'practising' entrepreneurship in some form – maybe as an entrepreneur.

So, who is my reader? Who are you?

Here is a story, an anecdote, about 'who' I think my readers are, and, 'who' I think I write to. I was just at a workshop where I was presenting and discussing customer value propositions to Lutheran pastors (I teach at California Lutheran University for part of the year, and, aspects of the University involve the life of Lutherans, as would be expected), and, the question during breaks in the workshop, to me, is often about what I do, and, often, more specifically, about my customer value proposition: what kind of value am I providing and who do I provide it to? My cursory answer, the one I have given for many years, to most people who ask about what I do as a scholar who does research on entrepreneurship is: 'I write for six people in the world'. What? Six people? And, then, I go on to explain that I do not write for the general public, or even a small segment of the public, but, rather, I am writing to a few scholars, at this present moment, I want to have a dialogue with. Because, for me, the entire point of scholarship is to engage other scholars in a conversation about specific problems and issues that we are researching together. So, 'scholarship' is indeed a 'ship' with other scholars on it. I am on a journey, not alone, always with others, where our voyage involves 're-search' (that is 're' – going back, which, simplistically, can be thought of as reading prior scholarship and knowing where my own scholarship fits into the context of ideas that have been discussed and dialogued in the past, and 'search' – which involves 'looking' and 'paying attention' to what is out there in the world, which simplistically, can be thought of as the methods used for paying attention). This book is, essentially, structured in that way: The first section being 'Re', and the second section being 'Search'.

Be that as it may, who, then, are my six readers that I am writing to today? Ted Baker, Denise Fletcher, Daniel Hjorth, Chris Steyaert, Kim Poldner and Friederike Welter. Four of these individuals have written chapters in the book you are reading (Friederike, Chris, Denise and Ted). The other two (Kim and Daniel) are colleagues that I have written with and worked with on various projects that have similar sensibilities to the idea of context that is the vortex of this book. (And, my apologies to friends and colleagues of mine if you did not make this specific 'list of six'. The list changes, often, depending on what I am writing, so, please trust me – you are probably on the 'list of six' for other articles I have written, just not on the list for this one.)

I try to write to this specific set of readers, and, therefore, I write to what I think they already know. The chapters written in this book, then, are reflections on aspects of their knowledge and interests, and, I would assume that they want to engage me as a reader of their work, as well. For writing to readers, then, I tend to consider their viewpoints and interests on the topic I am writing on, and, I desire to engage them in a way that will be: intriguing, amusing, entertaining, and, sometimes, I hope, informative. And, above all, I want my writing to be interesting to them. I want to engage them in a discussion, a discourse, a conversation that involves their ideas and insights coupled with my ideas and insights (as well as all of the other insights that occur through my and their referencing and recognizing other scholars on this 'ship' of research). That is the fun, really, of being a writer who writes for other scholars. It is about reading and writing to others as they also read and write to me. This effort, then, is essentially, about community. I seek to write to a reader who is also a writer and a researcher who reads me, and, writes to me, and, correspondingly, I read their work and I write to them.

The chapters written by Friederike, Ted, Chris and Denise (as well as all of the other chapters in the book), then, are the context for my writing about context. Assuming you have read those chapters, then, I hope you can see the connections between what I am writing and what they are saying. (But, as my chapter is a 'non-scholarly' 'non-contextual' text, I am not making the typical links to their work by citing them [more on this later when we get to the section 'Text'], that would clearly indicate where the connections are between what they are writing and what I am writing.)

Now, obviously, if my audience were only the six people I mentioned, there would not be many sales of this book beyond the copies the seven of us purchased. So, 'yes', I would like to have more readers than six. I hope, in some respects, that the six people I have chosen to be my readers might reflect a larger group of scholars and researchers with similar knowledge, interests and perspectives. Scholars who are interested in what I have to say. But, I cannot, often, specifically identify who those individuals might be. I do not write to them, per se, because I do not know their work well enough to dialogue with them. If I did, then, I would write to them as well. But, for now, I find the magic number of six readers to be enough of an audience to both focus my thoughts and provide a large enough scope of ideas to (I hope) be interesting in the conversation among scholars in particular segments of the entrepreneurship field.

The implication of this anecdote, and my musings about it, are that I write to identifiable readers. When I write I consciously consider the characteristics of my audience. I have some sense of their interests, their knowledge base, their research activities, and, their passions as scholars doing research on a particular topic. Therefore, I tend to write in a limited number of 'venues' where I think these scholars might be likely to read me. That means I tend to write in some journals and in some books, and, not in others, mostly because I think my readers read some journals and books, and not others, and, I want my readers to be able to find me and read me.

(And, that thought might be carried into an implication that if you know who your readers are, then, it would make sense to develop a list of them, and, send them your articles, book chapters and books so that you have a better chance that your readers are actually reading you! And, that thought might also be carried into the implication that with Internet web based search engines for finding scholarship based on key words and other forms of linkages, the effort to publish in a particular journal may be less of a way of connecting to a specific group of readers than has been in the past. And, that thought might also be carried into this question: How do readers find me? I am not sure.)

Finally, I want to re-emphasize that having a sense of 'who' my readers are requires that I be concerned with 'why' they might be interested in what I write. I began this section with an anecdote about a workshop on customer value propositions. My approach to considering the value of customer value propositions is to suggest that entrepreneurs find identifiable individuals (customers) who have problems (for those that know the customer value proposition literature, we could also talk about 'pains, gains and jobs' or any other set of words that might evoke ways individuals have desires that need to be satisfied) that need solutions. So, as a writer, I like to consider that there is a reader who has a specific problem that needs a solution. I write to that reader. I write to solve a particular reader's problems. I have that reader's problem in my mind as one of the purposes for writing what I write. Again, I write to other scholars who have problems they face as researchers, and, I write to offer solutions to aspects of their problems. And, they write to offer solutions to aspects of problems that I have as a researcher. My readers are other writers. Is that you?

So, the context of my writing, then, is the context of other academic researchers. A very limited number of people: we could probably all fit in a moderately sized room of a convention centre hotel.

Writer

So, who am I as a writer? Typically, this question is not addressed in academic writing. There is this tendency, I assume, that the combination of 'theory and data' presented in an article would lead to the same sets of ideas and conclusions. An author is merely delivering this message of facts and insights. And, given this, authors, could, in many respects, be interchangeable. By implication, if you encountered the same theories and facts, then, you too, would write the same article. Does authorship matter?

I think that the author matters in academic scholarship. Authors are part of the context of: what theories are offered, what research questions are posed to be interesting, what readers are selected to be addressed, what 'data' and methods are selected for exploring, what results are deemed relevant to report, as well as how and why those results will be discussed for insights and implications.

So, what do you know about me and the other authors who have written chapters in this book? Do you know us beyond the brief biographies that are included? Are you familiar with other work we have written? Does it matter to you to know what we have accomplished prior to writing these book chapters? I would assume that, in the context of the reader I have identified in the prior section, most readers are familiar with my work, and, the work of the other authors in this book, and, therefore, a reader would have some interest in reading what is written based on the writers. And, if this is the case, then, the reader would have some insights into why the writer is writing what is written. Authors have agendas.

For example, I know that I read whatever Karl Weick has written no matter what the topic appears to be. His work is interesting and his words tend to get my mind thinking in new ways, even though the topics he writes about are tangentially (in my mind) about entrepreneurship. Karl Weick tends to write with an agenda in mind. He writes about the nature of individual and social processes of sense making and the activities involved in dealing with the ambiguity inherent in all situations in ways that might make for plausible understandings of the past and future. This theme resonates with me, and my own problems, as a scholar (of trying to understand and explore how and why organizations emerge). I think the more interesting authors in academic scholarship tend to have a theme or themes that express a particular way of thinking about the nature of the world. Authors that quickly, come to mind, for me, would be: Howard Aldrich, Ted Baker, Denise Fletcher, Daniel Hjorth, Sara Sarasvathy, Scott Shane, Dean Shepherd, Chris Steyaert, Daniel Wadhwani and Friederike Welter. (Again, sorry, my dear friends and colleagues, if I did not list you as one of my examples, I could write many pages on, who, in the entrepreneurship area has a particular theme and how these themes are manifest through particular journal articles, book chapters and books.) If you have read any of these authors, then, I think you will know that they have an agenda: they have themes that they consistently write about, and, every aspect of the texts they write reflects specific issues and ideas. For the writers that have chapters in this book, you can see that they will offer citations of their own work as ways to demonstrate how a particular idea/issue has been carried forward through previous publications.

Is it fair to say that scholars write what they believe?

I assume, then, that all academic researchers have an agenda; they have reasons for writing what they write. The ideas they propose, the facts they marshal, are all intended to make a particular point and champion particular agendas and issues. Academic writing is not value free. While many academic articles are often written in the third person, academic articles are not written by disinterested third persons.

So, my own academic writing has a particular point of view. I bring to my writing a certain set of beliefs about the nature of the world I study. I believe that actions matter, and that what individuals 'do' shapes their beliefs and the futures they step into. I believe that situations are likely to be more fluid than we assume, and, that the boundaries of the constraints on possibility need to be challenged and tested. This is not to say that I think that there are no constraints on possibility, rather: futures are constructed based on the actions of individuals. There are no guarantees of happiness or success in this, or even that current constraints change. I do not assume that accomplishing anything is easy or without a significant cost. So, 'inaction' appears to rarely be the solution. And, I am not suggesting a process of 'Ready, Fire, Aim' as the *modus operandi*. Rather, whether it is 'Ready, Aim, Fire' or 'Ready, Fire, Aim' or 'Fire, Aim, Ready' or 'Fire, Ready, Aim' as sequences: all involve 'Fire'. Actions matter. We can think and think and think, but thinking does not manifest itself to others. Actions do. And, it is through action that the future comes into existence: We do not think it so. We make it so.

So, my research about the nature of entrepreneurship, therefore, tends to explore whether my beliefs have some validity in the evidence I find. Sometimes, I am surprised by how little support there is for my own beliefs. Sometimes, I am pleased that my views can be buttressed by confirming data. And, in nearly all of these efforts, I sense, for myself, a bit of surprise in the entire endeavour. Nothing ever conforms, exactly, to what I expected. What I find appealing in my own writing, then, is that sense of wonder about the world: the awe in curiosity.

(And, a note about the process of writing. I write to have such 'aha' moments as in writing the previous words: the awe in curiosity. That is, when we say 'curiosity' we say it with the 'awe' inside it. So, to be curious, then, is to wonder and to be in the presence of the wonderful. I hope that you will not be able to say 'curiosity', now, without thinking of the 'awe'. So, to be honest, if the only take away from this chapter is to savour this little amuse-bouche, I would be very pleased.)

I would assume that the authors in this book have a set of beliefs and values that they bring to their work. Writers all have agendas in writing. The work, the text, is not without the context of the writers who write these texts. What is fascinating in the chapters in this book is whether the authors state their agenda for writing their chapters, and particularly, the reasons and values that lead them to generate their work. I find that some authors, here, explicitly do, while others are not so obvious. And, my sense is, when reading academic writing in most academic journals, the values and perspectives of most authors are hidden. Indeed, it would seem out of the ordinary for authors of texts in journal articles to express their personal beliefs as the foundation for their research efforts. Typically, a reader would need to ferret out the beliefs and values of the authors by assuming that the literature review and the creation of hypotheses would somewhat reflect their viewpoints. And, then, this agenda, this viewpoint of the author(s) would merely be conjectures of the reader: guesses as to what authors actually believed.

It would be very interesting if every academic article started with a brief section on the author's beliefs and the author's agenda for writing the article. What if every article started with a statement of faith, the author's creed of what was believed?

So, I believe that authors matter in the context of researching context. Not one of the authors in this book is here by chance. They have been selected based on what we assumed they would offer readers: not only in terms of their knowledge about a specific aspect of context, but also in terms of how their own values and perspectives would be manifest in the texts, themselves.

Finally, one of the other issues that I think about, then, in terms of writers, is: why scholars? And, I guess, even more specifically, why me? Why am I the person who is privileged to have these pages in this book? Why am I the person who you would be willing to read? When we consider the context of this book, then, the legitimate holders of 'who' is valued to write these words are scholars, not any other group. So, while the context of entrepreneurship might involve entrepreneurs, or policymakers, or venture helpers, or customers, or any other type of individual embedded in entrepreneurial situations, why are they not writing these chapters? Where are their voices in the context of understanding the context of entrepreneurship?

Now, I am not saying the entrepreneurs or others, per se, do not have a voice in talking about themselves and the context of entrepreneurship. Indeed, entrepreneurs have plenty of opportunities to speak about themselves and their context. They speak through the creation of their organizations. They speak through what they say through their organizations: products, services, advertisements and so on. They have a voice in the media in news reports, society pages, magazine profiles and so on. They can author their own biographies and go on talk shows. They can tell their stories in: classrooms, public lectures and, any number of venues that might celebrate their gifts and successes. But, again, as I said, in talking about my readers earlier, I am, in this context (the context of this book) less likely to be writing to them (for example, to non-scholars). And, obviously, as they are not included as authors of texts in this book, they are not writing to me. The context of the dialogue is bounded. And, as we will soon explore in the next section, the format for whether they could hold a conversation with scholars, is, indeed limited.

I write for you. You write for me. Is this as it shall be?

Text

As Chris Steyaert (Chapter 3) covers many aspects of the text in con(text), my thoughts will segue towards the genre of academic writing, that is, the form of academic texts: the ways that academic texts are written. For example, this chapter has no citations in the text. It was, for me, difficult to actually write a chapter without citing other scholars. As I wrote earlier, the pretext of writing involves citing – making connections to other scholarship within the context of writing. I believe that scholarship actually requires this overt activity (that is, making connections to other scholarship through citations) in order to be scholarship. Texts with citations create this visible web of connections between the writer and other scholars (who are often the intended readers of the text). Citations become the way to say to other scholars (readers): 'I pay attention to your work, I see how your work relates to my work, and, now, how my work relates to your work'. Citations are a way to structure a form of dialogue between the writer and the reader. Academic scholarship is, therefore, very different from other kinds of writing in that the connections to other scholars (and, I would assume, the writer's readers) are made very visible. This ability to make visible the connections to other scholars (and readers) should not be minimized as a critical aspect of scholarly writing. I would hazard to suggest that the connections (citations) to other scholar's work is as important as the ideas, facts, findings and insights of the work, itself. Can you think of any other kind of writing where authors are, in the format they write, addressing specific readers and consciously making the reader a specific part of the text?

The other issue that I want to emphasize in the creation of texts that scholars write is the unique progression of ideas upon which nearly all scholarly manuscripts are structured. We offer an abstract (a brief overview of the entire paper), then, a kind of introduction and statement of the problem, followed by recognition of prior scholarship and the authors' reformulation of those ideas into a view of the world (for example, hypotheses and propositions), followed by a discussion of appropriate methods and data for studying one's conjectures about the world, followed by 'results' of analyses of the data, followed by a discussion of those results, and ending with conclusions. The sequence tends to suggest that the actual process of research followed this format. And, in very few instances in my own life, has the process of research ever mirrored how it was depicted in the journal article written. I find that individuals who are attempting to learn the process of scholarship tend to be confused and disoriented when their actual experiences of conducting research appears to have no relationship to the structure of journal articles they admire and use as templates for their own work. Journal articles are a particular genre, a particular way of formulating plots that are familiar and accepted ways of believing how research takes place. When I read a journal article I am often reminded of how the structure of these articles is like a murder mystery, something out of a 'Perry Mason' book or television show, where the formula for the book/show is always the same – for example, someone dies, a person is selected as the killer which requires a murder investigation and a trial, Perry Mason and his team uncover information that provides some insights into who might be the probable killer, and, then, with the presentation of compelling evidence (usually not obvious throughout the story), the real killer is identified and, often, publicly admits guilt. Case solved. But, does anything ever follow so easily the formula?

I would hope, at some point, to write out the actual experience of conducting a particular research effort (where it might start out with an idea, then, an initial foray into prior scholarship, then, an effort at collecting some data, then, some analyses that often contradict the original ideas, then, another foray into prior scholarship to find some way of making sense of what was found, then, another effort to look at the data through the new theoretical lens, then . . . it goes on and on and on and on and on . . .). There is a word for writing in this manner: autoethnography.

And, there are other ways to write about what we know, and, have discovered, as scholars: novels, short stories, magazine articles, essays, plays, poems. . . any particular way of writing might serve as text for the context of entrepreneurship. But, then, would these other forms be considered scholarship? Does the relationship of writers and readers (through some kind of form of recognizing the community of these individuals) through citations, necessitate specific kinds of texts?

Now, I am not sure about ways that might be helpful for breaking out of the typical genre structure of the academic article. I do not think that the journal article is big enough as the primary genre for channelling dialogue among scholars in the entrepreneurship field. At times, I find nearly every experience outside of the journal article (for example, books, weird papers that colleagues write that never get into journals but float around the Internet, blog posts, conferences, workshops, meetings on Skype, the chance conversation at an airport lounge) is more likely to engage me in the context of entrepreneurship scholarship. And, then again, maybe it is because of all of those journal articles that I continue to read, that I can even engage in other kinds of conversations.

Conclusions

I develop a strong feeling of ambivalence in reading and re-reading this book chapter. I doubt it is of interest to the six colleagues that I wrote it for. The chapter does not directly engage them: there are no citations, no direct connections to their own efforts. (To write to them is to show that I have read them.) And, I know they have already addressed many of these issues in their own work. So, the points I make are likely to be obvious rather than interesting to them.

The chapter comes across as lazy, self-centred and narcissistic. The lack of citations to other scholarship seems a lazy way to make a point about the inherent need for connections to a community of other writers and readers. Because I do not recognize other scholarship and authors, then, the chapter seems to be a self-centred and narcissistic journey into my own issues and concerns. Who would care about what I am thinking when it does not specifically relate to them? How boring. There is no scholar "ship" here, just a rowboat with me in it, gazing into the reflection of myself in the water. (Soon, I will fall in and drown.) Sigh.

So, one last thought. I have had a number of opportunities, recently, to consider how value (let us say that value, is, for scholars – insight) is acquired. At one point I had thought that in scholarly writing, one might construct a measure of value as: insights per 100 words, that more valuable articles and books have more insights packed into each page. For those of us that pour over hundreds and hundreds of pages of academic writing each month, it often seems as if there are few, very few insights that come from all of that reading. It often feels like sifting through thousands of tons of sand to find a small nugget of gold. And, therefore, in all of this sifting, only a few articles and books seem to tap into a rich vein of value that I so treasure. Yet, even in considering those high value touchstones in my life, I realize that insights do not surface so freely from those pages. For the articles and books I most treasure, the 'insight per 100 words' relationship is very meagre. Where I have found the most precious nuggets of insight have not necessarily been in pages where other gems reside so closely together.

The ability to offer 'insight' is a conundrum. And, so, with that, I leave you with this poem:

> I looked into the cave and realized
> The shadow came from the light behind me.
> I turned around
> And followed that.

Annotated bibliography

Orr, D. (2015), *The Road Not Taken: Finding America in the Poem Everyone Loves and Almost Everyone Gets Wrong*, New York: Penguin Press. The book is a close reading of the Robert Frost poem 'The Road Not Taken'. Nearly everyone is familiar with the poem and the ending lines:

> Two roads diverged in a wood, and I—
> I took the one less traveled by,
> And that has made all the difference.

The meaning of the poem, and, those lines, is shown to be both obvious and not. The book explores the poem, itself, as well as the context of both the poet, the events surrounding the creation of the poem, and, then, subsequent ways the poem has been interpreted and (mis)understood within the context of the past 100 years. It is easy to make a case that the poem has implications for how we understand the nature of entrepreneurs and entrepreneurship as the book explores the attributes of choice – contextually.

Vargas Llosa, M. (1984), *The Real Life of Alejandro Mayta: A Novel*, New York: Farrar, Straus and Giroux. This book is a novelistic attempt to offer various understandings of a failed attempt at a revolutionary uprising. The author explores a variety of stories and anecdotes of Alejandro Mayta that others tell about him, and, offers various interpretations of these 'facts' and insights through novelistic reconstructions of what might have been. The book is an elegant meditation on the nature of fact and fiction, stories and storytellers, and, the relationship of writers and readers in the construction of plausible insight.

References not referenced

Anderson, A.R. and M. Starnawska (2008), 'Research practices in entrepreneurship: Problems of definition, description and meaning', *International Journal of Entrepreneurship and Innovation*, **9** (4), 221–230.

Baker, T., A. Miner and D. Eesley (2003), 'Improvising firms: Bricolage, retrospective interpretation and improvisational competencies in the founding process', *Research Policy*, **32**, 255–276.

Barinaga, E. (in press), 'Engaged scholarship: Taking responsibility for the politics of method mediation', in H. Landström, A. Parhankangas and P. Riot (eds), *Challenging the Assumptions and Accepted Research Practices in Entrepreneurship Research*, Vol. 2, Routledge Series Advances in Critical Entrepreneurship Studies, London: Routledge.

Buttriss, G.J. and I.F. Wilkinson (2006), 'Using narrative sequence methods to advance international entrepreneurship theory', *Journal of International Entrepreneurship*, **4** (4), 157–174.

Davis, M.S. (1971), 'That's interesting', *Philosophy of the Social Sciences*, **1** (2), 309–344.

Downing, S. (2005), 'The social construction of entrepreneurship: Narrative and dramatic processes in the coproduction of organizations and identities', *Entrepreneurship Theory and Practice*, **29** (2), 185–204.

Fletcher, D. (2007), '"Toy Story": The narrative world of entrepreneurship and the creation of interpretive communities', *Journal of Business Venturing*, **22** (5), 649–672.

Garud, R. and A.P. Giuliani (2013), 'A narrative perspective on entrepreneurial opportunities', *Academy of Management Review*, **38** (1), 157–160.

Hjorth, D., R. Holt and C. Steyaert (2015), 'Entrepreneurship and process studies', *International Small Business Journal*, **33**, 599–611.

Kikooma, J.F. (2010), 'Using qualitative data analysis software in a social constructionist study of entrepreneurship', *Qualitative Research Journal*, **10** (1), 40–51.

Larty, J. and E. Hamilton (2011), 'Structural approaches to narrative analysis in entrepreneurship research: Exemplars from two researchers', *International Small Business Journal*, **29** (3), 220–237.

Lindgren, M. and J. Packendorff (2009), 'Social constructionism and entrepreneurship: Basic assumptions and consequences for theory and research', *International Journal of Entrepreneurial Behavior & Research*, **15** (1), 25–47.

Steyaert, C. (1997), 'A qualitative methodology for process studies of entrepreneurship: Creating local knowledge through stories', *International Studies of Management & Organization*, 13–33.

Welter, F. (2011), 'Contextualizing entrepreneurship: Conceptual challenges and ways forward', *Entrepreneurship Theory and Practice*, **35** (1), 165–184.

13 Advancing our research agenda for entrepreneurship and contexts

Friederike Welter and William B. Gartner

An invitation to our readers

We end this book by suggesting a number of points for a roadmap that we – personally – consider important for advancing a research agenda on entrepreneurship and contexts. But, we want you, the reader, to understand that by no means is this a fixed agenda. Rather, we see our final chapter as an invitation to all of those (entrepreneurship) scholars interested in contextualizing their own research efforts. We agree with Chris Steyaert's call to no longer hide behind the notion that 'contexts matter' (Chapter 3), but instead, do something with this notion. In fact, this book is about what we can and should do (and what we probably shouldn't do because other disciplines have discarded it. . .). We invite our readers to join forces and work together in developing the points set out below *and* revise and add elements you deem important. In fact, those of our readers who were present at the Professional Development Workshop 'Entrepreneurship and/in Context' at the Academy of Management Annual Meeting in Vancouver in 2015, have already contributed much to this research agenda.[1]

A roadmap for the future

Let's start with a simple point, but one which we believe has far-reaching consequences for the ways we contextualize (in) entrepreneurship (research): How do we talk about entrepreneurship and context? It is obvious, and cannot be repeated often enough – context matters. Now, we suggest a slightly different wording. It is not the 'context', but *contexts* that matter for entrepreneurship. The book, as a whole, describes multiple and diverse contexts. With the plural of the word, *contexts*, we fully acknowledge the diversity, heterogeneity and multiplicity required to adequately contextualize – in other words, the 'messiness' of contextualizing entrepreneurship. With this simple, but effective 'rewording', we hope to emphasize that contextualizing is not easy, but messy, noisy, complex and challenging – and at the same time, 'contexts' allow us to create real-life impressions of entrepreneurships, which will enrich our theories and our implications and allow scholarship to become much more relevant.

Next, we want to encourage seeing beyond the oftentimes 'context is the environment and nothing else' perspective of contextualizing. Context is not just the environment, it is not – only – 'situations' as older context definitions assume. Contexts are much more: They are 'inside' and 'outside' of us – they are 'subjective' and 'objective'. Most context-related research in the entrepreneurship field has focused on the 'objective' side of contexts, because what are assumed to be 'objective' constructs are easy to identify, observe, measure and study. Now, it is time to include other aspects of contexts. We believe that there is so much more to learn from studying the 'invisible' and 'subjective' facets of contexts; and in this we are supported by our contributors to this volume. Malin Brännback and Alan Carsrud (Chapter 2) relate contexts to cognitions, opening up the contextualization debate to the influence of individual interpretation and individual sense-making as touched upon also by Stephen Lippmann and Howard E. Aldrich in Chapter 5. Chris Steyaert, in Chapter 3, draws our attention to the importance of 'texts' and language – our ways of speaking, our intonations, our whole body language. Denise Fletcher and Paul Selden, in Chapter 7, highlight the relational aspects of contexts and contextualizing. Sarah Drakopoulou Dodd, together with Tobias Pret and Eleanor Shaw (Chapter 10) add the inter-subjectivity of entrepreneurial embeddedness. Ted Baker and E. Erin Powell (Chapter 4) take a look at the structural dimensions of contexts in relation to opportunities for entrepreneurship, deconstructing the notion of opportunity and drawing attention to its inequality which we 'normally' neglect to research. These chapters offer crossroads for many interesting avenues for future research!

And, once more, we offer a strong reminder that contextualizing is about acknowledging and working with variations in/of entrepreneurship instead of trying to equalize everything. We challenge scholars to reconsider the nature of generalizability in entrepreneurship contexts. Rather than look for similarities among various contexts as a way to generalize, we might find more insights by seeking to ascertain those differences and unique attributes of the contexts we study. Generalizability comes through developing theories of difference, and, freeing ourselves to see these variations (differences) in the contexts we study may provide us with acumen to forge new paths forward.

The next marker on our roadmap refers to the temporal aspects of contexts, a theme featuring prominently in several of the contributions in this book (for example, Chapters 3, 5, 6, 8, 10, 11 and 12) and also in the Professional Development Workshop discussions held at the Academy of Management Meetings in Vancouver, CA in August 2015. Contexts are not only fluid, they also are 'everywhere', both in terms of time and place: they are in the past, in the now and in the future and they are also: the past, the now and the future. Time matters, and Stephen Lippman and Howard E. Aldrich, in Chapter 5, show that this is, yet again, related to sense-making, in this case: our culturally and disciplinary understanding of which type of time matters and in which ways time influences our thinking and behaviours. Place matters also, and in Chapter 6, R. Daniel Wadhwani illustrates how historians contextualize by establishing the relationship between past events, the time and period they happened in, together with the place these events occur. In Chapter 8, Erik Stam introduces us to time-geography as an approach that seeks to integrate spatial and temporal perspectives of different disciplines. We need much more research that studies the temporal–spatial–historical contexts and their intersectionality as difficult as this may be!

This brings us to the challenges we face when contextualizing. As every coin has two sides, challenges are simultaneously opportunities for us as researchers. And the challenges here are twofold: How can we develop contextualized theory? And which methods and research approaches will help us to contextualize in our empirical studies?

We need more 'theories-in-context'. As a step forward, we encourage more work that is not shy in generalizing from contextualized entrepreneurship research, thus contributing to building theories-in-context. It is possible, and we have touched upon this in our introductory conversation (Chapter 1). In a way this also is a central theme of Chapter 4 by Ted Baker and E. Erin Powell, who argue for a reconceptualization of entrepreneurial opportunity, taking into account the inequality of opportunity. The authors demonstrate in an exemplary way what we can learn and theorize by understanding how opportunities are unequally distributed because of differences in how societies and economies are structured and 'regulate' access to resources. Along a similar vein, the authors of Chapters 7 and 10 show how we can re-interpret entrepreneurship by either taking a relational perspective on contextualizing or by using Bourdieu's theory of practice. And, the authors of Chapters 5, 6 and 8 suggest a plethora of ideas and approaches to theorize temporal and historical contexts: showing how to incorporate dynamics and a processual view into the contextualization debate. We believe these ideas are applicable to developing contextualized theories: Dig deeper than we usually do; step outside your own comfort zone and take a look at the 'other', the 'invisible' sides of what constitutes entrepreneurship. And, taking this further, there is room for contextualizing discussions about contextualization in the entrepreneurship field.

Stepping outside of what we know and use for studying contexts is also required methodologically. Simone Chlosta, in Chapter 9, illustrates how to consider contexts within each step of the research process. We support her call for a context-sensitive research approach; particularly in her demonstration of the value added in using 'other' – different – methods, variables, scales and so on. Sarah Drakopoulou Dodd and her co-authors suggest enacted methods. Another set of tools comes from historians, as shown by R. Daniel Wadhwani in Chapter 11. And, there are many more disciplines such as ethnology, anthropology and critical studies that may give us even more methodological options. Finally, William B. Gartner (Chapter 12) challenges us to consider the ways in which research is presented (as in recognizing researchers, readers, and the formats of the stories told) as an inherent aspect of the methodology of the research process. By 're-searching' (going back and looking) at the chapters in this book through a narrative lens, the contextualizing of contexts is more likely to be seen as discourses among the community of scholars. We (we include, you, the reader) are contexts for contextualizing.

This brings us to another point on the roadmap: contextualized research needs different understanding of what research is and how we 'do' research. We are confident that contextualization would greatly benefit from transdisciplinary work. (On a personal note, we might offer this view because we have had many enjoyable experiences working with 'others'. Or, our experiences have given us insights that working with others may be an unconditional requirement for getting the most out of contextualized entrepreneurship research.) The contributors in this volume illustrate, explicitly and implicitly, the importance of research beyond (disciplinary) boundaries. The biographies of the authors in this book illustrate this manifold disciplinary and business-related variation in backgrounds. To us, this is what makes contextualizing in entrepreneurship research so interesting. We are forced to talk to others beyond our own comfort zone, beyond what we know and can easily interpret, and – even more important – we have opportunities to listen to each other.

So, are there only positive aspects to this perspective on contexts? Are there no dark sides hidden in this debate? In Chapter 2, Malin Brännback and Alan L. Carsrud, while not denying the importance of contextualized research, point out that contextualization is a balancing act – balancing between inclusion and exclusion. They argue that we exclude some contexts and prioritize others. Put differently: This would imply that as soon as we start to conduct contextualized entrepreneurship research, we have to choose between being inclusive or being selective. In our view, this is not a genuine setback. We believe that the way we understand contextualizing is, per se, about being inclusive. Take a closer look at Chapters 4 and 10: in both cases, the authors demonstrate how our understanding of entrepreneurship changes and grows once we apply a more inclusive (that is, contextualized) perspective. Also, for us, contextualizing is having a holistic understanding and research approach, as difficult as this may be to achieve. Excluding contexts may reflect, to use some of Chris Steyaert's arguments in Chapter 3, on our own laziness (at times) as researchers.

Finally, we want to reiterate an important point which runs through the entire book, from our opening conversation in Chapter 1 to the other chapters: as soon as we include contexts into our research, we acknowledge differences and variations. To us, this is a constitutive element of any (further) research on entrepreneurship and contexts: There simply is no single model of entrepreneurship and entrepreneurial behaviour – and this is a point vividly illustrated by this volume: We interpret, make sense, talk in different languages and read 'con-texts' differently; the temporal dimensions of contexts differ across places such as regions, cultures and societies (and across our own disciplines); an awareness of cognitions, individuals, relations, time, place and history helps us to understand and explain where those differences in entrepreneurship originate from. The chapters in this book offer many more ways to think about contexts and methods as to how to contextualize (in) entrepreneurship than we currently are familiar with and apply.

It is no surprise then, there is much work left to do. A daunting task?

Trust us: we think that contexts in entrepreneurship present us with some of the most fascinating theoretical and empirical challenges we have come across. Advancing a research agenda on entrepreneurship contexts offers exciting possibilities and 'fun' as there are so many research avenues that have not yet been travelled down. We are convinced that contextualizing makes entrepreneurship research not only more relevant, as we have said before, but also so much more interesting.

Now it's your turn, dear reader!

So: the end of this book. We hope that the book offers some nuggets and insights for you. We, the editors, have learned much from the chapter authors and from all of the participants in many workshops and seminars where these ideas about contexts have been discussed and refined. The journey has been so much fun. Together with all our contributors, we want to thank you for having come this far with us. And, now, we are curious as to where you, dear reader, will go. So, let the journey towards contextualizing entrepreneurship research continue. . .

NOTE

1 We gratefully acknowledge the comments and suggestions from the participants at the Professional Development Workshop (PDW) at the Academy of Management Annual Meeting in Vancouver, 2015: Alan L. Carsrud, Alexander Fust, Alia Weston, Andrea R. Scott, Anna Jenkins, Anna Pastwa, Anusha Ramesh, Arjan Frederiks, Carla Costa, Carlos Morales, Carsten Nico Hjorth, Celeste Liu, Chen Fleisher, Chris Steyaert, Christina Lubinski, Christoph Winkler, Chrysavgi Sklaveniti, Claire Ingram, Daniil Pokidko, David Witt, Denise Fletcher, Derek Ozkal, Drew Gertner, E. Michael Laviolette, Emiel Eijdenberg, E. Erin Powell, Erik Stam, Ferran Giones, Ghazale Haddadian, Howard E. Aldrich, Huriye Aygören, Jessica DiBella, Julia Binder, Julienne Senyard, Karellos Pomagolis Nikolopoulos, Kilian Moser, Lutisha Vickerie, Maika Valencia-Silva, Malin Brännback, Margaret Clappison, Markko Hamalainen, Mary Kilfoil, Maximilian Rimbach, Mikko Jaaskelainen, Minet Schindehuette, M.K. Ward, Neil Thompson, Nguyen Bach, R. Daniel Wadhani, Renate Ortlieb, René Mauer, Richard Chan, Rob Mitchell, Ronit Yitshaki, Saras Sarasvathy, Sergio Janczak, Sharon Hunter Rainey, Steve Gaklis, Su Jing, Susan Marlow, Ted Baker, Todd Chiles, Tom Elfring, Trent Williams, Tyrah X.J. Li, Wu Jie, Yin-Chi Liao and Zhang Jiamin.

14 A reading list on entrepreneurship and contexts

For those readers who just want a quick overview of what we and our contributors deem important readings to make sense of the multifold aspects of entrepreneurship and contexts – if you are interested in why all of us recommend these particular readings, we refer you back to the chapters in this volume.

Abbott, Andrew (2001), *Time Matters: On Theory and Method*, Chicago, IL: University of Chicago Press.

Akman, Varol (2000), 'Rethinking context as a social construct', *Journal of Pragmatics*, **32** (6), 743–759.

Autio, Erkko, Martin Kenney, Philippe Mustar, Don Siegel and Mike Wright (2014), 'Entrepreneurial innovation: The importance of context', *Research Policy*, **43** (7), 1097–1108.

Bamberger, Peter (2008), 'From the editors: Beyond contextualization: Using context theories to narrow the micro–macro gap in management research', *Academy of Management Journal*, **51** (5), 839–846.

Baumol, William J. (1990), 'Entrepreneurship: Productive, unproductive, and destructive', *Journal of Political Economy*, **98** (5), 893–921.

Blommaert, J. (2001), 'Context is/as critique', *Critique of Anthropology*, **21** (1), 13–32.

Bucheli, Marcelo and R. Daniel Wadhwani (eds) (2014), *Organizations in Time: History, Theory, Methods*, Oxford: Oxford University Press.

Chalmers, D.M. and E. Shaw (2015), 'The endogenous construction of entrepreneurial contexts: A practice-based perspective', *International Small Business Journal*, published online before print 21 September 2015, doi: 10.1177/0266242615589768.

De Clercq, Dirk and Maxim Voronov (2009b), 'Toward a practice perspective of entrepreneurship: Entrepreneurial legitimacy as habitus', *International Small Business Journal*, **27** (4), 395–419.

Drakopoulou Dodd, Sarah, Seonaidh McDonald, Gerard McElwee and Robert Smith (2014), 'A Bourdieuan analysis of qualitative authorship in entrepreneurship scholarship', *Journal of Small Business Management*, **52** (4), 633–654.

Felski, Rita (2011), '"Context stinks!"', *New Literary History*, **42** (4), 573–591.

Gartner, William B. (2008), 'Variations in entrepreneurship', *Small Business Economics*, **31** (4), 351–361.

Gartner, William B., T.R. Mitchell and K.H. Vesper (1989), 'A taxonomy of new business ventures', *Journal of Business Venturing*, **4** (3), 169–186.

Grabher, G. (2002), 'The project ecology of advertising: Tasks, talents and teams', *Regional Studies*, **36** (3), 245–262.

Grusky, David (ed.) (2014), *Social Stratification: Class, Race, and Gender in Sociological Perspectives*, 4th edn, Boulder, CO: Westview Press.

Hjorth, D., C. Jones and W.B. Gartner (2008), 'Introduction for "recreating/recontextualising entrepreneurship"', *Scandinavian Journal of Management*, **24** (2), 81–84.

Huff, Anne S. (1990), *Mapping Strategic Thought*, Chichester, UK: Wiley and Sons.

Kipping, Matthias, R. Daniel Wadhwani and Marcelo Bucheli (2014), 'Analyzing and interpreting historical sources: A basic methodology', in Marcelo Bucheli and R. Daniel Wadhwani (eds), *Organizations in Time: History, Theory, Methods*, Oxford: Oxford University Press, pp. 305–329.

Koehn, N.F. (2001), *Brand New, How Entrepreneurs Earned Consumers' Trust from Wedgewood to Dell*, Boston, MA: Harvard Business School Press.

Komisar, R. (2000), *The Monk and the Riddle*, Boston, MA: Harvard Business School Press.

Lipartito, Kenneth J. (2014), 'Historical sources and data', in Marcelo Bucheli and R. Daniel Wadhwani (eds), *Organizations in Time: History, Theory, Methods*, Oxford: Oxford University Press, pp. 284–304.

Lippmann, Stephen and Howard E. Aldrich (2014), 'History and evolutionary theory', in Marcelo Bucheli and R. Daniel Wadhwani (eds), *Organizations in Time: History, Theory, Methods*, Oxford: Oxford University Press, pp. 124–146.

Maclean, Mairi, Charles Harvey and Stewart Clegg (2015), 'Conceptualizing historical organization studies', *Academy of Management Review*, published online before print 13 July 2015, doi: 10.5465/amr.2014.0133.

Mintzberg, H., B. Ahlstrand and J. Lampel (1998), *Strategy Safari*, London: Prentice Hall.

Orr, D. (2015), *The Road Not Taken: Finding America in the Poem Everyone Loves and Almost Everyone Gets Wrong*, New York: Penguin Press.

Pollitt, Christopher (2013), 'Context: What kind of missing link?', in Christopher Pollitt (ed.), *Context in Public Policy and Management: The Missing Link?*, Cheltenham, UK and Northampton, MA, USA: Edward Elgar Publishing, pp. 415–422.

Popp, Andrew and Robin Holt (2013), 'The presence of entrepreneurial opportunity', *Business History*, **55** (1), 9–28.

Powell, E. Erin and Ted Baker (2014), 'It's what you make of it: Founder identity and enacting strategic responses to adversity', *Academy of Management Journal*, **57** (5), 1406–1433.

Rowlinson, Michael, John Hassard and Stephanie Decker (2014), 'Research strategies for organizational history: A dialogue between historical theory and organization theory', *Academy of Management Review*, **39** (3), 250–274.

Schatzki, T.R. (2002), *The Site of the Social. A Philosophical Account of the Constitution of Social Life and Change*, University Park, PA: The Pennsylvania State University Press.

Shepherd, Dean (2015), 'Party on! A call for entrepreneurship research that is more interactive, activity based, cognitively hot, compassionate, and prosocial', *Journal of Business Venturing*, **30** (4), 489–507.

Shipp, Abbie J., Jeff R. Edwards and Lisa S. Lambert (2009), 'Conceptualization and measurement of temporal focus: The subjective experience of the past, present, and future', *Organizational Behavior and Human Decision Processes*, **110** (1), 1–22.

Stam, E. (2007), 'Why butterflies don't leave: Locational behavior of entrepreneurial firms', *Economic Geography*, **83** (1), 27–50.

Stevenson, H.H. and J.C. Jarillo (1990), 'A paradigm of entrepreneurship: Entrepreneurial management', *Strategic Management Journal*, **11** (5), 17–27.

Tatli, Ahu, Joana Vassilopoulou, Mustafa Özbilgin, Cynthia Forson and Natasha Slutskaya (2014), 'A Bourdieuan relational perspective for entrepreneurship research', *Journal of Small Business Management*, **52** (4), 615–632.

Ucbasaran, Deniz, Paul Westhead and Mike Wright (2001), 'The focus of entrepreneurial research: Contextual and process issues', *Entrepreneurship: Theory & Practice*, **25** (4), 57–78.

Vaessen, P. and E. Wever (1993), 'Spatial responsiveness of small firms', *Tijdschrift voor Economische en Sociale Geografie*, **84**, 119–131.

Van Gelderen, Marco, Enno Masurel and Karen Verduyn (2012), 'Introduction to "entrepreneurship in context"', in Marco van Gelderen and Enno Masurel (eds), *Entrepreneurship in Context*, London: Routledge, pp. 1–22.

Vargas Llosa, M. (1984), *The Real Life of Alejandro Mayta: A Novel*, New York: Farrar, Straus and Giroux.

Welter, Friederike (2011), 'Contextualizing entrepreneurship – Conceptual challenges and ways forward', *Entrepreneurship Theory and Practice*, **35** (1), 165–184.

Welter, Friederike (2016), 'Wandering between contexts', in David Audretsch and Erik Lehmann (eds), *The Routledge Companion to Makers of Modern Entrepreneurship*, London: Routledge, forthcoming.

Welter, Friederike, Candida G. Brush and Anne de Bruin (2014), *The Gendering of Entrepreneurship Context*, Working Paper, 1/2014, Bonn: IfM Bonn.

Wright, Mike, James J. Chrisman, Jess H. Chua and Lloyd P. Steier (2014), 'Family enterprise and context', *Entrepreneurship Theory and Practice*, **38** (6), 1247–1260.

Zahra, Shaker A. and Mike Wright (2011), 'Entrepreneurship's next act', *Academy of Management Perspectives*, **25** (4), 67–83.

Zahra, Shaker A., Mike Wright and Sondos G. Abdelgawad (2014), 'Contextualization and the advancement of entrepreneurship research', *International Small Business Journal*, **32** (5), 479–500.

Index